TRAGEDY
KENNY CARTER

TRAGEDY
KENNY CARTER

By Tony McDonald

Second impression April 2008
First published in England in June 2007
by **Retro Speedway**
Tel: 01708 734 502
www.retro-speedway.com

©Copyright Retro Speedway

Printed by Biddles Ltd, King's Lynn, Norfolk

Distributed by Retro Speedway
103 Douglas Road, Hornchurch, Essex, RM11 1AW, England
Email: editorial@retro-speedway.com

Set in Times Roman

ISBN 978-0-9551176-3-3

Cover photography by Ken Carpenter

Kenny before his first senior appearance for England – against Australasia at Swindon, July 1979.

CONTENTS

Acknowledgements

A special and sincere thanks to all the following for their help in making this book possible:
Jimmy Ross, Phil 'Ollie' Hollingworth, John Berry, Martin Neal, Richard Clark, Susie Muir, Jack McDonald and all the many riders, promoters, team managers and others from past and present who kindly gave up their time for interviews. Their co-operation is very much appreciated.

Photography
Ken Carpenter, Alf Weedon, Mike Patrick, John Somerville, Doug Booth, John Hipkiss, Alan Legg, Steve Magro, Clive Knowles, *Halifax Evening Courier*, Ross Parry Agency, WRNS Pictures.

Bibliography

Magazines and newspapers
Speedway Star, Speedway Mail, Backtrack, Vintage Speedway Magazine, 5-One, Halifax Evening Courier.

Books
Booey, Eric Boocock, Retro Speedway, 2006.
Confessions of a Speedway Promoter, John Berry, Retro Speedway, 2004.
Simmo: The Whole Truth, Malcolm Simmons, Retro Speedway, 2006.
The Complete History of the British League, Peter Oakes, Front Page Books, 1991.
Wheels and Deals, Ian Thomas, Pinegen, 2006.
When The Can Ran Out, Chris Morton and Brian Burford, Tempus, 2005.

Video/DVD
1982 World Individual Speedway Championship, World Class Inc, 1982.

INTRODUCTION

THE telephone in the Speedway Mail office at Walthamstow, East London rang one morning in May 1986 and the caller was abrupt and straight to the point.

"It's me," said the man in the broad Yorkshire accent, knowing full well that as editor of the weekly paper I would immediately recognise him as Kenny Carter, Halifax kingpin and self-proclaimed England No.1.

"Why have you got that w*****r Peter Collins on your front cover?

"You should've put me on there!"

About six weeks earlier Kenny Carter and Peter Collins, two big stars of English speedway, had been involved in a punch-up at Belle Vue. There was definitely no love lost between them. In fact, by then, they could not stand the sight of each other.

It did not seem to register with Kenny when I pointed out to him that he had featured on the cover of the Mail just a week or two before, and so it would be overdoing it to put his face on there again so soon.

It had been an uncharacteristically poor start to the season for the Halifax and England No.1, with injuries and a spate of bike problems adding to the stress he was under trying to make a success of his latest business venture. I was unaware at that time of the personal troubles boiling up inside him – not even the few people who were close to him knew about them until it was too late.

But you could not keep him down for long. He talked enthusiastically that day about his newly-founded Kenny Carter sports promotions company, and how he had just signed up the Olympic gold medal javelin thrower Tessa Sanderson as his first client.

I did not get to chat to Kenny, face to face, all that often, except at Test matches and World Championship meetings, because he was based in Halifax and I was in London. The last time I spoke to him at The Shay was one night the previous summer, when the Dukes announced their new team sponsorship deal with Coalite. I must have over-indulged in the hospitality bar before the meeting because I watched the second half from the centre green – on my back! I had lost interest and can recall being stretched out on the centre green turf, relaxing in the evening sun, as Kenny was making his way from the pits to the changing room.

We said 'hello', exchanged pleasantries and then he asked, with typical cheek: "What's up, Tony, have you been on Shawn Moran's marijuana?"

For all his self-opinionated intensity, aggression and arrogance, Kenny had a sharp sense of humour, too. We always got on well – he was just a year younger than me – and, as any reporter who covered speedway back then will tell you, he was always great for copy – a magnet for hacks. In fact, he was the best during my time at the *Mail* – always approachable (except when he was being carried off on a stretcher), chatty and invariably controversial.

After I had managed to placate his annoyance that Peter Collins had been pictured on the cover instead of him , Kenny finished his call with the words that I have never forgotten: "Anyway," he said, "I'll have a really big story for you next week . . ."

I did not know what he was referring to, and dismissed his teaser as nothing more newsworthy than another announcement of the next 'big' signing for his promotions company, which seemed to have absorbed him. Anyway, he would call again as soon as he had something he considered 'important' to say, I reasoned as I replaced the receiver and thought nothing more about it.

I never spoke to him again.

On the evening of Wednesday, May 21, 1986, probably within a week of our final conversation, I was visiting relatives, sitting on their sofa and chatting with ITV's News At Ten on in the background. No-one in the room was paying much attention to the telly – until the face of Kenny Carter suddenly filled the screen. Amid the shocking realisation that a speedway item had made the most watched national television programme broadcast across the nation, it was difficult to take in everything the presenter said.

But two words that stuck immediately were "shot" and "dead".

It could not possibly be true, could it? England's top rider, the undisputed King of Halifax, dead?

It was the speedway equivalent of a JFK moment.

Over the next few hours, days and weeks, the full horrific truth emerged. Kenny had blasted his wife, Pam, to death because he could not bear the thought of her leaving him, amid rumours that she was seeing somebody else behind his back, and then turned the gun on himself

Disbelief and horror in the farming community of Bradshaw, near Halifax, where the 25-year-old couple lived, turned to anger. How could Kenny have done this? How could he end the life of his childhood sweetheart, kill himself and orphan their two young children – a girl of three and a boy of two – in the process?

It was too unbelievable to take in.

More than 21 years later, people are still shaking their heads and quietly asking themselves those same questions.

We know how. But *why?*

Sadly, this book obviously cannot bring Pam and Kenny back, but it will attempt to explain who Kenny Carter – the person as well as the speedway star – really was. No matter what demons inside his head had sent him over the edge and turned him from father and husband into a callous killer, we cannot possibly forgive or condone what he did that tragic day at the couple's moorland farmhouse, and nor would we wish to. How can anybody forgive his murderous act?

There can be no justification for it – but there are contributory factors, unhappy and heart-wrenching experiences from his adolescent youth that probably go a long way to explaining what possibly possessed this very driven young man to finally lose it all in the shocking manner he did.

With help and contributions from Kenny's former friends and the people who knew him best throughout his eight full years as a rider – including team-mates, rivals, team managers, promoters, journalists and supporters, *Tragedy* examines the person behind the name. It is most certainly not a book intended to glorify the man, although it is only right that his many successes on the track, some of the biggest achieved with the most courageous, super-human efforts ever seen in a sporting context, are also fully acknowledged.

What I am sure will surprise many readers is the heartbreaking chain of family tragedies that devastated young Kenny before he had even become a speedway superstar. The loss of both his youngest brother, and particularly the mother he loved and cared for so much, no doubt left deep personal and psychological wounds that never healed and undoubtedly had a direct effect on his own personality.

Just as he did in his short life, Carter continues to divide people's opinion of him in death. Bruce Penhall, Kenny's biggest rival of all, did not even wish to talk about him when I called him up in California. He is still too sickened by the tragic events of Grey Horse Farm to be able to offer us much in the way of subjective analysis of their infamous battles that dominated the speedway headlines at the start of the 80s. But, very reluctantly, and because he knew that Pam and Kenny's children will benefit in a small way from the book's proceeds, Bruce did talk. And he was scathing.

So too was Kenny's biggest English adversary, Peter Collins. Not surprisingly, they both have very strong views of Carter the passage of two decades has done little to diminish.

The co-operation of these two speedway superstars of the 70s and 80s is appreciated, as is the time and help generously given by others who readily agreed to be interviewed for the book and who are all listed on an earlier page. Many of the ex-riders and personalities I have interviewed for *Backtrack* magazine over the past three years and more have their own, unique stories about Kenny to recall. You won't agree with the views expressed by all but I hope that some form of acceptable balance has been struck throughout the following pages.

Love him or hate him, it seems everybody has a view of Kenny Carter. And no-one can easily ignore him.

No-one I approached refused to speak about Kenny, although it is with regret and disappointment that representatives from both Kenny and Pam's families preferred not to give interviews, despite attempts to reach them via their acquaintances, letters, emails and phone calls. Some of them, we know, are aware of the book's existence and have raised no objection to it. Their reluctance to recall the past, however, is, of course, totally understandable in the circumstances and their right to keep their own private thoughts to themselves must also be respected. The Carter and Lund families have all suffered far too much in one way or another.

I am particularly indebted to two of Carter's closest friends – Jimmy Ross, who became a father figure to Kenny, and Phil Hollingworth, KC's former main mechanic. They have recalled their memories – good, bad and sad – of many shared experiences they had with the man they knew better than anybody outside the immediate family possibly could.

This book would not be what it is either without the time and advice offered by John Berry, for his constant encouragement and prompting, and for the ever-willing efforts of my old mate, Martin Neal, for providing some of the ex-rider interviews.

Can any good possibly come from such an awful tragedy? I think and hope so. Two young lives were needlessly wasted and the devastating effect the deaths of Pam and Kenny had on their families is beyond comprehension. But there is a legacy left by Pam and Kenny for the relatives and close friends to preserve and nurture now and for many years to come. I feel sure that everyone who reads *Tragedy* will join me in wishing the couple's two offspring, Kelly Marie and Malcolm, a happy, healthy and fulfilling life. God knows they deserve it.

Tony McDonald
June 2007

Kenny's first major title – British Junior Champion at Canterbury, 1979.

Chapter 1

DAMNED FROM THE START?

IMAGINE how devastated you would be, as a normal happy nine-year-old with two younger brothers to play with, if your mother's life was ruined in a car crash that left her paralysed from the neck down.

Imagine the sheer horror of hearing that in the same road accident that crippled your mum, your little four-year-old brother had died.

Imagine how sickening it must be to see your helpless mum bedridden for years, wracked with unremitting pain, living on an endless supply of tablets and relying on you and her dedicated carer to attend to even her most basic feminine needs.

Imagine what it would be like to suddenly find yourself head of the family, trying to look after her and your remaining younger brother as best you could because your parents have parted – this enormous burden having been thrust upon you because your father had moved out to rebuild his shattered life elsewhere with his new love.

Then imagine all this happened to you well before your adolescence. Before you had much chance to enjoy doing all the many other things most 'normal' young boys do in their formative school years.

And then, nine years after the fatal car crash that has devastated your family, you popped out very briefly and arrived home to discover, to your horror, that the mother you loved very deeply and who you would do anything for, had committed suicide.

Imagine what a living nightmare that scenario would be. It's unthinkable, isn't it? Too horrendous for any mature adult to even dare contemplate, let alone a kid with a younger brother to think about.

But this chain of events was no fiction. Kenny Carter did not have to try and imagine this heartbreaking string of tragedies, any one of which would be enough to seriously affect a young boy's view on life.

The skinny, little kid from Halifax experienced this living hell before he had even started shaving.

No wonder he skipped his youth and grew up very fast, independent and fiercely driven by an incredible inner strength and desperation to prove – to himself and perhaps most of all, a strong-willed father – that he was the best at whatever he did.

It all started to go terribly wrong for Kenny and his family when he was nine-years old. To be precise, it was the afternoon of Saturday, October 24, 1970.

That is when Kenny's mother, 26-year-old Christine Carter, set off from their house at 15 Brickfield Lane in the Holmfield area of Halifax, just north of the town centre, in her Cortina car with his little brother, Malcolm. Brickfield Lane is a short, ordinary looking street lined with a combination of old terraced houses and the kind of two-bedroom semi-detached property that Mal and Christine bought relatively new after moving from their previous home at 90, Elizabeth Street, Elland. Previous to that, they lived at 176 Westage, Elland at the time Kenneth Malcolm Carter entered the world at Halifax General Hospital on March 28, 1961.

In his early married days Mal worked as an overhead linesman for Yorkshire Electricity Board. Christine Margaret Carter (née Hanner) stayed at home to bring up their three sons, Kenny, Alan and Malcolm.

By the time the family moved to Ovenden, Mal was well on his way up the business ladder as a self-made man running the thriving Pharoah Garage in Keighley Road, Ovenden Cross, just a two-minute drive from the Carters' second home.

Brickfield Lane is a slightly inclined no-through road. At the top end the road is joined by several acres of lush, tree-lined fields where Kenny and his brothers used to play on their little bikes and kick a football around. At the bottom end, marked by what is now a small sub-post office-cum newsagent, is the junction with Shay Lane which, despite what its name may suggest, is in fact a couple of miles away from the local speedway track.

It was while driving along Shay Lane, a meandering, single carriageway route, on that autumn Saturday afternoon that the first of numerous tragedies struck the Carter family. The car Christine was driving suffered a puncture, spun out of control and was in a collision with another vehicle and a parked car.

The car had apparently turned on its roof and in the ensuing carnage, it is believed a man decorating the front of his house was seriously injured, if not killed.

Christine was rushed to hospital suffering what the local newspaper described as 'multiple injuries'.

Poor Malcolm, almost five years younger than Kenny and two years middle brother Alan's junior, did not survive the crash. He died of chest injuries in the Royal Halifax Infirmary the following day.

The following Monday, with Christine still lying heavily sedated in her hospital bed and unable to move, her life turned upside down, the front page headline in the Halifax Courier read: 'BOY DIES AFTER 3-CAR SMASH'.

Kenny's life would never be the same again.

His mother had suffered such horrendous injuries that had left her paralysed from the neck down and unable to ever walk again.

Christine spent the next year receiving treatment in the spinal injuries unit at Pinderfields Hospital, Wakefield – where doctors saved the life of triple speedway World Champion Erik Gundersen after his near fatal crash at Bradford in 1989. As soon as she returned to the family home in Brickfield Lane, her husband Mal moved out and subsequently bought a farm at Barkisland.

She continued to be looked after by male nurse, David Wood, who had cared for her during some of her time at Pinderfields, although Kenny and Alan would continue to run errands for their mother and generally help out as best they could.

Mrs Mary Parker, a neighbour who lived opposite the house where the Carter boys grew up, said: "Kenny and Alan did everything for her and if they couldn't do it themselves they asked neighbours. Everyone rallied round to help the family.

"Kenny wouldn't let anything happen to her. He really cared deeply for his mother."

There are friends of Kenny's who still insist today that, psychologically, he never got over what happened to his mother, or the way his parents parted – at a time in the early 70s when divorce was still frowned upon – so soon after she came home from hospital.

Was his life damned more or less right from the start?

How the young Kenny coped with the double tragedy, plus the break up of his parents' marriage all in relatively quick succession, we can only speculate. He had always displayed less emotion than Alan and would keep his most personal thoughts and fears bottled up inside. This was a worrying personality trait that never changed.

What we know for sure is that he found solace by completely immersing himself in motorcycles and racing, a world his father already knew well. The thrill of riding small motor bikes must have helped ease the pain inside the kid and Mal Carter, though a typical Yorkshireman and never one to show his sons any outward sign of love and affection, certainly made sure his boys were the best equipped young riders in the whole of West Yorkshire.

It was on the hills behind his father's garage at Ovenden Cross, where Mal earned a good living selling used cars and vans and running a motorcycle dealership as main agents for Suzuki, that Kenny first learned to ride a motor bike. A pupil at Moorside Junior and Infants School in Keighley Road, his dad bought him a 50cc machine at the age of six.

Mal said: "He became so good at handling it, it was not long before I got him a Suzuki Falcon 80cc, specially made for him.

"He joined the Youth Motorcycle Association and he was outstanding in the juniors and intermediates. I then got him a Yamaha 100cc moto-crosser and he was brilliant on that too.

"He shot from juniors to seniors in eight weeks, and he did so well I put him with the experts. Some of them resented a lad so young doing so well against them and they started to knock him around, so I decided to make moves in other directions.

"At first he was reluctant to give up scrambling but there was not much money in that. I wanted him to be a hero in his home town. I decided he was better off being a hero in speedway, where he would get paid for it, so I bought a bike and that was the start of it all."

Big Mal Carter's passion for bikes manifested itself in road-racing – firstly as an enthusiastic local rider and, later, as a prominent sponsor of motorcycle racing legend Ron Haslam, the former double Formula One TT World Champion. However, Mal had watched speedway at The Shay before his involvement with 'Rocket' Ron.

He got to know Eric Boothroyd, who was well known in his home-town as captain and then promoter of the Halifax Dukes speedway team.

Eric said: "I had known Malcolm since the early 70s, when he was a road-racer on the local club circuit and I tuned and repaired motorcycles for a bit of extra money

Mastering the art of the wheelie on a moto-cross bike, aged 15, in 1977.

in the winter close season while I was still riding at The Shay. He brought his bike to me one day because he complained that it kept stopping – not surprising really, because he was a big bloke, weighing about 18 stone.

"He won his next three races the following week and said I'd done a brilliant job but, as he'd not bothered to do anything else to the engine since I'd tuned it, the motor blew the next time he rode it!

"I saw him fairly regularly at his car sales business and one day he mentioned that he wanted me to take a look at his young son, Kenny. I didn't take too much notice at first but he insisted I saw him ride and an opportunity presented itself when Kenny was competing in a local junior moto cross event, held at the Wainstalls scrambles course. 'Have a look – he's brilliant!' Malcolm kept telling me.

"By the time I arrived at the meeting Kenny had already ridden a couple of times and fallen off once. 'Get back on, lad, and go out and show Eric what you can do,' Malcolm demanded of his son, but the kid was clearly unfit and pointed out that he'd probably broken his wrist in the fall! Malcolm was very insistent, though. He was a very hard man to please," said Eric.

Boothroyd kept his ear to the ground and knew something of the trauma Kenny had already endured at such a tender age. "I'd heard about what he'd been through in his childhood," he said.

Christine Carter had enjoyed no quality of life since being confined to a wheelchair and then, in time, becoming completely bedridden. All she could do was keep taking the painkilling tablets to try and ease her suffering as best she could while watching her two surviving sons, Kenny and Alan, grow up without being able to enjoy with them a normal mother-son relationship most of us take for granted. All she had to cling on to were happy memories of the kids and her most cherished possession was the pair of little red shoes four-year-old Malcolm had last worn before the fatal crash, which she kept with her at all times.

She still had the house – Mal signed it over to her as part of their divorce settlement – and, at first, she also had the love and devotion of David Wood, who she married at Halifax Registry Office on June 5, 1976. The boys got on well with David – they were at least happy for a while that their mother had found another companion in her life – although this relationship was not without its problems.

Hard-nosed Yorkshiremen tend to take life's disasters in their stride, at least on the surface, but you sense the huge understatement in Eric Boothroyd's voice when he says: "Kenny had a pretty traumatic young life."

Mal started pushing his son towards the shale sport that attracted a regular 5,000 crowd to The Shay on a Saturday night back then. The Dukes had not won anything since they were crowned British League champions in that famous sporting summer of 1966, when Eric Boocock, Dave Younghusband and veteran skipper Eric Boothroyd were the three local stars. Even though the team with the red-and-blue halves and distinctive white elephant on its race jacket had struggled to recapture those glory days, speedway was still the most attractive sport the West Riding town had to offer at the time. The alternative spectator sports in the immediate area were a second rate rugby league team and an ailing fourth division Football League club

Mal Carter

whose pitch was laid inside the oval speedway track. But they did not compare to the thrills and excitement served up by the bikes, and the intoxicating aroma of burning methanol fuel, at The Shay every Saturday from March until October, when the best riders in the world would race flat out, risking life and limb at speeds of up to 70mph.

Eric Boocock had been England's No.1 for a spell in the late 60s and early 70s. He reached three world finals and in 1974 put the town on the map by winning the British Championship in front of the ITV *World of Sport* cameras. Everybody in Halifax had heard of 'Booey'.

Mal Carter made it his business to make sure the people of Halifax would hear a lot more about his eldest son before long. Whatever anybody may think of the larger-than-life character some have described as bullying, aggressive and obnoxious, others would argue that he never wanted anything but the best for his two young sons once he had set them on the path to motorcycle glory – Kenny in speedway, Alan in Mal's favoured bike sport of road-racing.

Sporting history is littered with sons and daughters who have owed a large part of their early success to ambitious and overbearing parents, relentlessly driving them on to become the best and to always believe that they are. Speedway itself has seen the coming and going of plenty of youngsters who, when pushed too hard by fathers trying to live out their own unfulfilled dreams through their kids, have fallen by the wayside. It's still happening every week on the football playing fields throughout Britain, where parents forget that their boys are primarily there to have fun and want them to become the next David Beckham . . . and berate them mercilessly when they don't attain their expectations.

Mal loved road-racing and even if his affection for speedway soon dwindled once the riders he sponsored failed to show him the appreciation he thought his generous support deserved, he pushed Kenny towards a career that would bring him success and a lifestyle that he could never have dreamed of achieving among the blue collar workers of Halifax. The town could not even count its sporting heroes on one finger until Kenny Carter emerged from nowhere – Boocock was from Coxley, near Wakefield – and became an overnight teenage sensation, a genuine superstar in the making.

Boothroyd said: "I could see Kenny had something about him, because he was already a successful moto-crosser against top blokes who were older than him.

"Malcolm kept on telling me how good his son was and before long he wanted to bring him to The Shay to show me what he could do on a speedway bike. I always worked on repairing the Halifax track on a Monday afternoon following the Saturday home meeting, so one day I agreed to let Kenny come down for a few laps before I started work on the track at 2pm.

"But Malcolm then had another request. As well as his son, he also wanted to bring along Ron Haslam, the top road-racer he sponsored.

"I brought the track spare to the track for them to ride and although Kenny didn't look too bad, Haslam was easily the pick of the two and could slide the bike better.

"A week later, Malcolm was back in touch with me again about giving Kenny another chance, so I agreed he could have a second try-out the following Monday. Now I don't know what he had been doing during that week, whether he'd been practicing elsewhere or what, but Kenny looked 100 per cent better the second time he rode at The Shay – much more impressive than Haslam."

Those first private practice sessions took place in September 1977, a few months after Kenny had been glad to leave the former J.H. Whitley secondary school in Holmfield behind him. He only had thoughts of racing motor bikes, although there was a pretty girl he took a fancy to as well.

Her name was Pamela Lund, a black-haired, dark-eyed farmer's daughter from the semi-rural village of Bradshaw, where she had attended the local infants school. Kenny and Pam were in the same school year, though not the same class, but he did talk to his future wife despite being one of the "toughies".

After they were married, Pam – who was born just 28 days after Kenny, on April 25 – told Alyson Lanning in a 1982 interview for *Speedway Star*: "He was always getting into trouble but I did like him because he talked to me at break time!"

The couple drifted apart but met up for a date at the age of 16 when Kenny was working at his dad's garage as a mechanic.

"He didn't seem that interested in speedway then," recalled Pam, "but he was spending a lot of time scrambling. In the end I think it was his dad who suggested he started riding at Halifax."

The speedway season was nearly over by the time Kenny had impressed Boothroyd with his much improved second practice spin, so he would have to wait until the following March, the start of the 1978 campaign, before making his competitive debut.

"I don't think he had been interested in speedway before then but his father started to bring him along to our home meetings," said Boothroyd. Further rides round The Shay helped Kenny to familiarise himself with the shape and demands of a big, grey granite circuit with its long straights, steeply banked bends and imposing steel fence that could be lethal if you hit at 70mph.

The Halifax boss, a former England international and world finalist himself in 1956, knew he had a special talent on his hands and Mal Carter was only too eager to see his boy snapped up by his local club.

"He said that if I agreed to sign his son, he'd buy him a new bike and get him all geared up and ready for the following season," said Boothroyd. "Malcolm had plenty of money and was already sponsoring two of our riders, Chris Pusey and Eric Broadbelt, with bikes and cars."

No-one was splashing the cash around more at The Shay in those days than Mal Carter, whose backing of Broadbelt alone was reportedly worth £3,000. Boothroyd

Mal Carter with his sponsored riders, Eric Broadbelt and Chris Pusey, and a young Kenny in 1978.

was understandably keen to cultivate the major benefactor's interest and signing his son was the perfect way to keep him onside.

"In the meantime, I advised Kenny to practice as often as he could," said Eric.

Kenny's first speedway bike was a British Weslake his dad bought from Halifax's Danish star Mike Lohmann for £600 and he spent the winter of 1977-78 riding it at regular Saturday morning sessions put on at Ellesmere Port and run by the local Gunners' promoter Joe Shaw. Other hopefuls who also showed up at the Cheshire venue to learn the art of sliding their 500c machines with no brakes included 16-year-old Neil Collins – the fourth in line of the famous brothers – plus Pete Ellams, Paul Embley and the outstanding 14-year-old Peter Carr. In time all four ended up signing for Port's National League (second division) team.

Dukes' Australian team manager Dennis Gavros would regularly drive Kenny from his Halifax home to Merseyside, while Boothroyd would also go along to check on the rapid progress of their future starlet. Even then, it was immediately obvious that Kenny had what it took to become an outstanding speedway rider.

"He was so outstanding that the Newcastle promoters, Ian Thomas and Bryan

Larner, tried to snatch him from us by offering him inducements behind our back," said Boothroyd.

Thomas' memory of Carter's first season in the sport is hazy but he admitted: "I can't remember it, but I wouldn't deny what Eric told you and certainly wouldn't be surprised if it was true – we nicked a few good lads over the years!"

"Kenny liked money and he did actually consider joining Newcastle. But we had already agreed to sign him and, fair play to his dad, he stuck by our agreement and told Thomas and Larner that his boy was already committed to Halifax."

As Kenny was still only aged 17 when the 1978 season began, his father agreed the terms and countersigned the contract forms. Although Mal clearly knew how to make a bob or three, even he perhaps underestimated how fast young Kenny would rise through the ranks. Kenny's first contract, over three years (1978-80), was for just £4 per start and £8 per point, which was around the basic going rate at the time.

Few people beyond the management of Halifax, Newcastle and the handful of trainees and enthusiasts who showed up at Ellesmere Port each weekend throughout the winter of 1977-78 realised just how good the 16-year-old Carter really was.

Or what a ruthlessly determined streak he possessed for one so young and inexperienced.

When 20-year-old novice Stuart Shirley crashed during a practice session at Ellesmere Port on December 3, 1977 and died as a result of his injuries, his death was given only brief coverage in the speedway press the following week. It was understandable, for very little was known of Stuart who was still trying to make his way in this fast and dangerous sport after having made just one appearance for the Gunners in '77.

What those brief reports in *Speedway Star* and *Speedway Mail* did not mention was that the rider whose robust riding onlookers said had contributed to the fatal crash was . . . Kenny Carter.

Speedway Star quoted an 'eye-witness' as saying: "Stuart Shirley and another rider seemed to collide and he hit the fence before swerving on to the centre green and then falling."

Shirley's tragic misfortune was to crash into a metal mechanical object – a tractor or a roller – on the inside of the track. Joe Shaw and Dennis Gavros immediately rushed to his assistance but the poor lad was dead on arrival at hospital.

Carter has never been publicly linked to Shirley's accidental death before now. And there was no evidence that it ever preyed on the youngster's conscience.

He knew, all too sadly, what it was like having to deal with tragedy. For him it meant bottling it up, burying the bad stuff deep inside and getting on with things. There was no room in his world for sentiment or self-recrimination. After all, he had not deliberately caused the crash – to him, it was a pure racing accident; four inexperienced youngsters going fast and maybe losing a little control.

Kenny realised very early on that speedway is a tough and highly dangerous sport – people get badly hurt, an unlucky few are killed. He did not need anyone to remind him what the nightmare ordeal the parents and family of Stuart Shirley would be going through – he had already faced enough tragedy himself to last him a lifetime.

Unsure if he would be signing for Newcastle, Kenny turned up for their first pre-season practice in 1978 wearing his own race jacket to promote his dad's garage . . .

. . . But for the opening night (below) he was a settled member of the Diamonds squad – on loan from Halifax – and about to show the National League just what he could do. Standing, left to right: Kevin MacDonald, Peter Moy, Robert Maxfield, Robbie Blackadder, Neil Coddington, Tom Owen. Front: Paul Cook (mascot), Robbie Gardner, Kenny, the tragic Chris Prime, David Bargh, Nigel Crabtree.

Chapter 2

DIAMOND GEEZER

THE determination of Halifax to tie Kenny Carter to a contract as quickly as possible was fully justified but it would have been asking too much of the precocious kid to put him straight into top flight British League racing before he had even turned a competitive wheel.

Newcastle Diamonds co-promoter Thomas invited Carter, accompanied by Eric Boothroyd, to the Diamonds' pre-season practice in March '78 but Kenny did not commit himself to Newcastle until after he had ridden the Byker circuit aboard a brand new Weslake paid for by his dad.

George English's family – his late father, George senior, and mother, Joan, have been a vital cog in the backroom staff at Brough Park for many, many years – are steeped in Newcastle Speedway. George junior is the Diamonds' promoter today but he can recall Kenny Carter's first visit to the north-east venue as if it was yesterday.

He said: "When Kenny arrived at Newcastle in 1978 I was 19. My dad used to run the supporters' club and I was working on the turnstiles and things like that.

"On press day he refused to wear a Newcastle race jacket, simply because he didn't know if he was coming to stay. He wanted to see what the track was like before deciding if he was going to join the team or not.

"He rode the press day in his Pharoah Racing race jacket but he settled down straight away, loved it and was in the team for the opening meeting a few days later.

"We'd heard about him before he joined us. We knew that Halifax had this young kid who was something special and in those days Newcastle were the Second Division track to be at so they were quite prepared to let him come on a year's loan.

"We didn't know quite how good he was until we saw him, but just watching him on that press day you could see he really was something special."

Halifax and Newcastle agreed a one-season loan deal for Kenny to spend his first full season learning his trade in the less demanding waters of the second division before attempting to swim among the big fish. It was agreed that the Brough Park track – at 361 yards, smaller with much tighter turns compared to the very fast and sweeping 400-yard Shay circuit – would benefit Carter in terms of broadening his experience.

Boothroyd recalled: "Ian Thomas and Bryan Larner approached me directly to ask about Kenny and I agreed it would be a good idea for us to loan him to them at Newcastle.

"Apart from the complete contrast between the Newcastle and Halifax tracks, I also considered it would do him no harm racing against lesser riders in the National

League. I was happy for him to double up between Halifax and Newcastle in his first season."

Even so, Boothroyd knew he had a very special talent on his hands. "Kenny has made sensational strides in such a short space of time and has the ability to make the same kind of progress as Michael Lee," he predicted at the time.

Kenny went straight into the team at Newcastle, who staged their home meetings on Monday nights, but he would also continue to gain experience by riding in second half events at Halifax after the main senior match had finished. His public debut followed the Dukes' 44-34 Gulf British League win against Bristol where his initial opponents in the 'Shay Stampede' included Alan Stansfield, Paul Wood and Peter Wilson. No-one paid much attention to the diminutive, slightly built brown-haired, blue-eyed lad programmed as 'Ken' Carter. Most of the opening night crowd had come to see the team's new signings – Eric Broadbelt (from Poole) and Mitch Graham (from Hull).

The following Monday (March 20), Kenny made his official debut for Newcastle, scoring four (paid six) points in their 45-33 home challenge match win over Ellesmere Port. Kenny's debut ride came in the reserves' race, heat 2, which started embarrassingly for him when he parted company with his bike at the tapes.

But, showing a steely determination that would characterise his career, he re-mounted, chased after the other three and got his reward by collecting a third place bonus point behind his partner, Chris Prime, and race winner, Louis Carr, after Gunners' Pete Ellams had packed up.

Afterwards, the teenage duo of Carter and Prime, who was just starting his second season of racing and his first in the main team, earned rave reviews for their opening night efforts in the black-and-white jacket.

In the third meeting of the season at Brough Park, the Diamonds' opening home league match against Mildenhall on April 3, the 18-year-old Prime crashed into the fence in his first ride and later died as a result of his injuries. No other riders were involved in the fatal incident – in fact, the leading Fen Tigers pair of Mel Taylor and Neil Leeks had already crossed the line ahead of third placed Carter when young Prime, some 40 yards behind, lost control and crashed.

After the worst possible news had been confirmed from Newcastle Royal Victoria Infirmary, a devastated Ian Thomas broke the tragic news of the Hull-based youngster's death to a stunned Geordie crowd and immediately cancelled the second half as a mark of respect.

George English said: "To this day I have still not met anyone who saw the accident. Chris was so far at the back that nobody saw it. We were all watching Kenny.

"I was standing up in the bar and the crash happened more or less in my line of vision but we were all looking the other way."

The thrilling 40-38 NL win – and Carter's match-winning two points contribution – had been rendered totally meaningless as, for the second time in a matter of just four months, Kenny's embryonic speedway career had been touched by human tragedy.

His mum, his little brother, Stuart Shirley . . . Chris Prime. Was he jinxed? Damned from the start?

If Kenny had been in any way affected by the death of his fellow reserve and opening race partner, he certainly did not let it interrupt his progress. When newcomers Barrow visited on April 17, he recorded his first race win in his opening ride, on his way to a best yet seven points in the 52-26 win. In fact, by following home Blackadder in his two other outings, Carter registered his first-ever (paid) maximum.

At Halifax five days later, he was given an unexpected senior debut for the Dukes against

Getting to know the tighter turns at Newcastle.

Swindon, as a late replacement for the Australian, Mick McKeon, who went down with gastro-enteritis. Kenny claimed third place in heat 2 ahead of David Ashby but behind his partner Mitch Graham and the other Robins rider, Geoff Bouchard. He finished in front of Ashby again in heat 4, but this time he also picked up a bonus point behind Eric Broadbelt, with Swindon's Bob Kilby winning the race.

Mick McKeon, who had made his name on the massive Claremont track in Perth, Western Australia before joining Halifax for his first taste of BL racing in 1977, recalls how Kenny had been shaking up the moto-cross scene riding with – and beating - the local senior men when he was only 15. So when word spread that the young Carter was going to try his hand at the shale sport, McKeon, not a star rider by any means in the Dukes outfit, was concerned for his own position.

It seemed that concern was more than justified as soon as the Aussie watched the young local whizzkid take his first few laps around The Shay. Never one to mince his words, McKeon admitted that he was initially as jealous as hell of what he describes as "the young whirlwind who didn't look a day over thirteen."

He just could not believe how good the young tyke was. More importantly, he could not understand how anyone so young could have so much talent or self-confidence.

Speaking from his Perth home in 2007, McKeon said: "Even at 16, Kenny was afraid of nobody and laughed at reputations. Very soon my jealousy disappeared and I found myself watching and learning from the kid. Yes, he could be a bit too up-front, but during the time we rode together we became firm friends. I don't mind saying, I really loved the little fella."

McKeon laughs at claims Carter never team-rode. "He was incredible at making space for his partner and didn't demand the best gate all the time, as some have suggested. I well remember him dropping back to let me cross the line first and complete my own maximum at The Shay."

With Diamonds' co-promoter Bryan Larner after getting filled in at Mildenhall.

Carter grew in stature with Newcastle and Ian Thomas said: "His form as a kid coming into his first season was blooming brilliant and it was obvious he was going to be a star. But he wasn't a superstar then – Tom Owen was the top dog at that time and he didn't see Kenny as a threat. Kenny got on well with everybody at Newcastle.

"I had no problems whatsoever with any other riders in the team over anything to do with Kenny and he never caused me any problems himself. I never had any trouble either with him or his father, who I had very few dealings with anyway."

Newcastle and Thomas might not have had a problem with Mal Carter but the Wimbledon's rising star Colin Richardson did when Kenny received another senior league call-up by Halifax to race against the famous Dons at their plush south London venue. Richardson could have given young Kenny lessons in arrogance and the home rider was clearly incensed by the visiting youngster's hard riding style when he kicked out at him at the end of a particularly hostile race.

Richardson's act of petulance did not go unnoticed back in the Wimbledon pits. As soon as he rode back to his position and prepared to dismount, beneath the main glass-fronted grandstand, he soon found an irate Mal Carter confronting him. Even before Richardson had time to remove his crash helmet and goggles and prepare to defend himself, Carter senior knocked him spark out with one hammer blow from his meaty fist. Mal would not stand by and see anybody try to take advantage or inflict harm to his lad, as more than a few would come to realise in the years ahead.

In the bedlam that ensued, Wimbledon manager Cyril Maidment threatened to have Kenny's dad arrested, and it took the calming influence of Reg Fearman – the southern-based co-director of the Halifax promotion and deputising for Boothroyd as team manager on the night – to restore order.

Even after peace broke out, an unhappy Mal went looking for a couple of loud-mouthed Wimbledon fans who had been yelling abuse at him from the terraces following his unprovoked attack on Colin Richardson. Mal was accompanied on this trip by Jimmy Ross, another Halifax hard case who also ran a used car garage and petrol filling station in the town. Jimmy, who says he has mellowed a lot since those days, did not want to get involved in any trouble but felt he had to support Kenny's dad when two Wimbledon fans threatened to set about him. He recalled: "We went looking for the two Wimbledon fans who had been having a go at Mal up in the grandstand bar after the meeting, but we never found them.

"I think the general view that Kenneth was someone not to be messed with stemmed from what happened with his father at Wimbledon that night. Word seemed to go around speedway that Kenneth always had a couple of 'minders' with him, but it was really not the case."

Mal would usually drive his 17-year-old son to Newcastle's home meetings in that first season, Kenny also invited along another good mate of his from Halifax, Phil Hollingworth. Phil, who was three years older than Kenny, would compete in the second half and they hit it off as friends straight away.

Phil, who still lives in Halifax, recalled their early days together:

"I started riding locally at the same time as Kenny. He asked me to go up to Newcastle with him. I'd been riding in second halves at The Shay and Sheffield but when Kenny got in the main team at Newcastle, he got me a second half ride there. One night when Boston were the visitors, I was on the outside of Tom Owen, Gary Guglielmi and somebody else and ended up going through the fence on the first bend!

"Kenny's first mechanic was Gary Docherty, who was probably his best mate from school. But Gary didn't know much about bikes, but then neither did Kenny. His

Setting the pace at Brough Park with Ellesmere Port's John Williams giving chase.

Kenny drives hard under Barrow's Chris Roynon, with Kevin MacDonald and Chris Bevan behind.

first set of bikes were painted red, white and blue and looked a mess, really shocking, although they went all right.

"We used to thrash around the Halifax track together after meetings, bumping into each other and having a laugh like mates do.

"As Kenny progressed up the ladder, he needed someone who could do more than just dope and oil for him, so that's when Richard Pickering came on the scene. I'd signed for Sheffield at that time but didn't get to ride in the main team and then spat my dummy out after a row with promoter John Dews.

"I gave up trying to make it in speedway and became a joiner instead, although later on I worked part-time for Kenny as his back up mechanic when Richard couldn't make it to meetings, and later I worked for Kenny on a full-time basis. I was never that fantastic with engines but I knew the rudiments of the job. I used to knock around with Kenny and go to meetings with him before I actually started working for him."

With Newcastle still clinging to the hope that they could catch NL pacesetters Canterbury and Eastbourne, Kenny came good in the closing stages of the Diamonds' match at Berwick to beat the home top scorer, Mike Fullerton, and notch seven vital points in a 41-37 away win. Even more satisfying for the Geordie fans, Carter's nine (paid 10) points at Cleveland Park ensured a 41-36 victory to keep the championship challenge going a little longer.

Newcastle's fading hopes of regaining the title they had last won in 1976 virtually disintegrated in a 45-33 defeat at Rye House – the only team to complete a league double over the Diamonds – on Sunday, October 1. Those two defeats by the Rockets proved too costly in their quest to catch Canterbury, although it could hardly have been closer at the finish. Newcastle matched Canterbury's 60 points tally, lost one match fewer than the Kent club, won one less, but paid the price for drawing two matches (at Crayford and Oxford, where Carter scored a creditable seven points each time). Canterbury snatched the title thanks to their superior race points difference of just 42 over 38 matches – 479 points compared to the Diamonds' 437. It was the tightest finish in NL history.

Newcastle actually beat Canterbury both home and away (by 42-36 each time) fairly early in the campaign but those home defeats by Rye House and Oxford proved crucial in the final analysis.

Despite having just missed out on a league winners' medal, Kenny had to be highly satisfied with his first season in speedway and an excellent average of 7.58 a match from 41 league and cup appearances. He had risen rapidly from rookie reserve to talented heat leader with Newcastle in the space of a few months and it was largely thanks to his emergence that the Diamonds went so close to winning the title. In a season in which they suffered a succession of injuries, Carter was the only Newcastle rider not to be sidelined by a knock at one stage or another – a remarkable fact given his lack of experience and the catalogue of serious injuries he would suffer in the future.

George English spoke for many Diamonds' supporters who consider themselves fortunate to have seen the start of Kenny Carter's career.

English said: "He was tremendous on and off the track. He was such a lively character – fantastic to be around.

"He integrated straight away with everyone else and desperately wanted the team to win and he was up for as many supporters' club functions as he could make. He really mixed in well with everybody.

"In those days we used to take two, three or four buses to away matches and he had this idiotic trend of passing them all on the way, then immediately turn off at the next junction and wait for them to go past, and then do it again. He was absolutely crackers!

"He was very lively and on one occasion there was a function in the Cornerhouse, which is a pub in Newcastle, and he decided to pour a pint over his co-promoter Bryan Larner's head, which didn't go down too well!

"Why did he do it? He was just Kenny being Kenny and having a laugh. I think someone had said he wouldn't dare do it, and that was a good enough reason. Never dare a fool!

"What impressed everybody about Kenny on the track that year was that he'd come in very much as a raw talent but produced an excellent season and sustained it all the way through.

"You would expect a youngster to have highs and lows but he didn't – he was excellent all the way through and we would have loved to have kept him for another year."

Unfortunately for the Geordies, they reluctantly had to accept that Carter would return to Halifax and remain full-time with them in the senior league the following season. Eric Boothroyd was never in any doubt that his young find would be stepping up into the big-time in 1979 and he moved swiftly to quash rumours that Carter might be persuaded to spend a second season on loan at Newcastle.

Many 17-year-olds would have opted to spend at least one more season in the

A taste of the big time . . . a proud Kenny in the colours of Halifax Dukes, 1978. Left to right: Dennis Gavros, Mick McKeon, Klaus Lohmann, Ian Cartwright (on bike), Tormod Langli, Mike Lohmann, Graham Plant and Kenny.

second tier, rattling up easy wins and basking in the relative glory of being big fish in a small pond. But Carter was fiercely competitive and ultra ambitious. He wanted to prove himself among the elite – against the likes of then World Champion Ole Olsen, Ivan Mauger, Peter Collins and Michael Lee.

Lee had emerged as PC's main rival for the title of England No.1 and it was only a matter of time before he would become World Champion. Like Kenny, he had a very ambitious, strong-willed father behind him.

Soon after the end of the 1978 season, Mal Carter was among guests who attended Eric and Bonnie Boothroyd's silver wedding bash at the Laithe Restaurant in Halifax. It was on this night that he announced he would not be continuing his sponsorship of Eric Broadbelt and Chris Pusey for the following year and, instead, all his speedway efforts would go in to supporting his son's push for glory. "I didn't realise there was so much aggro in speedway," said a disillusioned Mal.

For his part, Kenny knew he had a long way to go before he could challenge Collins and Lee and become the best in England, let alone the world, but patience was never one of his virtues. His season with Newcastle had provided an excellent foundation but he wasn't hanging around in Division Two. He had his sights set firmly on the big time and no-one was surprised when he reverted to his home-town club.

As Halifax legend Eric Boocock, by then the manager at Belle Vue, observed at the time: "Kenny is the best British rider at his age."

Eric Boothroyd said: "He's following the example set by England's leading riders, Collins and Lee, by moving up before becoming the dominant force among the Nationals.

"I believe he will go just as far in the sport as those two."

Chapter 3

'I'LL WIN IT FOR MUM'

KENNY and his friend, Jimmy Ross, had only been gone from the house at Brickfield Lane for little more than half-an-hour on the evening of Tuesday, September 18, 1979. They had gone to look at a possible new car for Kenny but the 18-year-old did not take a fancy to this particular motor he viewed, so they returned home for tea.

At around half-past six Jimmy walked into the kitchen to put the kettle on while Kenny went upstairs just to check that his mother, Christine, was all right and to see if she needed him to fetch anything for her. Kenny was always running around after his bedridden mum who had been left paralysed from the neck down in the car crash that killed her youngest son, Malcolm, nine years earlier.

But Kenny was in for the most horrendous shock and found his mum slumped, limp and lifeless, on the bed. He shouted to Jimmy to 'come quickly'. While Kenny at first thought she might still be alive, Jimmy knew differently – there was no sign of a pulse.

They phoned for an ambulance but by the time the medics arrived at the house in Holmfield, Christine had already stopped breathing.

Three months short of her 36th birthday, the poor woman had decided that she could take the pain, discomfort and sheer hopelessness of her tragic situation no more. She took her own life by swallowing the pain–killing tablets that, by a twist of cruel fate, Kenny had gone to the local pharmacy to collect for her.

Christine Margaret Wood died of barbiturate poisoning –'killed herself while the balance of her mind was disturbed', it stated on her death certificate – and was pronounced dead on arrival at the Royal Halifax Infirmary.

Naturally, Kenny was utterly devastated.

Jimmy got in his car and drove as fast as he could to find Kenny's 15-year-old brother, Alan, who was enjoying a night out with friends at the local school disco. Jimmy said: "Alan could immediately tell from the look on my face that something was seriously wrong and you could have heard the scream he let out from the other side of Halifax."

Although deeply saddened at this latest tragedy to blight his young life, Kenny's reaction showed little outward sign of emotion. He went quiet, whereas Alan was clearly distraught and showed his distress at the loss of their mother far more visibly.

In the days and weeks that followed Kenny would turn to Jimmy occasionally and express his guilt that he had not always immediately done as his mother had asked. Described as being of average build, pretty and with slightly fair hair, Christine was more reliant on her children than most mothers because she was unable to do most things for herself.

Jimmy said that she would sometimes call out: 'Kenneth' – the name she always called her eldest son by. 'Can you come in and do this for me?' She used to moan at him at times – but then she had plenty to moan about, didn't she?

"After his mum died, Kenny would tell me how guilty he felt when he remembered those times when he either ignored her calls or was too busy playing football outside the house and he cursed her because she had interrupted his game. He'd get a bid fed up with her calling him and say: 'Oh, give it a rest, mother'.

"After she died he felt very bad about it but, of course, he had only reacted in the same way many other young children would have done to a demanding mother who needed constant help from those around her."

He might have been irritated when his mother called out to him to run yet another errand as the head of the house in the absence of his father, but no-one could ever doubt the genuine love Kenny had for Christine. Her death would haunt him for the rest of his life – he never got over it.

Carter rarely showed any emotion but Jimmy Ross revealed: "Pam told me later that Kenny went to bed after his mum died and never stopped crying all night."

No-one, apart from possibly Eric Boothroyd, in speedway circles realised the full devastation and heartbreak the new, young Halifax Dukes whizzkid had endured for one so young. Most other 18-year-olds in his shoes would have asked for time out to grieve, especially as there were only about seven weeks of the 1978 season left.

So what did Kenny Carter do?

He went out in his very next meeting, on September 22, just FOUR DAYS after his mum had committed suicide, and scored a brilliant, unstoppable 12-point maximum in the home win against Yorkshire rivals Sheffield – only the third full house he achieved in his second season in speedway. He led the Dukes to a 47-31 Gulf British League victory, winning all of his four races from the back, including the only two defeats Tigers' No.1 Reg Wilson suffered all night.

The *Speedway Star's* match reporter, Peter Hale, could not possibly have known the background to this stunning performance by the lad they were already calling the 'Golden Boy' of Halifax Speedway. With a sentence that must rate as one of the understatements of the century, he unwittingly wrote: "Kenny Carter's maximum came the hard way, as he had to pass Sheffield riders in all his races."

Kenny had always been obsessively determined to be 'a winner' but the loss of his mother in such sad circumstances elevated his burning desire for success to a whole new stratosphere. Driven relentlessly beyond belief, Carter vowed to the world: "I'm going to be World Champion for my mum".

Given the tragedies and dramas going on in his private life away from the glare of the public eye, it was astonishing that Kenny should have enjoyed such a successful first full season of top flight racing. It was obvious to everyone who saw him race that England had a new major star in the making.

By mid-April, Carter had progressed from the No.6 reserve berth to the main body of the Dukes' team and did well partnering new crowd favourite Tormod Langli.

Leading Les Collins at Belle Vue in 1979. Kenny always looked forward to his visits to Hyde Road.

They combined for a 5-1 in their first outing in the home win over Belle Vue but Kenny still wasn't ready to take points off the Aces' big two of Peter Collins and Chris Morton.

Kenny was less than happy, too, the following week at Wolverhampton, where he fell after being the victim of some hard riding by Hans Nielsen, Denmark's World Cup-winning hero from the previous year. He realised quickly that the British League was so much more faster, ruthless and physically demanding compared to the National League.

His confidence and stature growing rapidly by the day, Carter went to Wolverhampton and won the World Championship-Berger Grand Prix round with 14 points. Despite a surprise defeat by Poole's Peter Prinsloo, he produced the ride of the night to take home No.1 Jimmy McMillan from the back, and seal victory a point clear of the experienced Scot.

He had blasted his way to the British semi-finals – featuring the top 32 Brits – and made it to the final of the domestic Grand Prix at Wimbledon, where there was no pits aggro this time. Suddenly, people beyond Halifax were sitting up and taking more and more notice of the 18-year-old with the cherubic face who had a job to even convince traffic cops he was old enough to drive.

Kenny gravitated more and more to Jimmy Ross, who became a close friend and confidant. Rather than ask his dad to drive him around or accompany him to speedway, Kenny would badger Jimmy to drive him to away meetings. "The usual routine would be to call in at the newsagents in Halifax, where Kenny would pick up a copy of the evening paper, buy himself a bottle of Lucozade and two Lion bars and then he'd say: 'Let's go, Jimbo!'

"On the way home back up the M1, he liked to stop for something to eat at the Leicester Forest services and play the pinball machine.

"There were times when I was too busy running the garage to have the time to take him to away meetings but he'd insist. He'd sit in my office nagging me for hours before I'd finally give in and then I'd have to phone my wife to say I was off

Animal-lover Kenny leading Billie, the buffalo, on his dad's farm at Barkisland.

somewhere with Kenny to another meeting."

Jimmy recognised the winning mentality in Kenny from an early age. "He had to win at everything," he said. "At lunch times we would often go the Braziliana coffee bar in town, where his favourite meal was meat and potato pie. Or we'd go to The Millers pub, which was run by the father of Halifax junior Kenny Young, and usually he'd eat sausage, eggs and chips.

"If we went to the pub, he would want to play pool or darts and we had to keep playing until he won. It would start out as a best-of-three contest but if I won, it became the best-of-five. In the end, the lunch break was lasting more than two hours – and I had a garage to run, so I'd end up letting him win just to get back to work! 'See, told you I'd beat yer!' he'd say as we left the pub."

Eric Boothroyd was another who witnessed the relentless competitive nature of Kenny at first hand. "He would come round to our house to play snooker with me on my half-size table. He'd phone up and say: 'I'll just come round to thrash yer!' He beat me a few times at first but, one day, I managed to beat him and he couldn't wait to return the next day to try and put one over on me again, to get his revenge if you like. But after I beat him for a second time he stopped coming round to play!

"He had to win at everything he did."

After winning the Wolverhampton individual World Championship round, Carter gave his first interview to *Speedway Star*. He told reporter Bob Radford: "For some time during the winter I wanted to have another season at Newcastle. I loved the fans at Brough Park – they were real. And I still prefer the smaller tracks. Not that I mind the big ones – I beat Chris Morton at Belle Vue, and I enjoy them – but not as much.

"Now when I look back I realise I'd have been a fool to have stopped down in the National League."

Radford – who described Carter as having a voice like "the little lad on the Bird's Eye beefburgers TV advert – questioned the teenager about his relationship with his father, who towered over him like a giant shadow. Kenny said: "He sponsors me with two machines, that's it. Anyone who thinks I have an easy life is daft. Dad is hard with me – always has been, and probably just as well."

Recalling that first ever public interview today, Radford said: "While not afraid to speak up, and be sure he was heard Kenny was still a youngster in a dressing room and pits full of older men.

"As his confidence grew, of course he got louder. I think the clue to his relationship with his father was alluded to in his quote about not having had it easy. I suspected, but could never know, that he father had been, or maybe still even was, a physical bully and undoubtedly a financial one."

Carter's outstanding display in the qualifier at Wolverhampton earned him a return invite to the Black Country track the following month to contest their annual Strongbow Olympique handicap event. He managed to win a couple of races but suffered a fall and exclusion when he came up against Bruce Penhall. Not only did the ankle injury he suffered at Wolves fail to keep him out of the following night's home match against Birmingham, but Carter – now partnering Mike Lohmann in the opening heat – led the way to a 44-34 victory with his first 12-point maximum for the club. A last lap bike failure for Brummies' Ray Wilson in heat 10 allowed him through to record his maiden max and he completed a memorable night by winning his second half heat and final.

Afterwards, Kenny revealed the most unlikely of mascots. He loved animals and while he was recording his first-ever Halifax maximum against the Brummies, he had his pet lamb, Bimbo, tucked up safely in a wooden box on the back seat of his car, which was parked on the banking overlooking the first bend at The Shay!

As word of Carter's fondness for animals spread, Dave Lanning reported in his *Speedway Star* diary column that as well as the lamb, Kenny also kept a buffalo, a pea hen and acquired from Peru a long-necked llama. The family did, however, lose its eight-foot long python -– apparently they switched the television off on a cold night and forgot the snake's thermostatically-heated cage was on the same circuit!

Carter's first tilt at the World Championship ended inauspiciously at Leicester, where he scored just two points in the British semi-final won by Peter Collins. Still, considering he had only started riding speedway competitively 13 months earlier, Carter had done well to progress that far in the competition. He was still learning the ropes – his time would come.

He soon put the disappointment behind him, however, top-scoring with nine points in Dukes' 10-point defeat at Eastbourne, one of the tightest and smallest tracks in the country and a place where Halifax inevitably struggled. The eternal problem for the vast majority of Halifax riders through the years was their failure to adapt themselves and their machinery from what was required at their big home track to the more subtle requirements of smaller venues, where more deft throttle control, more brain and less brawn were essential ingredients of success.

But Carter's outstanding performances in his first full BL season at small circuits like Wolverhampton and Eastbourne showed that he did have the class and adaptability to excel on tracks of all shapes and sizes.

Jimmy Ross said: "I recall Klaus Lohmann going up to Kenny in the pits at

Although not a fan of watching speedway, Kenny looks interested here with Mike and Klaus Lohmann, Tormod Langli and Dennis Gavros.

Eastbourne and asking him for advice on the best way to get round the tight and tricky corners. He was hoping for something inspirational but Kenny just told him: 'Screw it on and turn left!' It all came too easily to Kenny and he couldn't understand why his team-mates had problems adjusting to away tracks."

Despite Carter's inexperience, he received a call up for what would have been an historic first full England cap in the opening Test against world champions Denmark, scheduled for The Shay on June 18. He would have become the youngest England international at senior level. Alas, the four-match series was scrapped after the BSPA failed to reach a pay agreement with their counterparts at the Danish Motor Union, who were demanding an additional £1,000 fee per match on top of the basic £6 per start and £8 per point deal that already been agreed between the two governing bodies.

The late cancellation of the series against Denmark meant Carter had to wait another 19 days before making his official Test debut, against Australasia at Swindon. By then, he was two days older than Peter Collins had been when he rode against Scotland in 1972.

But Carter was not to be denied his share of the limelight in that summer of '79. On Saturday, June 23 he lived up to his pre-meeting red-hot favourite tag to win the Junior Championship of Great Britain with 12 points after a three-man run-off at Canterbury. The 'junior' tag tended to devalue an annual event that boasted some illustrious past winners in Peter Collins (1973) and Michael Lee (1976), who used their victory at the Kent track as a springboard to much bigger things.

Kenny had to earn his first major title the hard way, however, after being excluded

Kenny and Nigel Flatman after the British Junior Championship – they became good friends on trips to Australia.

from his second ride for his part in a first bend melee that saw Mark Courtney bite the Kingsmead dirt. But four straight victories, including back-to-back wins in heats 16 and 17, kept him in contention. Ipswich's Nigel Flatman – on loan to Peterborough – could have snatched the title if he hadn't finished second to Boston's Dennis Mallett in heat 18. And when Mildenhall star Mel Taylor eased home in heat 19 ahead of passive team-mate Richard Knight, it called for an extra race to decide the title.

With the pressure on, Carter roared away first from the outside grid to comfortably win from Flatman – who would become a good friend to him in the near future – and Taylor.

With impressive figures in excess of eight points a match, Carter had climbed to heat leader status by July and after returning from a trip to Poland with the England under-23 party, he marked his elevation in the Dukes' rankings by claiming the scalp of Ipswich's recent signing, 1974 World Champion Anders Michanek, in the return league clash at Foxhall Heath.

Then, on July 27, came his delayed first senior international appearance – against Australasia in the second Durex Test at Swindon. As one of England's reserves, Kenny had to bide his time in the Blunsdon pits until heat 12, when he received the call from team manager John Berry to replace the out of touch John Davis. And to show he was not overawed by the occasion, he led home newly-crowned British Champion Peter Collins for a home 5-1 against Aussie pair Billy Sanders and John Boulger. His only other ride, in heat 14, saw him finish third behind Larry Ross and Phil Crump, with the struggling Collins left trailing.

Leading Peter Collins and Billy Sanders on his senior Test debut against Australasia at Swindon, July 1979.

To the speedway world at large, Kenny Carter was still the cocky, fresh-faced kid who loved to race at every opportunity. What separated him from many of his contemporaries is that he wanted to win the relatively meaningless second half races at Halifax as much as he did a vital World Championship qualifier – and that burning hunger for success never left him. In fact, at the end of the season, Cockhill Motors presented him with a cheque for £100 as the highest scoring rider in second halves at The Shay.

As the sport was about to enter a new decade, well informed observers sounded the warning bells that problems lay ahead. Actually, Stevie Wonder could have seen the writing on the wall for many tracks whose most profitable days were behind them. In a climate of high interest rates and with the cost of petrol having quadrupled in the previous 10 years, fans were not travelling the distances they once did and they complained that there were too many 'filler' meetings padded around the official Gulf British League and KO Cup fixtures.

There was still in-fighting among promoters who were faced with rising VAT charges and having to pay their riders more. Admission prices in the senior league were creeping towards the £2 mark. The riders, in turn, were forking out £25 for a new tyre. Costs were escalating but the entertainment value was not. On the contrary, faster bikes on slicker tracks produced less overtaking – a gripe that is still all too common today.

The fans always got their full value for money when Carter was on track, though, and the worrying economic climate would not have concerned him. Carter was the best of the 1979 BL newcomers, ahead of Cradley Heath's Phil Collins, and veteran scribe Eric Linden summed up his outstanding first season in *Speedway Star*: "Carter came into the league like a rocket, with less respect for reputations than a berserk baboon would have for Women's Rights, and tore the league apart. We didn't expect another 'Michael Lee' so quickly. They generally only shoot up once every five years or so."

Kenny Carter had to grow up faster than any other lad his age. The death of his mother had given him more determination than ever to make it all the way to the top.

Next stop Australia.

Chapter 4

WHEELER-DEALER

KENNY began the 1980s a long distance from home – 12,000 miles away in Perth, Western Australia. He was joined on his first trip Down Under by Nigel Flatman, the Peterborough No.1 he had pipped to the British Under-21 Championship the previous summer. In fact, by then Carter and Flatman had become good friends, having ridden together as a pair in the Nigel Wasley Memorial meeting that brought the curtain down on the previous British season at Cradley Heath in early November.

That freezing night in the Black Country seemed another world away from warm and sunny Perth, home to the massive 620-yard Claremont track. It made The Shay seem so small in comparison and racing there each week for a couple of months would not only keep Carter in peak fitness, it broadened his horizons. The scale of the tracks in Australia were in stark contrast to the tiny, 118-yard, glazed concrete bowl Kenny had ridden on during the first-ever indoor speedway event to be staged at the Wembley Arena a month earlier.

Not that he had it too easy in Perth. Top of the bill at Claremont in the first couple of weeks of 1980 was reigning World Champion Ivan Mauger, who won the CIG Solo International meeting on January 4 with a faultless 15-point maximum – three ahead of Flatman. Carter finished on 10 points, the same as his Halifax team-mate Mick McKeon, although he did push Mauger all the way, to within 0.2 of Michael Lee's track record.

Carter and Flatman's friendship brought them both success on the track in that 1979-80 Aussie season when they combined to win the Castrol International Pairs title, ahead of a quality field that included Bruce Penhall, Bobby Schwartz, Ole Olsen and Hans Nielsen. Flatman, who emigrated to Perth in 1991 and now runs a successful stretch limousine business in the city, still cherishes the picture he has of him and Kenny holding their trophies after what was for Nigel his biggest claim to fame in a speedway career of unfulfilled promise with Peterborough and Ipswich.

Speaking in 2007 from his home in Perth, Flatman said: "Kenny and me came out here to Perth two or three years on the trot. We just clicked and became good friends. I thought he was great. We stayed with different people – I stayed with Paul Johnson, the flag marshal who worked at Ipswich and Swindon, and Kenny lodged with former rider Robbie Cox and then Bill Cato, the ex-speedcar driver.

"The Claremont crowd loved us – they called us the 'Terrible Twins' – but I don't think we took it too seriously. It was more like a holiday for us both.

"We'd go to the beach almost every day at Rottnest Island, a 45-minute boat trip from Perth. We went there to swim and scuba dive."

Flatman, with his bleached blond hair and brightly coloured leathers, was one of the more flamboyant riders during his racing days in Britain. He was not a complete show off, though!

Nigel explained: "Kenny and me also visited the nudist beach at Swanbourne but we were so frightened to show our wares that we just covered ourselves up and lay face-down in the sand!

"We'd drive around in a Ute and go to drive-through cinemas. We also liked to go to parties and chase the chicks. There were a few wild parties, lots of great laughs but I guess I'd better not say anymore!

"Kenny obviously wasn't into drugs but he liked a drink. He wasn't a heavy drinker, just a beer to wind down, or he'd stick to soft drinks.

"Once Kenny tried to take an engine back with him from here to England but he was stopped by customs at Singapore airport, where it was confiscated because it was way over the luggage weight allowance. He wasn't happy about leaving it there, he was going off his face about it. Come to think of it now, that engine might still be sitting somewhere in Singapore airport awaiting collection!"

After racing at promoter Con Migro's Claremont raceway on Friday nights, Carter and Flatman would routinely travel around 130 miles to Western Australia's No.2 speedway venue, the 585-yard Bunbury circuit, the next day. They would spend time on the beach and then race in the evening.

As well as delighting the Perth crowds with his exploits on two wheels, Carter also showed his all round motorsport skills by successfully driving the Offenhausen speedcar of Bill Cato, a local hero.

When Kenny went out to ride in Perth as a 'resident international' thanks to his friendship with Mick McKeon, he found the easy going, free-wheeling Aussie, just a second string rider with Halifax, an entirely different proposition on his own home track. McKeon was known as the King of Claremont and was virtually unbeatable there.

Part of the difference between the Mick McKeon in Perth and the Mick McKeon in Halifax was the influence of his brother, Graham. Not only was he an expert engine tuner, but also a good mentor.

In subsequent years, Kenny and his young family stayed at Graham McKeon's house and the mechanical wizard recalls how he had an effect on the popular Brit.

In their early Claremont meetings McKeon blew the Englishman away, after which Graham offered to help Kenny with his engine. Finally the young Englishman agreed and Graham did very little other than adjust some of the settings and clearances to help cope with the excessive size and speed of the track. He also suggested the fastest lines for Kenny to ride. It seems strange in this day and age for the brother of one rider to help another, but such was the camaraderie of the time.

From then on the racing between Mick McKeon and Kenny Carter around Claremont was as close as it gets, and Carter actually broke the track record.

Graham is quick to point out the actual changes he had made to Carter's motor were marginal. He cheerfully explains half the battle with a speedway rider is to

Making the Aussie connection with Merv Janke (left) and Mick McKeon in 1980.

convince him he is on the best possible equipment.

Kenny rarely asked for, or accepted, help and perhaps found it strange that Graham McKeon should have volunteered it. Graham was offered a full time job as Kenny's mechanic in England by Kenny's father, Mal, but turned it down, although he accepted invitations to spend time in the UK helping Kenny and was also asked to attend the World Pairs Final in Sydney and then the individual World Finals in Los Angeles (1982) and Norden (1983).

Graham explains it as being a mental issue, Kenny wanting somebody around who he felt he could trust to give sound advice and to check the engines. At this time Carter had a full-time mechanic in fellow Yorkshireman Richard Pickering. Graham says Richard was very good at doing the basics and a hard worker, but by no means a mechanic in the accepted sense.

Carter started the new British League season on the same double-overhead camshaft Weslake engine that had carried him to great success in Australia. Mounted on two new Comet frames, with the double tube design that did not suit many riders, it was a measure of his growing stature in the sport that team manager Dennis Gavros elevated Carter to number three in the riding order, which made him the senior rider in his pairings with the Dukes' reserves of Ian Westwell and Paul Sheard.

Carter's flying form at Belle Vue and Hull, where he scored his first maximum of the season, could not escape the attention of Eric Boocock and Ian Thomas, who, as well as being the respective promoters at those two northern tracks, had also just been appointed the new co-team managers of England. "He stood out, he'll be one to watch this year, definitely a lot of potential," noted Thomas after seeing his Vikings beaten 41-37 at The Boulevard, where Carter was promoted to the top of the riding order. He relished wearing the number one race jacket, it meant a lot to him personally, and it was more firm evidence of his meteoric progress.

Carter did not appreciate or have time for anyone who attempted to stand in his way. His relentless pursuit of success, and indignation at any perceived injustice, surfaced for the first time publicly during the marathon 16-lapper meeting at Ipswich in June. The first attempt to stage the race, a great test of skill and endurance, had to be stopped when Kevin Jolly fell on lap 11. It had to be halted again after Peter Prinsloo slid off and Carter appeared to lay his bike down to avoid a collision with the Zimbabwean.

Referee Reg Trott saw it differently, though, and harshly excluded the Halifax star. It didn't end there, however.

Kenny was involved in a heated protest at the starting gate and had to be physically removed from the track by staff before the race could be re-started without him for the third time.

Ipswich promoter John Berry, who has railed against the powers that be plenty of times himself when he felt the victim of injustice, recalled Carter's first notable scrape with authority. He said: "It was one of those annoying times when the ref was correct under the regulations – but Kenny had every reason to feel hard done by."

In fact, Poole's Zimbabwean Peter Prinsloo admitted afterwards that Kenny had not been to blame for his spill.

Berry continued: "He staged a demo on the track. He wouldn't allow the racing to continue – and the crowd loved it. Half were booing him and the other half cheering. It was pure theatre, and I would have been happy to let things run their course, except that it had started raining and I needed to get the meeting over with. It might also have occurred to me that there was perhaps a little more mileage to be gained…

"I had my track security man pick him up, like a spoiled child having a tantrum, and carry him off, all arms, legs and mouth. Fabulous . . . we were guaranteed a front-page picture in tomorrow's local paper!

"I prevailed upon the ref to take no action, and later Kenny, showered, dressed and still full of disappointment at not winning the meeting, took the trouble to come into the speedway office in order to seek out the security man and apologise for a swinging fist that had landed during the melee.

"That was one of the problems with Kenny. Everyone wanted to beat him – and tried just that little bit more to do so."

The drama of the 16-lapper at Foxhall Heath was by no means the last time Carter was convinced the whole world was against him. But rather than dismiss him as a disruptive troublemaker, British promoters were suddenly putting the brash, young kid at the top of their booking lists when it came to assembling a top field for individual meetings. Carter was the new big box office attraction. Yes, he wanted to be paid as much as he thought he was worth but he was not greedy. He had a tendency to ask what Peter Collins was getting to appear – and then ask for the same money as him.

"If PC is getting £36 per point at Belle Vue, then I should be paid as much as him," Kenny would complain.

Berry admits: "He was always the first rider I booked in to open meetings. He was never too greedy and as far as I am aware, never failed to turn up for a booking.

"Nobody received booking fees for the Golden Sovereign we staged at Ipswich every year. They raced for the sovereigns. Likewise the 16-lapper, where the winner received a new engine. Kenny was still happy to ride, although he wanted a fee for our Star of Anglia meeting when all the biggest names were invited."

A seized Weslake engine had put paid to Carter's 1980 World Championship progress in the British semi-final at Sheffield. Carter had to bide his time before he would become an England No.1 but he was very much on the threshold of international stardom. The 1980 season proved a brilliant one for English speedway in terms of on-track success. Peter Collins and Dave Jessup won the World Pairs title, Mike Lee briefly shrugged off his 'Bad Boy' tag to become the individual World Champion in Gothenburg and the grand slam was complete when England (Collins, Jessup, Lee, Chris Morton and John Davis) avenged their Test series loss to America by winning the World Team Cup Final in Poland.

Carter hadn't been included in the squad for the final, although Boocock and Thomas had previously called him up as reserve for the Inter-Continental Final round of the team event at Vojens. "It was a really big surprise and I'm chuffed," had been Kenny's reaction to being included in the five-man squad for the meeting in Denmark where he was un-used in the team that qualified alongside the USA and at the expense of the hosts and Sweden.

Thomas was highly critical of the hospitality (or rather, lack of) afforded by the Danes to their visitors, who were cramped together in dressing rooms while the Denmark team had a room to themselves. And at the end of the meeting, staged in dreadfully wet conditions, it was left for Thomas and Boocock to present the medals to the winners and runners-up! Thomas also complained that the Danish authorities at Ole Olsen's Vojens track didn't have the courtesy to pay the unused reserve for four starts, which, though not in the rules, was accepted common practice by most other speedway federations. At 1980 pay rates, Thomas reckoned Carter should have received at least £25 as a goodwill gesture.

And £25 then was a lot of money in Kenny' eyes. In fact, an extra 50p in his pocket meant the world to him if he thought he had made a profit on the deal.

He bought and sold his own cars from a young age, and would advertise them for sale in the local paper. 'Buy Kenny Carter's car' the message would say. Kenny's first car was a Mazda 1800 but he progressed to a Fiat and then a Mercedes 220.

Jimmy Ross said: "Kenny was tight-fisted with money. His brother, Alan, would give you a tenner if you really needed it. Kenny might lend you it, but if he did he'd want 12 quid back in return.

"If you made a tenner between you on one kind of deal or another, he'd want £5.50 of the profit – even if the idea had been yours!"

"I never got involved in his financial affairs as far as speedway was concerned but I never heard of him having any problems with the tax office. The only time he asked me for advice is when he received a visit from people querying his National Insurance contributions. But I managed to save Kenny a few bob when I pointed out that he had been out of the country, in Australia, during the weeks when he hadn't paid his NI, so they were happy with that explanation – and Kenny was tickled pink that his bill had been reduced."

Jimmy recalls the trips he made with the entrepreneurial Kenny to the wholesalers at Cheetham Hill Market, Manchester which perfectly illustrated the young man's reputation as a wheeler-dealer of Del Boy proportions.

"We both went there one November and bought loads of cigarette lighters that played the tune, Yellow Rose of Texas. I used to give them away at my garage whenever customers bought at least four gallons of petrol. I had ladies compact mirrors and then there was the time when Smurfs were all the rage.

"Kenny was in his element at the wholesalers and for the next year he couldn't meet anybody without selling them a cigarette lighter that played the Yellow Rose of Texas – that bloody tune drove me mad and I can't bear to hear it now!

"He would sell them to his friends, everybody he knew and complete strangers. When he walked into a chip shop he wouldn't come out before he'd sold one. Even if you didn't smoke, Kenny would pester you so much that you had to buy one from him in the end – just to get rid of him!

"We bought 20 lighters at first and then when we went back to the warehouse the next time, he bought another 200 – he'd worked out that by buying in bulk the unit price came down from, say, 5p to 4p. I can't tell you how much it used to please him when he sold out of his box of 20. 'I've stuffed another 20 away, Jimbo,' he'd boast to me. It was earning him peanuts and he couldn't seem to see that he made more from winning one race at Halifax than he did selling a box of these bloody lighters!

"The next time he came with me to Cheetham Hill it was to buy sets of Christmas fairy lights, which we would buy for, say, £1 each and sell on for £2. I couldn't give them away in my garage, but he would try as hard as he could to shift them all – selling them to Pam's mum, her sisters, the neighbours . . . everybody he came into contact with had to buy one from him. He loved it until he once got left with 10 sets of lights and had to throw them away!

"Kenny wasn't clever, academically, but he was smart and was good at weighing people up quickly.

"He used that ability to good effect in speedway as well. John Davis was one he always thought he could psyche out. He'd say: 'Watch me and Mavis next time we're against each other. I bet if I click my clutch he'll go straight through the tapes – and usually that's exactly what happened. Everyone would refer to John Davis as 'Mavis' behind his back, but Kenny always called him that name to his face.

"Kenny didn't really use psychological ploys to try and beat his opponents – in fact he hardly ever knew who he was riding against in the next race. We were at White City one night and he just slammed the programme over a nail hanging on the wall in the pits. He turned to me just before the first race, as he was putting his helmet on, and said: 'Who've I got in this one, Jimbo?'

"I told him: 'Gordon Kennett'.

Halifax Dukes, 1980. Left to right: Merv Janke, Craig Pendlebury, Ian Cartwright (on bike), Dennis Gavros,
Ian Westwell, Mick McKeon and Kenny.

"Kenny said: 'Who's he?'

"I pointed out to him that he was the home number one and was used to scoring maximums there week in, week out.

"Kenny said: 'Watch this . . .' And he went out and beat him twice that night!

"But he never thought much about the psychology of speedway. The only occasion when it seemed to work for him was when we were at Coventry for, I think, the Brandonapolis. All the top riders were there . . . Olsen, Penhall, PC, Nielsen, Gundersen, Lee . . . everyone who was anyone.

"I said to Kenny, 'did you notice how they all looked over when you walked in with your bikes?' There was always the feeling that whenever Kenny arrived at a track, especially for the big meetings, the atmosphere in the pits went up 20 per cent. And the bigger and better he got, the more noticeable it became.

"He hadn't noticed the riders giving him the eye, so I walked him to the pit gate and said: 'You see that crowd out there, well 3,500 of them have come here tonight just to see you get beaten, so make sure it doesn't happen'. Kenny just smiled and said, 'yeah I will'.

"The thought that all those people disliked or hated him never bothered him at all.

Following the death of his mother the previous September, Kenny took over ownership of 15 Brickfield Road. The house was then valued at £6,500, so Kenny gave half of that amount to his brother, Alan, and kept the house for himself. David Wood, who had looked after and then later married Christine Carter, left after she died and made no claim on the house.

Previously, Kenny and his girlfriend, Pam, spent many intimate moments at a

Ivan Mauger clinched the Northern Riders' Championship at Sheffield in August 1980 . . . and then loaned Kenny his bike so that he could pip Dennis Sigalos to second place.

caravan Kenny owned, which was located within the successful mobile home complex his father and stepmother, Janet, owned at Elland. But once Kenny had his mother's old house to himself, Pam was there much more often. They were in love with each other and in the summer of 1980 they became engaged.

Even so, Kenny confided in Jimmy Ross that on one of his visits to Belle Vue a couple of the Aces riders had teased and ribbed him mercilessly about his love life and other private issues. It was well known in dressing rooms around the country that Kenny was very well endowed and while it was the type of good-natured banter inevitably heard in the showers and changing rooms of male-dominated sports everywhere, and is usually a cause for amusement and bragging rights, Kenny was embarrassed by the unwanted attention he was getting.

He was also unhappy when a couple of rivals suggested to him, while he was getting changed after one meeting, that he could 'do a lot better' than Pam. Kenny knew he would not be marrying Miss World but he had been obsessed with Pam since they were at secondary school together and he had every intention of spending the rest of his life with her.

He turned to Jimmy Ross for reassurance: "What do you think, only they're saying I could do better for myself?"

Jimmy said: "I asked Kenny if he really loved her, as I knew he did anyway, and he said 'yes'. So I told him, 'it doesn't matter what anybody else thinks then, if you know she is the right one for you then go ahead and marry her'.

"Pam was just an ordinary farmer's girl who happened to be in love with a boy who became a speedway star."

Even at 19-years of age, Kenny had a clear vision of what he wanted, on and off the track. With the first of many bold pronouncements to follow, he said: "My aim is first to be England's number one and then go on to be World Champion."

Being based hundreds of miles away from the Weslake factory in Rye, Sussex, did not help him to ensure he always had the best equipment at all times. The big, fast Shay track was also demanding on engines. He was nevertheless grateful for the sponsorship backing he received from Mike Daniels and the Weslake concern. When his engines were flying – he preferred the overhead camshaft motor for the bigger tracks and the pushrod 'Wessie' for smaller circuits – there was no stopping the Halifax number one.

"By and large the Weslake backing is magic," said Carter, before claiming: "I should have been Halifax number one with well over nine points a match, but I've had quite a few engine failures and, believe it or not, three punctures while I've been leading. I've even had a fuel filter cost me a maximum this season."

He had set his sights on winning the Northern Riders' Championship at Sheffield and looked on course to do so until his engine seized as he crossed the finish line while leading his fourth ride. He borrowed team-mate Mick McKeon's bike for his fifth outing but the motor lacked the power he had been used to and he had to admit second best to the old warhorse, Ivan Mauger, who triumphed with an impeccable 15 points.

Then, in his determination to at least finish second overall in the meeting, Carter borrowed another machine for the run-off against Dennis Sigalos and Peter Collins after all three had completed their programmed five rides on 13 points. So who did he turn to for help? Who better than the champion himself!

On a bike loaned to him by Mauger, Carter duly won the three-man run-off and so began a relationship between the sorcerer and his apprentice.

Kenny said after Sheffield: "Whatever some people may think and say about Mauger, I have always found him a great sportsman and to be very helpful."

It is not known if Sigalos – Mauger's team-mate at Hull – would have appreciated the Vikings skipper helping a Halifax rider to beat him, but Ivan did not worry about offending a team-mate – he was already making future plans.

Carter respected Mauger – like him, a very single-minded, fiercely driven individual who knew what he wanted and, nine times out of 10, he earned it. Kenny also appreciated the fact that, for all his raw talent and his ability to go faster than most, he still had a lot to learn.

As if to prove the point, Mauger – who had turned 40 and just failed to reach the World Final for the 15th successive season – beat Carter again when they met in the final heat of an inter-league four team tournament at Newcastle the following week. Kenny made it his business to learn as much as he could from Ivan Mauger over the next couple of years.

Where did it all go wrong? A ponderous Kenny (left) after his bizarre mix-up cost him the BLRC title.
Right: Receiving last minute adjustments from mechanic Richard Pickering.

He was also looking forward to renewing his developing battle with Bruce Penhall. When Halifax and Cradley Heath met home and away at the start of October, Kenny won their heat one clash on each occasion. With 13 (from five rides) in the Dukes' 40-38 BL defeat at Dudley Wood and a flawless 15 in the return rain-affected match the next day, he was also the most outstanding performer in both matches.

Carter got the better of Penhall again in the season's last big annual event, the classic British League Riders' Championship at Belle Vue. His reward for overhauling Ian Cartwright at the top of the Halifax averages was a coveted place in the BLRC, where he started the meeting in style by winning the first race from Jan Andersson and new World Champion Michael Lee. Victory over Penhall by a tyre's width in heat 7 put him among the leading contenders but then he became the victim of a bizarre mix-up that smashed his hopes of becoming the youngest winner in the event's 16-year history.

With a third straight win in his grasp – Carter had surged from last to first, past Scott Autrey, Malcolm Simmons and defending champion John Louis – he suddenly slowed, appearing to suffer yet another engine failure. It was not until he had finished the race, pointless, that Carter explained he had deliberately slowed at the start of the last lap because he thought he had seen a chequered flag waved on the home straight. But no-one else saw it – it was inexplicable.

Chapter 5

FACING THE PAIN

IT was the worst crash they had witnessed at The Shay for many years. At one point, Bonnie Boothroyd, devoted wife of Halifax boss Eric, feared that the Dukes' number one rider had been killed.

The night of Saturday, April 4 began ominously for Carter when he suffered an engine failure while leading Birmingham's new star signing Hans Nielsen in the first race.

But it was about to get a whole lot worse for him when the respective number ones clashed again in heat 4. This time Kenny's partner, Craig Pendlebury, led from the gate, followed by Nielsen, but Carter was pushing him hard in a determined effort to join his Halifax team-mate at the front. At the end of the first lap, just as he was closing in on Nielsen, he ran into the Dane's back wheel, pitching himself, face-first, into the fence along the home straight.

It looked serious and immediate concerns for Carter's health were not eased when the St John Ambulance staff went to his aid. An ambulance was brought onto the track and, accompanied by the track doctor, rushed him to hospital.

Eric Boothroyd recalled: "Kenny flew up into the air and came down on his face. He broke his jaw in eight places and when the doctor got to him, Kenny's helmet was full of blood.

"The doc – not our normal one, but a stand-in from the football club – came into the office where Bonnie worked during the meeting and, when she asked how Kenny was, he just gave a desperate shake of his head and said: 'It's bad'.

"From the look on the doctor's face, Bonnie thought Kenny must be dead!"

Phil Hollingworth recalls that his friend never, ever forgot or forgave Hans Nielsen for his part in that spectacular high speed crash that could have ended Carter's life, never mind his racing career. He said: "He totally detested Hans Nielsen with a vengeance for what he did to him that night."

Hollingworth says that Kenny was convinced Nielsen deliberately knocked off the throttle going into the turn, leaving the following Halifax No.1 unable to avoid hitting his back wheel.

"When I went to visit Kenny in hospital, I walked straight past him because I didn't even recognise him. His jaw was so swollen, he looked like Desperate Dan.

"Kenny told me: 'The bastard knew what 'e were doing, 'e just rolled it off'. It was obvious Kenny was going to pass him but he hit him straight up the back end and went over the top into the fence.

"I'd stand up in a court of law and say it was deliberate on Nielsen's part.

"He didn't get on with Bruce Penhall, but he didn't dislike him – he just wanted to beat him out on the track. But he totally hated Nielsen. If he'd had a chance to 'do'

Nielsen after that, he would have killed him. But Hans never got involved in anything like that with Kenny again – he knew what would come his way."

I recently telephoned Nielsen in Denmark to get his take on the crash and the four times World Champion, only the second former rider after Ivan Mauger to become a millionaire from his illustrious speedway career, said he had no recollection of it. Hans, who is now semi-retired with a large property portfolio and a nine hole golf course in the grounds of his luxury farmhouse, was just about to tee off for a leisurely round with his wife, Suzanne, when I called him on his mobile. "I can't honestly say that I remember the crash – it was a very long time ago," he said, sounding genuinely puzzled.

"I remember some fuss about Kenny Carter but nothing specific. I certainly never thought he hated me.

"I can tell you for sure, though, that I would never have deliberately 'rolled off' the throttle in the situation you've described. Yes, I would have taken Kenny wide, as you do, " he admitted, "but not shut off the throttle in that way."

The first bad smash of Carter's career came after the year had started so brightly for him. He had returned to Perth for a second spell under the Australian sun and a few weeks after leading a Great Britain team to victory against Rest of the World in the second indoor event at Wembley Arena, where he also picked up the individual King of the Concrete trophy, Carter was again displaying his versatility on the wide, open spaces of the Claremont track where he renewed his battles with friends Mick McKeon, Nigel Flatman and Ivan Mauger.

When the new British season got underway in mid-March after another very wet start, Carter claimed the first individual success of '81 – the Second City Trophy at Birmingham, where he finished a point clear of . . . Hans Nielsen.

Off the track, his father had organised sponsorship of a new Mazda van, although the colourfully signwritten vehicle left no-one in any doubt who was paying for it. Emblazoned on the side were the words 'Malcolm Carter – Pharoah Racing'. With a renewed deal for partial sponsorship from Weslake – Bruce Penhall and Dave Jessup were their two fully-backed works riders for 1981 – Carter was well set for continued progress towards the elite.

Before returning to the saddle, Carter raised eyebrows by testing his fitness on the 120-miles per hour straights at the Cadwell Park road-racing circuit. An exasperated Eric Boothroyd was not amused, having warned his prized asset before about taking unnecessary risks in previous road-racing jaunts at Oulton Park and Croft.

Carter, though, was simply irrepressible. A mere 35 days had passed since his jaw had been shattered in eight places and yet he not only made an astonishing comeback at home against Cradley Heath on May 9, he also beat Bruce Penhall on his way to a stunning 17 points from six rides. The 42-54 defeat paled into insignificance for the Halifax fans and management, who were just relieved to welcome back their main man.

Carter celebrated his return after a five-week break by beating Penhall in the opening race and though he dropped his only point to the American when they met next, in heat 4, Boothroyd was full of praise for his heroic efforts in very difficult track conditions. He said: "People have talked about how brave Lester Piggott was in coming back so quickly after his starting stalls accident when he had part of his ear sliced off. But Kenny's fractured jaw was much worse and his comeback was more courageous than Piggott's.

"He practiced on the Friday as if he had never been away. It took a lot of guts for the lad to go out and score 17 points in his comeback match against Cradley in the worst conditions we have had at The Shay for a long time, with mist and drizzle coming on top of heavy rain earlier."

Five days later, and with one wire still in place due to the damage to his teeth, Carter sailed through the British semi-final with 13 points – just one behind winner Les Collins. It didn't matter that he was beaten by Chris Morton in a run-off for second place overall. All that counted at Sheffield was that his world title dream was alive again.

He was also delighted to finally be able to eat solids again after having his jaw wired together for the previous five weeks, which he spent on a diet of soup and milk consumed via a straw.

Given the seriousness of his facial injuries, it was a brilliant performance by Carter in the British Final at Coventry, where he only lost out to Steve Bastable in a three-man run-off for the title that also included his Halifax team-mate John Louis. Kenny could not feel too disappointed at second place. He had confounded medical opinion and other doubters simply by riding in the meeting – to go so close to winning his first British Final at the age of 20 was a fine achievement in itself, as ITV commentator Dave Lanning and pits interviewer Gary Newbon were quick to point out. Talking for the first time in front of national television cameras, Kenny's boyish face appeared chubbier than usual as a result of the operations and wiring of his jaw. "You don't notice the pain when you're racing," he smiled, and to prove it his thrilling heat 10 victory to pass Halifax team-mates Ian Cartwright and John Louis had provided one of the best races of the night.

Louis, who had seen the Dews Trophy snatched from his grasp when Carter powered past him, had nothing but respect for the team-mate who was half his age.

Louis faced a long weekly drive from his Ipswich home to West Yorkshire and he was grateful to Carter for the mutual friendship and respect they shared during his two seasons with the Dukes.

Now promoter at Ipswich, Louis recalled: "Kenny didn't mix with the rest of the team at all, he was a loner, but I got on very well with him.

"I liked to arrive in Halifax two hours before the meeting, to give myself time to relax, and I'd often go straight to

After snatching victory in the Dews Trophy at Halifax from John Louis (left). Ian Cartwright was third.

Kenny's place to see him before a home meeting.

"He impressed me with his attention to detail. People thought he was just a mad-head but he was very clever in the way he kept detailed records of every track he ever rode at. I kept a little book in which I jotted notes about tyre and gear ratios at different tracks, but he had it all written out neatly in charts. He recorded every engine set-up he ever used at a track.

"He had a super way of conducting his business that surprised me," said Louis.

The summer of '81 marked Carter's return to the international scene – and England boss Len Silver welcomed him into his fold with open arms. Silver, who was appointed England team manager for the second time (he quit at the end of 1976) after both Eric Boocock and Ian Thomas had resigned the previous winter, never underestimated Carter's value to England. Admitting that he was somewhat surprised to see his Lions extract revenge over the USA with a 4-1 series win while Carter was still sidelined in late April and early May, a result that was all the more creditable in view of Peter Collins' retirement from British speedway, he told Speedway Star's Peter Oakes: "I considered Kenny's injury a very serious blow – I didn't really think I could afford to have that sort of bad luck."

"I looked upon Kenny as the new Peter Collins," said Silver..

"The last time I was England manager PC had more or less arrived on the international scene and used to do magic things for me.

"I was hoping Kenny would fill that role – when the chips were down I could put a lot of pressure on his shoulders and because he was not frightened of anybody and because he was young, hc would do it for me like PC did."

Silver said how very impressed he had been by the courage Carter had shown in making a rapid return from his bad jaw break. "I am always impressed by a man who comes back from very serious injury and starts scoring straight away. That, to me, is the stamp of a champion.

"Anyone who can come back riding a very fast track – Halifax can be a bit frightening — and score 17 points has got to be something a little bit special. There's a man with absolutely the right character.

"I think Kenny has the kind of mental make-up that will always make him a winner."

Jimmy Ross said that Kenny had no interest in picking up a second place medal, as he did in the British Final. "He used to say, 'who the f*** remembers second?' He saw the silver medal as a waste of metal," said Ross. "Kenny would rather finish fifth than second."

And there was nothing Kenny Carter hated more than to finish second to Bruce Penhall. The Overseas Final round of the World Championship was scheduled for London's White City and his simmering rivalry with the American was about to get dirty.

Chapter 6

CARTER v PENHALL – Part 1

THERE had been scores of bitter on-track rivalries and feuds before but it's doubtful if any have been more intense or sustained than those bruising battles between Kenny Carter and Bruce Penhall that were the talk of speedway in the early 80s and are still remembered today by those who witnessed them.

Kenny disliked most of the American riders and never made any attempt to disguise his feelings. He didn't care much for their bubbly, happy-clappy approach to racing, their showing off and generally boisterous demeanour.

What few realised in 1981 is that the ill feeling between Carter and Penhall had in fact first surfaced three years earlier – Kenny's first season and Bruce's debut year in the British League for Cradley Heath.

Carter recalled: "When I first started in speedway in 1978 I rode at No. 8 for Halifax against Cradley and I trapped on Bruce when he was unbeaten. He tried to take me on the inside and fell off on to the grass. He said I chopped him and ever since then there has been a bit of rivalry between us."

The first major incident involving Carter and Penhall to reach the attention of a much larger audience became the biggest talking point of the Overseas Final – a new round of the World Championship at White City in West London on July 12, 1981.

Heat 18 brought him together with Penhall, who was two points behind meeting leader Dave Jessup and still had hopes of winning the qualifying round. The title of Overseas Champion meant relatively little in the grand scheme of things – see how many past winners you can name – but victory was good for confidence and sent out a message to rivals that you were a serious contender for the Big One – at Wembley in September.

Carter had six points going into his last ride, two less than Chris Morton. Scott Autrey was there just to make up the numbers with only three points.

Starting from the outside grid, Carter seemed agitated by the presence of top photographer Mike Patrick in close proximity, just the other side of the wire safety fence. He waved his right arm in the direction of the *Speedway Star* snapper, shouting to him to back off, just before the tapes rose. This distraction probably contributed to Carter's untidy start, as he clattered dangerously into the side of Morton who found himself sandwiched between his England rival and Autrey, leaving Penhall a clear run to the first bend from the inside position.

Penhall knew Carter would not give up that easily, although even he was startled by the express train as it came hurtling past him on the back straight. They brushed elbows as Carter surged into the lead going into the third bend but rather than steam

Kenny is already down as Bruce Penhall (left) slides into the fence. You can't miss Kenny's van in the background.

on, Kenny tried to close the door on Penhall, locking up slightly as he tried to cover Penhall's anticipated challenge from the inside.

Their bikes hooked up, became almost welded together and, inevitably, Carter and Penhall both headed for the fence around the pits turn. It was not a frightening-looking crash – more a slow motion collapse that sent the kickboards at the foot of the fence flying – and no-one was hurt. In fact, after seeing Penhall lay his machine down to avoid injury, Carter quickly jumped to his feet and twice angrily pointed an accusing finger in Penhall's direction before shaking his head in disgust as he walked back to his corner of the pits.

To Carter's fans, it looked as if Penhall had caused the incident – the rider on the inside usually cops the blame in these instances – and referee Kjell Kristensen, from Denmark, agreed with them.

Penhall, incensed at his exclusion from the rerun and the end of his Overseas title bid, was adamant that the collision was the fault of his opponent. "There was nothing I could do," he told ITV's Gary Newbon who interviewed him seconds after the decision was announced.

"We came into the corner and Kenny dropped it on me. Our bikes locked together and the referee's excluded me for foul and dangerous riding, but I think it's unfair. There was absolutely nothing I could do. Nothing."

If the Danish official had ruled against Carter, his World Championship dream would have ended there and then. But this time luck, and the referee, was on his side.

Not surprisingly, Carter saw it differently to Penhall. After comfortably collecting the two points he needed – behind Morton, who re-passed him to cap a brilliant tactical ride - to guarantee qualification among the top 10 riders, he gave Newbon his version of events. As he watched a replay of the dramatic incident on a small TV monitor in the pits, Kenny revealed his outspoken nature to the world with a full and frank assessment that had Newbon drooling and Penhall and his fans up in

Explaining to ITV's Gary Newbon how Penhall "had to be the superstar".

arms: He said: "Bruce was a bit selfish there. If he rode normal he would probably have beaten me, or I might have past him, but he tried to be a superstar and put me through fence, didn't he?"

Carter simply ignored Newbon's point, raised a few minutes earlier by Penhall, questioning whether he had deliberately 'dropped' it on the American as they raced into the bend at the end of the first lap. Turning to the TV for evidence of his innocence, he continued: "I'm coming down straight…I got passed him and I'm going across…I'm in front…look, now watch Bruce there, right…he hits me, takes me out and keeps me out…he doesn't turn. Look! He . . . he just rode me out all the way, two-wheeling me…it's on television to prove it.

"I don't have to lie. If he'd have just turned hard he would have passed me, but he had to knock me off, didn't he?"

While Penhall was perhaps justified in protesting his innocence in what was not an entirely straightforward call for the referee, who could easily have excluded either rider, there was a more personal edge to Carter's comments. By referring to Penhall in such sarcastic, derogatory tones, Kenny was revealing his growing resentment of the colourful Californian and all that he believed he represented.

Penhall was clearly unhappy with the nature of Carter's comments when he subsequently told the press: "Carter called me a show-off and made other accusations, and there was no need for it. He tried to make a fool of me, and that just isn't on." Cradley Heath team boss Peter Adams supported his skipper and described Carter's outburst as "childish."

Some time after the dust had settled on the incident, Penhall admitted that the referee was right to have excluded him. Having watched several replays of the incident, the Cradley and USA captain said: "What happened wasn't deliberate. I'm not a dirty rider.

"I owe Kenny an apology for the spill, and I think he owes me one for what he said on the radio mike and on TV. Our bikes locked together, and anyway there are enough accidents without deliberately riding someone into the fence."

The ultra consistent Dave Jessup was deservedly crowned the first Overseas Champion but no-one was saying or thinking much about the neat, steady but unspectacular England skipper.

This will forever be remembered as Carter versus Penhall – Part One.

Their controversial White City spat was great news for speedway, though, and it made entertaining viewing too. Suddenly, Carter was no longer just the King of Yorkshire, the Cock o' the North. He was now big on a national basis thanks to ITV. Back in 1981, the sport was still enjoying much broader coverage on terrestrial television, reaching millions who tuned in to the popular Saturday afternoon *World of Sport* programme on the number one commercial channel – the speedway normally going on air before Dickie Davies introduced wrestling from Wolverhampton!

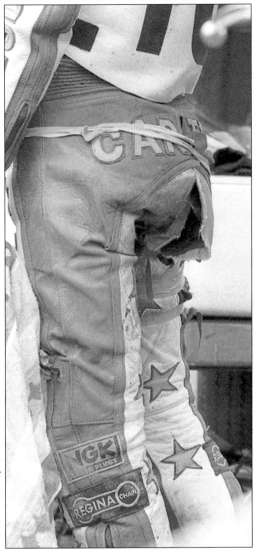

After his White City tangle with Penhall, Kenny was annoyed that his unscheduled fall had ripped a hole in his brand new leathers.

Thanks to ITV, who did much to turn Peter Collins into a national hero in the 70s, British speedway had a new star to take on the best the rest of the world could offer. Unlike the more universally popular PC, fans from all over Britain would view Kenny Carter in black or white. They either loved him or hated him. And he claimed not to care either way.

This first much publicised row between Penhall and Carter briefly lit up a dreary, grey corner of West London but it ignited a personal feud that would continue to unravel until Penhall's retirement from the sport.

Chapter 7

MAUGER TURNING POINT

TWO weeks after the explosive Overseas Final at White City the World Championship trail moved on to Denmark, where Kenny comfortably qualified in fourth place with 11 points at the Inter-Continental round – the last stepping stone to the World Final itself.

The meeting at Vojens, the purpose-built track part owned by Ole Olsen, was again badly affected by rain – as just about every meeting held there seemed to be. Not that the rain and the 90-minute delay it caused troubled Bruce Penhall, who dominated with an unstoppable 15-point maximum. Five starts, five wins, he dealt with the tricky conditions better than everyone but for the five who missed out there was only misery. They say today's Grands Prix are high pressure occasions but the pre-GP days of World Championship qualifiers were often much more tense. One mistake, one bike failure or fall, a tapes exclusion, or a dodgy refereeing decision and a year's planning and hard work could vanish down the drain.

This time, though, there were no fireworks between Penhall and Carter when they met in a tame heat 11 which saw Michael Lee and Ivan Mauger relegated to the minor placings. Lee managed to get himself together to secure a place among the 11 qualifiers for Wembley but with only four points to his name, the 41-year-old Mauger announced afterwards that he had finally called time on the speedway World Championship he had dominated like no other since Barry Briggs and Ove Fundin in the first half of the 60s.

Mauger was in the final weeks of his fourth, and final, season with Hull Vikings and though he wished to continue racing on the continental long-track scene where he remained a force, he also needed to devote time to organise the 1982 World Final in Los Angeles with fellow Kiwi Briggs and the American promoter, Harry Oxley.

But, of course, Mauger still had a lot to offer speedway in one way or another. After an amazing 14 individual speedway World Final appearances and a record six victories to his name, he knew better than anyone what it took to scale speedway's greatest heights. His experience would prove invaluable to any aspiring young rider and it made perfect sense when Mauger agreed to become Carter's manager and mentor in the build up to the '81 World Final.

Carter and Mauger were kindred spirits. Both possessed an unshakeable belief in themselves that few of their peers could ever match on a consistent basis. They were both fiercely driven, highly self-motivated individuals able to focus on their goals without distractions. They craved success but didn't mind upsetting people on the way to achieving it. They weren't in speedway to win popularity contests; they were in it to win it.

Carter recognised Mauger as a man who could help him fulfil his ultimate dream, add a few more coats of polish to his rough edges. In Carter, Mauger saw a lot of himself and, no doubt, the chance to bask in some reflected glory beyond his own racing days.

Mauger said: "I was up at Newcastle one night, doing something for Ian Thomas, when I first met Kenny Carter. I immediately took to him. We got on well together."

It seemed a match made in Heaven, and for a while it was, with the maestro handling the youngster's contracts and sponsorships, as well as looking after his bikes.

Ivan arranged for a private practice session for Carter at Belle Vue, where he had attained legendary status following his move to the Aces from Newcastle in 1969. In the weeks leading up to the team and individual World Finals of 1981, Kenny also experimented with different engines – including a Jawa – and carburettors. Further after-meeting practices were organised for his benefit at Halifax. Kenny asked John Louis, the veteran whose opinion he trusted, to try out his Weslake, to gauge his view on whether it was powerful enough.

Mauger has always prided himself on fine attention to detail. Another similarity between him and Carter was a shared knowledge of their true worth in pound notes. It rankled with Kenny for some considerable time that he was paid much less than his fellow number ones and international rivals, and at one time he even threatened to walk away from speedway and join his younger brother Alan on the road-racing circuit, where sponsors were more readily attainable.

Soon after becoming Carter's manager, Ivan made it his business to open talks with Eric Boothroyd about improved terms for the following season.

Another early piece of advice Mauger gave Carter was to bury the hatchet with Bruce Penhall. Ivan, the Svengali figure, reasoned at the time: "You cannot have a feud with a guy you are racing against, especially in the World Championship. I told Kenny that Bruce was just trying to win the race at White City, not to knock him off, and he accepts that now."

As the highest placed Englishman at the Inter-Continental Final at Vojens, Carter earned his first crack at the Golden Helmet, one of the oldest and most traditional competitions in the sport's history. He was nominated as the August challenger for the monthly match-race title sponsored by Motor Cycle News and had little difficulty in beating Gordon Kennett, 2-0, in the decider at neutral Reading after each rider had won their respective best-of-three home legs.

One who did not agree with Carter being given a shot at the Helmet was Cradley Heath boss Peter Adams, who complained that the in-form Penhall should have been nominated by the BSPA instead. With perhaps a hint of paranoia that his club was being punished for their success, the deep-thinking Adams argued: "I was of the opinion that a rider had to win something before getting a nomination. This is what happened with Steve Bastable after he won the British Final.

"But Carter has won nothing while Penhall has just won the Inter-Continental Final and is top of the averages – but he still cannot get the nod."

Adams' provocative words only fanned the flames of burning desire within Carter, who won the Star of Anglia event at Ipswich and then all of his five rides to become

Racing flat out with King's Lynn's Michael Lee – the rider Kenny succeeded as England No.1.

Northern Riders' Champion at Sheffield – the first Halifax man to win the NRC since Eric Boocock in 1970. Carter, Billy Sanders and Chris Morton all went into the last heat unbeaten but after Hull's Australian star Sanders led from the start, Carter burst through on the inside to clinch his maximum in front of the Yorkshire TV cameras.

Afterwards, he revealed that he had used Mauger's bike to win the vital last heat at Owlerton, after team-mate Louis had also offered his machine to Carter. This was 24 hours after Halifax had drawn 39-39 with Hull at The Boulevard, and Kenny and Ivan had practiced together after the meeting. Carter, who won all of his five rides in the match, was so impressed with Mauger's Weslake that he declared he would be using the same engine in the World Final.

No-one could question all the good Mauger brought to Hull, guiding them to within a whisker of the league title in 1979, and not only in terms of his scoring power but also his professionalism and team spirit. But he was caught up in an unfortunate conflict of interests when the Vikings visited The Shay and were beaten, 46-32, in the BL. Although Carter had beaten Kennett 2-1 in the first leg of the MCN Golden Helmet, the third race was necessary after the Weslake Kenny had borrowed from Mauger 'dropped' a piston and caused him to stop.

It meant Kenny reverted to his own bike to score 11 out of a possible 12 points in the league match that followed . . . while Mauger, who contributed an uncharacteristically low seven, had to make do with his spare machine!

Carter was the top Brit again at Wimbledon, but had to settle for the silver medal when Hans Nielsen romped to a perfect 15 to win the annual Embassy Internationale, rearranged after being rained-off on its traditional spring Bank Holiday slot and worth £1,250 to the classy Dane.

Carter's 12-point performance at Plough Lane did at least give England some encouragement ahead of the World Team Cup Final in Germany a week later. Lions boss Len Silver initially named the four English riders who had reached the individual World Final – Carter, Jessup, Lee and Morton, with Kennett replacing Bastable at reserve – but had to bring in John Davis for Lee, whose personal problems were piling up fast. On top of a number of lame excuses for missing a series of King's Lynn matches and meetings at other tracks, the defending World Champion had just landed himself in court for a drugs conviction – possessing a pipe containing a small amount of cannabis. There was growing concern for his future in the sport. Officially, Lee missed the World Cup final through 'illness' but his private life was beginning to unravel faster than his factory-sponsored Jawas.

It wasn't the first time that the spectre of drugs in speedway had raised its ugly head. George Barclay, secretary of the Speedway Riders' Association, had previously drawn his concerns to the attention of the authorities and urged the Speedway Control Board to act in response to growing rumours that illegal substances were becoming the staple diet of several riders. The Americans, in particular, were being blamed, behind the scenes, for introducing a drugs culture to speedway in Britain in the early 80s. Although in fairness to Lee, he has since accepted full responsibility for bringing about his own self-destruction.

Without the wayward Lee, England were never in the hunt on the long, flat and wide Olching track that was very much to Denmark's liking. Nielsen continued where he left off in the Internationale, top scoring as the Danes sizzled in the sun to win by eight points from England, who had to scrap to take second place ahead of the Germans, with the Soviet Union beaten out of sight. Chris Morton revelled in the dusty conditions to score 11 hard-earned points, while the ever-battling Carter won two races for his nine points, including an absorbing win from the back against local Bavarian hero Georg Hack in heat 4. But it was not enough.

In the inquest that followed England's second World Cup final defeat in Germany in four years, Speedway Star editor Philip Rising called on the BSPA – or SCB – to appoint an independent team manager, or, ideally, a pair in the mould of the successful Thomas-Boocock partnership of 1980. He also criticised the amateur approach to the meeting that saw the England riders left to organise their own transportation of bikes and equipment. And as if to underline the chaos that surrounded the weekend, Carter even missed the original flight out of London and arrived later than his team-mates.

As well as running the show at Hackney and Rye House, Len Silver had other very important business to attend to which were an understandable distraction from his England duties. He had again been charged with the enormous responsibility of building the Wembley World Final track.

A week before the biggest night of the year, Carter signalled his intent by turning up at Belle Vue with five engines and three bikes . . . and then going out to beat home favourite Chris Morton FOUR TIMES in the match and second half.

He was looking forward to Wembley . . .

Chapter 8

WEMBLEY BLOW

PLENTY of speedway riders dreamed of winning the World Championship at Wembley and Kenny Carter was no different. For most it remained no more than a very distant fantasy. For Kenny, being crowned beneath the famous Twin Towers on Saturday, September 5, 1981 was a distinct possibility.

He had visited the national stadium only once previously – to watch the 1978 final, won by Ole Olsen. Now he was back there in north-west London, wearing the No.5 Union Jack body colour and carrying the hopes of many Yorkshire folk and fellow Brits among the 90,000 near capacity crowd. As well as his manager Ivan Mauger, who had won two of his six world titles at the Empire Stadium, Carter would also have his Halifax team boss, Dennis Gavros, for company in the cramped pits at the mouth of the inclined Wembley tunnel.

Carter thought he was as well prepared as anyone could be for the big occasion. To overcome the lack of seating for the riders within the cramped pits area, he even took a fold-up garden chair with him to Wembley, so that he could sit and concentrate comfortably while Mauger and mechanic Richard Pickering got to work between races.

Phil Pratt, the renowned South London-based Weslake engine tuner, was also hovering around Kenny's corner. Carter had been introduced to Pratt by Mauger and it was some recommendation because the former Eastbourne and Wimbledon hopeful had been preparing Ivan's engines since 1977 – and was still tuning them for him when he finally retired from the British League in 1984.

Before Pratt came on the scene in 1981, Kenny's Weslakes had previously been tuned by Essex-based Alex McFadzean, who also did motors for several Hackney and Rye House riders.

"I'd been doing Ivan's and a lot of other riders' engines for many years and when Ivan became Kenny's mentor he introduced me to him. Ivan wasn't impressed with Kenny's previous tuner because he didn't have anything special or better than anybody else. Kenny's engine reliability wasn't good either.

"He first rode an engine I'd prepared for him at Reading and cleaned up. From then on we just had a fabulous relationship."

Pratt confirms Carter had little mechanical knowledge himself. He said: "He was very much like Ove Fundin – he didn't want to know the technical side of engines. He just wanted to know that when he dropped the clutch, he would be faster than everybody else.

"Kenny wasn't a technical guy, not a good mechanic as such, but with everything he had on his plate – promoting himself and chasing sponsorship – even if he'd wanted to get more involved on the mechanical side, he wouldn't have had time for it."

Brighouse-based Richard Pickering was Kenny's main mechanic for most of his career, especially in the early years. Phil Pratt appreciated Pickering's strengths as a loyal and capable spanner man for Kenny. He said: "He was Kenny's right-hand man and a very level-headed, sensible person. He was very, very professional and well organised. Richard always knew where he had to be at any given time – he would have to deliver engines back and forth to me at Teddington – and he would never let you down.

"He was an excellent spanner man, very much a hands-on person and he was dedicated. He worked hard and the good thing about him was that he wasn't a bullshitter.

"I think he and Kenny had a bit of a bust up in the end but there was a time when he would have walked through fire for Kenny."

Pratt relished the chance to be part of the Carter pit crew, along with Mauger and Pickering, at Wembley. "I didn't usually go to World Finals – it can be a bit awkward for tuners, because you have invariably tuned engines for two or three different riders in the meeting and you don't want to be seen too closely associating with one in particular. Ivan had invited me to places like Katowice before but I'd always said 'no.'

"But it had always been my ambition to be in the Wembley pits on World Final night – I'd ridden there myself as a kid in a match for Wimbledon and got paid eight points in place of Ronnie Moore, so when the chance came up in 1981 I took it."

Carter was in typically bullish mood as he prepared for his first big test of nerves on the biggest stage of all. "I'm going there to win. I want to finish top, not second or third," he declared.

Before the meeting Mauger gave his usual rider-by-rider predictions and gave his talented, young understudy a "90 per cent chance" of winning and reckoned that only Bruce Penhall and, to a lesser extent, Dave Jessup – the bookies' two clear-cut favourites – could have genuinely fancied their chances of winning. Mind games? Was it Ivan's way of provoking a positive response from the young man under his wing? Surely Carter, a somewhat generous 14-1 shot for the championship according to Coral, didn't need any motivating on this, by far the biggest night of his blossoming career.

If Mauger made little secret of his belief that 1981 would probably be Penhall's year, he offered Carter strong words of encouragement when he added before the final: "Kenny's a young racer, a tiger, and if he doesn't win it now, he's going to win it in the next two or three years anyway."

But patience and Kenny Carter were words that never co-existed in the same sentence.

The presence in the pits of Mauger, dressed immaculately in white overalls, guaranteed that even more attention would be focused on the 20-year-old Carter. Kenny looked quite pensive on the pre-meeting parade truck, sitting alone on a

Alone with his thoughts under the glare of the Wembley floodlights.

Above: Getting down to business in the cramped Wembley pits with a word from Ivan Mauger, while Gary Newbon looks for his next interview subject in the background.

Far left: Watching the racing with Ivan.

Left: Strategy talks with Dennis Gavros.

Flying start . . . getting ready to charge under Zenon Plech.

single seat between the RAC Range Rover and the trailer it was pulling, away from the other 15 riders who were all standing, but he displayed no nerves once the lengthy preliminary introductions to dignitaries were completed and the bikes began to roar above the klaxons and whistles from the crowd.

Forget Malmo, Gothenburg, Katowice and Wroclaw, where speedway's greatest occasion had been staged before, this was Wembley – the spiritual home of the World Final. And there was nothing that could compare with it. Kenny's blue eyes widened beneath his bright yellow cap supplied by NGK spark plugs and he could not wait to get going.

When Zenon Plech rocketed from the gate in heat four, it took Carter – from gate one – only until the end of the back straight to seize his moment, charging underneath the helpless Pole to claim an unassailable lead over Chris Morton. Three points in the bag.

There was little time to bask in the glory of winning his first-ever ride at Wembley. In heat 5 he made a reasonable start from gate three but could not catch Michael Lee, trying to put his recent troubles behind him in a vain attempt to hang onto his crown.

In heat 10, Carter made a flying start from gate two to force the pace and leave young Dane Tommy Knudsen trailing in his wake. Eight points after three rides left him one behind the undefeated Penhall after all 16 riders had completed three rides apiece.

But something wasn't quite right. With Knudsen breathing down his neck, just two bike lengths behind, Kenny signalled to his team back in the pits that there was a possible problem with his motor.

He told them his bike did not seem to be handling right.

The response to that setback was to wheel out Mauger's bike for Kenny's fourth ride, in heat 15 – the next race after Penhall had taken his unbeaten tally to 12 with a brilliant narrow win over the impressive Knudsen.

His well-founded fears were about to explode before his eyes.

With Dave Jessup moving sharply in to an early lead, disaster struck Carter when the bike he had borrowed from Mauger developed an ignition problem and spluttered to a halt along the home straight on lap two. In those few seconds his dream of winning his first World Final had been well and truly shattered. It was of no consolation to him that on the very next lap, Jessup would also suffer a costly mechanical failure, leaving Danes Erik Gundersen and Ole Olsen to collect easy points.

The break down had cost Carter what looked like two certain points. All he could do at that stage was keep going . . . and pray that Penhall would also run in to trouble when they met in their last ride.

It said much for Carter's incredible spirit and resilience that he did not allow that heartbreaking fourth ride stoppage to affect his desire to finish the night as a winner. But there was a big anti-climactic feel to his heat 20 clash with his old adversary Penhall. With four consecutive wins under his belt, the Californian needed only a point to clinch his first individual world title. It meant he needed only to finish in front of either Larry Ross or Jiri Stancl, who had mustered just four and two points respectively between them in their previous four rides, to be certain of lifting the title.

Much as Bruce always loved the challenge of trying to beating Carter, there was no way he was going to mix it with him this time – not with so much at stake. He could afford to concede the win to Carter and that is exactly what happened.

The tapes rose and while Carter – back on his own engine – trapped sharply from the inside grid, pulling alongside Penhall around the first turn, the American drifted wide and was content to let Kenny race ahead of him unchallenged. The Californian was happy to maintain a safe distance of some 50 yards between them as Kenny took the chequered flag, waved frenetically by the flamboyant Paul Johnson.

It was the only point Penhall dropped but it did not matter in the slightest to him as he showboated on one wheel and 90,000 fans stood to salute the new champion.

Carter was the first to offer a hand of congratulation to the new champion as they slowed on the back straight at the end of the race. An elated Penhall accepted his arch rival's hand before being engulfed by the throng of well-wishers waiting to greet him at the pit gate. Bruce could not have cared less what Carter was thinking beneath his crash helmet that night but he believes now that the outstretched hand was no more than an empty gesture on Kenny's part, a formal and expected gesture rather than a genuine token of sportsmanship.

Knowing the full and tragic circumstances surrounding Carter's death, Penhall now freely admits that he "does not have two good words to say about Kenny Carter". Talking recently about the moments immediately following his first World Championship victory from his home in California. He said: "He came to a slowdown before I did, so I don't think he had any other choice but to offer me his hand. It was a nice gesture. Did he really mean it? I'd say no, zero. "Kenny didn't come over to congratulate me, verbally, in the pits afterwards. Ivan did, but not Kenny," added the double World Champion.

Of course, we will never know how heat 20 would have panned out had the destiny of the 1981 World Championship rested on the outcome. When the World Final draw was first made and it pitched these two big rivals against each other in the final heat of the night, there was a buzz of great anticipation among fans and everybody else heading for Wembley. It was effectively billed as the Carter v Penhall re-match, a chance to settle old scores following their White City fracas a couple of months earlier.

Penhall wasn't racing Carter at Wembley – he was simply keeping out of harm's way and protecting his comfortable two points in second place. But one of the great unanswered questions of World Final history is, how would Kenny and Bruce have handled the enormous pressure if there had been only one point between them going into their last ride, which would have been the case if Carter had not stopped in his fourth ride? Kenny would undoubtedly have fancied his chances from gate one.

While Carter's supporters argue that he was robbed, Penhall and his admirers would point out that to have won the meeting, Kenny would have had to beat the American TWICE – in heat 20 and then also a run-off.

Mauger said: "Kenny was good enough to have won the world title in '81."

But a lot of people tend to forget that Carter and Jessup were not the only two riders who suffered costly mechanical failures. Although little Dane Erik Gundersen profited from Carter's misfortune in heat 15, he was close to tears after his bike had stopped when he was leading his easiest third ride.

However, it has to be said Penhall was simply superb on the night and fully deserved the title. And he won it in considerable style, including two exceptionally breathtaking on-the-line wins over Olsen and Knudsen, who joined him on the rostrum after their run-off to decide the runners-up positions.

But 11 points and fourth place – the highest of the four Englishmen – in his first final, just three-and-half years after his first competitive ride on a speedway bike, was a performance Kenny could be proud of. But as he stated before the final, he did not go to Wembley to finish anywhere other than first.

He was upset at his bike breaking down while very well placed in his fourth ride and left the old Empire Stadium cursing his wretched luck and wondering 'if only'. It certainly cost him a place among the top three and, in all probability, second place, if not the title itself.

Phil Pratt, who tuned the two different Weslake engines Carter rode at Wembley, is still disappointed now about how mechanical problems denied him a rostrum place, if not the title itself. He said: "I couldn't believe it when Ivan offered to lend Kenny his bike and he took it.

"All that happened in his third ride was that the points had closed up on the ignition, which cause it to not work properly. His engine had been popping and banging simply because they hadn't done the points.

"Depending on whether a track was slick or grippy, riders altered the ignition timing of the engine by the points, according to what is required at the time. They would either close them or open them to get either advance or retire ignition.

"I would have prepared Kenny's engine beforehand but Ivan's philosophy always was, 'whatever engine you're going to use for the World Final, you try out first in a

Another point dropped to Michael Lee.

league or open meeting', to avoid those sort of things happening on the most important occasion.

"Obviously, in the course of their general maintenance, they had altered it – but not correctly. It took me about 30 seconds in the pits at Wembley that night to guess what they had done and then to alter the points to how they should have been set up in the first place.

"Kenny was obviously bitterly disappointed and wanted to make it clear to everyone in earshot that it wasn't his fault that he stopped – the bike was the problem. Whereas if that had happened to Ivan he would just have said nothing, got on with it and sorted the problem out later.

"There was a discussion about what went wrong after the meeting, but Kenny didn't blame me for his break down at Wembley."

Carter's performance, typical of his bulldog spirit, had brought him to the attention of a whole new viewing public, for ITV later revealed that more than seven million people had watched their 35-minutes highlights show that went on air an hour after Penhall had been crowned.

No-one would have believed it at the time, but that was the closest Kenny Carter would ever come to winning the World Championship.

Chapter 9

HATS OFF TO HELMET HOLDER

THE fact that Bruce Penhall had become World Champion at the age of 24 only served to intensify the rivalry between him and Kenny Carter, who would rather have seen the Wembley World Final won by anyone other than his most bitter rival.

Penhall's Cradley Heath promoter Peter Adams was keen to promote the rivalry between the two British League stars when his Heathens team were due to face Halifax two weeks after the dust had settled on Wembley . . . so he was most unhappy when Kenny failed to appear for the clash at Dudley Wood, rearranged for a Wednesday night after rain had forced a cancellation the previous Saturday.

The day before the meeting at Cradley, Carter reeled off a five-ride maximum for the Dukes at Leicester. But 24 hours later, instead of renewing his rivalry with Penhall, he was busy opening a garage dealership in his home-town for sponsors Cable Motors. Kenny's explanation was that in the course of the meeting at Leicester he had aggravated ankle and thumb injuries originally sustained the previous week while road-racing with brother Alan. And he produced a doctor's certificate to 'sign him off' for 48 hours' rest.

An indignant Adams complained to the authorities about Carter's uncharacteristic absence and to underline his point he said he would bar Kenny from being offered any future open bookings at Cradley. A dour, deadpan character at the best of times, Adams didn't hold back when he said: "There is no doubting Carter's ability – he is an exceptional rider. But it seems he has some growing up to do. I intend to take this as far as I possibly can. I have nothing against the rider but he mustn't be allowed to get away with this. This kind of behaviour is not on."

Carter was not one to decline any invitation to race anywhere and his argument that he wanted to honour his commitment to attend the garage opening was a valid one. Adams was understandably aggrieved that the Cradley public were denied the opportunity to see a major drawcard but speedway's habitual rearranging of fixtures at the drop of a hat is a problem that has continued to plague the sport for years, and still does today..

Carter, whose medical note was accepted by the BSPA, was completely unperturbed by Adams' verbal attack on him, saying: "I'm not short of extra meetings. If Cradley want to lose spectators, that's up to them."

In fairness to Adams, he knew just how good Carter was. In fact, while resisting one of many calls to take over as England manager, Adams once said: "If England had seven Kenny Carters the job would be easy."

Taking advice from the injured Ivan Mauger during his first BLRC victory at Belle Vue . . . which earned him pride of place on the front cover of Speedway Star for the first time.

Adams' mood lightened when his dominant Heathens were crowned worthy British League champions in the first week of October. For Halifax, as usual, there was nothing to celebrate by way of silverware. The Dukes climbed three places to seventh in the final table but failed to win a single away league fixture.

The season did, however, end on a high note for Carter, who raised his average (including all matches) to 10.17 – the first Halifax rider to burst through the 10-point barrier since Eric Boocock in 1974. Only Bruce Penhall could boast a superior CMA in the BL and Kenny's figures were not helped by his early season injury.

The highlight for Carter in 1981 was winning the British League Riders' Championship at Belle Vue. Back then, the BLRC was still a prestigious meeting and one all the top riders wanted to win – tougher, in terms of the depth of quality of riders who competed in it, than the World Final itself. With every team's top rider in contention, this annual October classic was always an event to whet the appetite of riders and fans alike. The same cannot be said for today's ELRC, which has been consistently undermined by too many rider withdrawals in recent years.

The meeting had lost a lot of his lustre by the mid-80s but it was still a title the top riders wanted when Kenny first got his name on the trophy alongside those of early winners such as Briggs and Mauger. With the Aces' Hyde Road track – arguably the finest racetrack in world speedway – incorporated in the Belle Vue funfair and leisure complex, it provided a great night out before the sport entered its winter hibernation period.

After the bizarre mix up that proved so costly to Kenny in the BLRC of 1980, he made no mistake this time. Guided from the pits by Mauger, who had to hobble around on crutches after breaking his right ankle in the World Longtrack Final, Carter produced a superb performance to win with a blistering maximum, two

Maximum man at the 1981 BLRC, with Chris Morton and Shawn Moran for company on the rostrum.

points clear of home favourite Chris Morton and Sheffield's American Shawn Moran. Kenny flew past Mort on the back straight and victory was all the sweeter for the fact that he clinched the title by heading home Penhall, who scored just eight points, in heat 17.

Carter was on fire, completely demolishing the strongest line-up seen on any British track all season, and it didn't worry him that a section of the Manchester crowd – and not just those wearing green-and-white Cradley colours – were booing him as he collected first prize. Mauger, who never let his universal unpopularity bother him while he reigned supreme, said afterwards: "He listens to everything he is told and then acts on it. He reminds me so much of the young Ole Olsen in the way he always wants to learn."

The next day, Carter not only beat Penhall three times at The Shay, he won them all from the back. Penhall took the first race in their MCN Golden Helmet, second leg clash but Carter won the next two races from the back and then repeated the feat when they met for a fourth time in the opening heat of the Halifax v Cradley Heath league match.

There was no way Carter would allow Penhall to take the Helmet away from him. he was so confident he would retain the title that he did not even bring the headgear to Dudley Wood. Jimmy Ross explained: "We were about five miles down the road on our journey to Cradley when we suddenly remembered that we'd left the Golden Helmet at home. But Kenny said: 'Don't worry about it . . . he ain't having it off me anyway!'"

Afterwards, Kenny was full of praise for the work put in by his engine tuner Phil Pratt and Gordon May of Comet Frames, who made him a new frame for the BLRC and the Helmet match-races. "The new frame gave me extra drive," explained Kenny.

Who needs the Golden Helmet, too, when you've got the BLRC trophies to show off after beating Penhall!

Pratt got to know Carter quite well having worked with him in 1981 and found him to be nothing like his public persona. "He was not the type of aggressive person we'd all heard about at the speedway track. There was no silliness about him. He was a true professional," said Pratt.

He also gained an impression of the volatile relationship between Kenny and Mal Carter.

"I got on OK with his dad," said Phil. "Although his old chap was a bit of a rough diamond, a bit of a car-dealing, ducker and diver, he loved motorcycles. He was very much into his road-racing.

"As a person, I suppose he was a bully, a typical Yorkshireman. He didn't mollycoddle anybody, he told it like it really was. As a southerner, I found that a bit difficult to understand at times but I also did a lot of work for Eric Boocock – another Yorkshireman who told it like it was. If you didn't like it, tough shit!

"Malcolm and Kenny had a typical father-son relationship and there were times when he made his point quite firmly with Kenny. The impression he gave me was that I wouldn't want to rub shoulders with him too much.

"To be honest, I think I only actually met his dad once. Yeah, there were times when Kenny would mention 'my bloody dad this' or 'my bloody dad that' but I've seen other kids who were as good, or nearly as good as Kenny, and their fathers have been there too, pushing them all the way.

"Kenny told me that his dad once brought home a monkey. Because they had nowhere to put it, they took the doors off the wardrobe, put some chicken wire up and kept it in there! That's the type of guy his dad was."

No-one was going to make a monkey out of Kenny Carter, though. With a 2-1 first leg win over a jetlagged Penhall at Cradley already in the can, he ensured he ended the season as the winter holder of the Golden Helmet.

Penhall's World Final win further boosted his appeal and superstar status but Carter had enjoyed a brilliant 1981 too. With Mike Lee's career teetering on the brink of self-destruction, many – including the tabloid *Daily Star*, who signed him up for a regular newspaper column – recognised Carter as England's new big hope.

Even in America they got to hear of Carter's exploits and his well chronicled rivalry with their No.1 rider. As soon as the British season ended, Kenny flew out to the States to compete in a Superbikes challenge event at Carlsbad, California, where his skills as a moto-cross exponent were tested alongside Penhall. Neither speedway rider was able to get the better of the local moto-cross heroes but it was an enjoyable experience.

Kenny flew back from America in time for his biggest match of the year. On Saturday, November 7, he married his childhood sweetheart, Pamela Lund, at St. John's Bradshaw Parish Church, Halifax. Kenny's Best Man duties were shared between his brother, Alan, and Pam's brother, Adrian. Pam's sisters, Heather, Diane and Wendy, were her bridesmaids.

Pam, the second eldest of the Lund sisters, joked that there were no bikes present on the couple's special day and that the only horsepower was provided by the horse and carriage that delivered her and Kenny to their wedding reception at Halifax's

Soaking up the sun in America, where he was invited to attend a motorcycle challenge event.

Warren Club, owned by Bachelors singing star Con Cluskey.

It was an exciting time for the 20-year-old couple. Having taken over ownership of the two-bedroom, 13-year-old property at 15 Brickfield Lane after his mum died, Kenny sold it for £17,500 to Mike and Sue Condon and he and Pam prepared to move into their dream home.

Kenny bought the derelict premises of the Grey Horse Inn, off Perseverance Road, on the hillside above the village of Bradshaw, where Pam's family lived. It was just five miles north-west of Halifax, further up the Keighley Road. The building, registered as a pub from about 1905, had been closed since January 1941.

The couple planned to have the main building renovated into a modern luxury farmhouse, but the work would take until the following summer to complete. Kenny tried unsuccessfully to delay the sale of their Brickfield Lane house, so until their new abode was ready the newly-weds had to sleep in a caravan that stood on what used to be the old pub's car park.

Pam could oversee the building operation every day having recently given up her job as a VDU operator in the data input office of the Provident Finance Group in Hayes Lane, Mixenden, Halifax, where she had worked since 1978.

After their brief honeymoon in Wales the couple were then parted again as Kenny again jetted off to Australia – this time as a member of the Young England tour organised by Nigel Boocock.

While he was enjoying himself Down Under, Pam remained at home in Yorkshire, watching progress on their farmhouse and continuing her new part-time job of delivering 'fizzy pop' to the people of the local farming community. She made her van deliveries on Wednesdays, Fridays and Saturday mornings. When she wasn't out earning a few extra bob for herself, she liked to enjoy a game of squash with a girlfriend she knew from school. An athletic youngster in her school days, Pam was a competitive runner before marrying Kenny.

The vast Claremont circuit in Perth was the venue for the first Test, where Kenny set the pace with a new track record of 61.3 seconds en route to a six-ride, 18-point maximum. John Davis and Andy Grahame produced thrilling overtakes in the last two races to earn Booey's boys a hard-fought draw against an Aussie side spearheaded by Billy Sanders, Glyn Taylor, Phil Crump and Gary Guglielmi. England's tour side was completed by Alan Grahame (Cradley Heath), Kevin Smith (Poole), Phil Collins (Cradley Heath) and his younger brother, Neil Collins, who had just moved from Edinburgh to Leicester in a £15,000 deal.

A week earlier Carter had become the newly-crowned King of Claremont with a 24-point maximum, seeing off nearest rivals Andy Grahame, Phil Collins, Smith and Taylor. As Ivan Mauger had won the title for the third time 12 months previously, he kept the trophy and Carter received a new one.

As well as Perth, the Test series also took in matches at Mildura, Liverpool – where Kenny scored another unbeaten 18 – Newcastle and, early in the new year, Brisbane. Tour organiser Nigel Boocock, the former Coventry and England star, said: "Brother Eric recommended Kenny to me. He was very confident of himself but he wasn't a team man – he led from the front and did very well for the Lions."

Although Kenny was riding as a member of a team as opposed to the individual freelancer he had been on his first trip to Australia a year earlier, none of the Lions thought he appreciated the difference.

Booey said: "In Sydney Kenny kept the garage door of my workshop closed while he was in there. He didn't help his team-mates, nor did he expect any from them.

"He didn't want to share his secrets," added Boocock.

Alan Grahame was very critical of Carter's self-absorbed approach to the England tour of 1981-82. He said: "I remember one incident, which not many people know about.

"We had two meetings in Brisbane on consecutive Saturdays, so we all booked into a hotel and stayed there all week.

"The promoter, Bill Goode, got in touch with us and suggested that, because we were there all week, he could put a meeting on just for us on the Wednesday. He said it would give us some extra wages and help us with our hotel bills.

"The only thing was that we'd have to ride for less money but, we were riding there on the Saturday before and the Saturday after, so we thought it would be a good opportunity – after all we weren't doing anything else.

"We had a vote on it but Kenny, very craftily, didn't vote. The rest of us thought everyone was in agreement but, come the day of the meeting, Kenny went to see the promoter and said he wanted more money.

"We told him that we thought we were all agreed – we'd had a vote. But he told us

The black sheep among the England tourists. Standing, left to right: Neil Collins, Alan Grahame, Nigel Boocock, Phil Collins and Kenny. Front: Andy Grahame, Kevin Smith and John Davis.

he hadn't voted. We asked him why he didn't say anything and he said: 'Well, I'm saying it now'.

"I don't know what went on, and we'll probably never know, but Kenny rode in the meeting, so one would presume that he got his deal.

"We all got to know about this so, on the night we were all anti-Kenny Carter. Why was he getting more money than us?

"Prior to the meeting there were a couple of riders who were struggling for money and the rest of us weren't. so we decided to pool all our earnings from the meeting and split it equally between us. Except Kenny, who didn't want anything to do with it.

"The meeting took the form of heats, semi-finals and a final. In the final was John Davis – who was in our syndicate – Kenny Carter – who wasn't – John Titman and another Australian rider who I can't remember.

"Kenny broke the tapes! He was up in the referee's box arguing his case, so Phil Collins and I ran out onto the track, grabbed his bike and pushed it into the pits!

"We wanted the referee to know that we knew Kenny had broken the tapes and that he deserved to be excluded. The referee did exclude him and, to make it worse for him, John Davis won the race.

"There was a prize of something like $1,000 for the winner, so that money went into the syndicate which, when it was shared out, meant we all got more money than Kenny!

"To me that was justice done. That was the sort of person he was. I admired him 110 per cent as a rider but, as a person, I had no time for him at all," said Grahame.

Chapter 10

QUESTION OF MONEY

IT spoke volumes for Kenny Carter's standing in Yorkshire sporting circles that he won Pennine Radio's Sports Personality of the Year poll for 1981. In January of the following year the local commercial radio station, based in Bradford but with listeners in Halifax and Huddersfield, announced that Dukes' golden boy had won a phone-in vote ahead of more well known names from mainstream sports like football, cricket and rugby.

He gained more fan support than former England centre-half Roy McFarland, who guided Bradford City FC into the promotion stakes as player-manager; Yorkshire and England opening batsman Geoffrey Boycott; and Peter Fox, coach of rugby league first division champions Bradford Northern.

When Kenny received news of his award in Australia, it gave him another lift as the start of the new European season approached. Whatever Andy Grahame and his other England team-mates thought of him, the single-minded Carter continued to rattle up lots of points. On January 9, he recorded his third 18-point maximum of the series to lead the tourists to a 62-46 victory at Brisbane that clinched a 2-1 series win, with two other matches drawn.

After returning from his winter racing in Australia and New Zealand, Kenny signed a new, improved contract with Halifax. Eric Boothroyd admitted his deal with Carter had to reflect his new status as England's No.1. No doubt Kenny had been heavily influenced in his pay demands by his manager, Ivan Mauger, who looked after his financial interests as well as acting as advisor and mentor at the track on the most important race nights.

To help pay for Carter's increase Halifax raised adult admission prices at The Shay by 30p, to £2.20, although the cost for kids and OAPs remained at £1.00. Fans had to pay a 30p transfer to the seated areas on the home and back straights, while the programme price rose by 5p, to 25p. They seem such minuscule amounts now for two hours of Saturday night fun and thrills.

Kenny did not waste time in hitting the headlines. In the first week of the new season the national press had their first major speedway story of 1982 when Carter refused to accept an open meeting appearance at Birmingham, saying: "It's just not worth it. I think I'm worth much more than they offered."

Critics saw the influence of Mauger manifesting itself as Kenny started to make more and more headlines for negative reasons. While some saw his absence from Perry Barr as greed on Kenny's part, he had every right to say 'no' to what was no more than an invitational event – a low-key challenge match between the Brummies and the Young England side that toured Australia the previous winter. As it happened, the match at Perry Barr was rained-off – but Carter had still made his point.

If promoters were not willing to pay what he believed he was worth – he would haggle with them over pennies when negotiating his petrol allowance before accepting a guest booking – then it was his prerogative to either accept or turn down their offers.

Kenny took the opportunity to explain himself in his first regular column for *Speedway Star* magazine. Through his ghost-writer, the *Sunday Express* journalist Richard Bott, he wrote: "If you think I'm getting greedy, forget it. I've got commitments with other promoters and it wouldn't be fair on them if I rode somewhere else for a lot less."

For all Carter's sheer will to succeed on the track and the adulation of his supporters, even those close to him claim now that he never loved speedway. According to friends, although he was obsessed with winning and desperately craved the world title, he was no natural speedway enthusiast like Ivan Mauger, who has always retained a passion for the sport that made him a wealthy man.

But friends of Carter claim he simply saw speedway as his job, a means to an end.

Jimmy Ross confirmed: "Kenny didn't enjoy speedway as such, he just loved winning. That, and making money.

"To him, points meant money and at the end of the night he wanted to know how much he'd earned.

"In his early days with Halifax, I invited him along to watch a meeting at Sheffield, with myself and the Lohmann brothers, Klaus and Mike. But the first time Kenny came with us, he moaned after 20 minutes that he was 'bored silly' and wanted to go home.

"Even after meetings he'd ridden in, he wanted to be straight off home afterwards. I told him that he should socialise with the other riders in the bar but he just wasn't interested. He saw it as a job and nothing more."

If anything, it was often said that road-racing appealed to Kenny as much as speedway did. On the eve of the 1982 shale season he was seen flying around Donnington Park – where his father entertained from a hospitality box – and riding flat out at speeds approaching 180mph on a Honda 1100R borrowed from Ron Haslam. There is no doubt, had Kenny chosen road-racing instead of speedway for his living, as his brother Alan did, he would have been very successful at it. Some say he would have been better than Alan. Even in the occasional 'fun' ride around Donnington and other top road-racing circuits, he clearly had what it took to at least compete on level terms with Haslam and other leading British road-racers of that period, such as his brother, Mick Grant and Roger Marshall.

Doug Wyer, who was a team-mate of Carter's at Halifax from 1981 until '84, said: "Kenny's brother was a road-racer and won a 250cc grand prix, but Kenny used to tell me he'd been to Cadwell Park or Donnington with him and that he could beat him easily. Whether he could or not, I don't know, but I wouldn't have been surprised if he could!"

With old hands Dougie Wyer and John Louis, 1981.

One shrewd move Kenny did make at the start of the '82 season was to re-employ his trusty mechanic, Richard Pickering, on a more permanent basis. Pickering, who bore a distinctive black moustache or occasional beard and amused Kenny with his relatively 'posh' Yorkshire accent, was one of Carter's most loyal allies.

Phil Hollingworth, who helped Kenny on a part-time basis alongside Richard before replacing him in 1984, said: "He was a good mechanic, very efficient but pedantic. You either liked him or you didn't and he was hard to get on with because he kept himself to himself. He was quite a bit older than Kenny and me, so there was an age gap and he just didn't fit in after a while.

"Richard was more of an employee than a close friend to Kenny, whereas I was Kenny's mate as well as his mechanic. But I wouldn't knock Richard. He was all right and I couldn't really say a bad word about him."

March 1982 was a time for celebration in the Carter family. To mark Kenny's 21st birthday on the 28th of the month, 24 hours after his first maximum of the season at The Shay against Sheffield, and just days after his father's birthday, a combined father-son party was arranged at the local squash club.

The Halifax fans and management were bitterly disappointed when World Champion Bruce Penhall failed to return from a visit to the States and missed Cradley Heath's League Cup match at The Shay. It was a testing time for the World Champion whose popularity began to wane when he came under fire from all quarters for his protracted pay disputes. Firstly for pushing Cradley into a corner over a better deal and then for demanding an appearance fee from the BSPA before agreeing to lead his country in the Test series against England. In fairness, Penhall was simply trying to maximise his earning potential as the sport's new No.1, just as Carter would have done, and the matter was soon resolved by the promoters' association agreeing to pay him a £1,500 fee. When you consider what top sports

Kenny looking the part at a Yorkshire grass-track prize-giving ceremony. Don't know who the two lads are to the right, but that's former Sheffield favourite Sean Wilson in white on the far left of picture.

men and women were paid in other sports, it was nothing less than the charismatic Penhall deserved.

Carter was not sorry to see Penhall lining up against him again. He cast his mind back to their well-publicised clash in the 1981 Overseas Final and said: "I'm still annoyed at what happened at the White City – if someone wrecked your best bike and ripped a pair of brand new leathers, you wouldn't be too happy either!

"That crash cost me a lot of money and could have put me out of the World Championship. But there is no vendetta. If there was, I'd have knocked him off at Halifax in the Golden Helmet last season!

"Let's put it this way. I don't like him to beat me and I don't reckon he likes me to beat him, so we both tend to ride a bit special when we meet."

Yet again, England went into the international campaign under new management after Len Silver resigned, claiming he was fed up with all the back-biting he endured from fellow promoters. Eric Boocock and John Berry, who had both had previous spells in charge of the national team, were persuaded to return and form a new partnership.

The first thing the chalk-and-cheese duo of Boocock and Berry did was to hand Carter the No.1 race jacket for the forthcoming Test series against the Americans. He was by then easily his country's top rider anyway but, for Kenny, there was nothing like rubbing-stamping it with the actual number one on his back. It signified another stepping stone on his way to the top as he revelled in the added responsibility and his new found status.

Did increased fame and fortune with Halifax and England go to Carter's head? Doug Wyer, an experienced former England international and 1976 world finalist, said: "I liked the kid, I got on well with him. To be honest, he was on his way up and I was on my way down, so he didn't have to worry about me. I was no threat to him.

"When I rode with him, he was a lot better than I was at that time. He was one of the best riders you could wish to see and he did some fantastic things on a motorcycle.

"He used to arrive at Halifax in his mate's helicopter which used to land on the centre green. I suppose he was being the superstar but it didn't bother me.

"He had a reputation for being self-centred but you've got to be self-centred. I wanted to win every race and I wanted my team-mate to come second – you never wanted to come second and him to win it, and that is self-centred.

"People said to me sometimes during my time at Sheffield that I wasn't a very good team rider, but I did my best for the team by trying to win every time. To me, that's three points in the can and at least you've drawn your race and it's then up to your mate to pick one point up. If I was going out trying to beat Ivan Mauger or Peter Collins, I couldn't hang around looking out for Craig Pendlebury or whoever. I used to tell those critics that if the team had seven blokes who could ride like me, we'd win every meeting easily.

"Kenny was like that – he wanted to win every time because he wanted Halifax to win, and that meant doing his bit for the team."

Wyer echoed the earlier comments of Mick McKeon when he confirmed that Carter would offer the use of his bike to team-mates if required. Dougie said: "He would lend you his bike if you needed it – I've borrowed his bike on occasions and he'd nick yours if he needed it.

"We rode at Wimbledon once and Kenny's bike wasn't very good so he borrowed Billy Burton's. He won every race on it and when Billy asked for it back, he wouldn't give it to him for the rest of the night!

"He'd team-ride if he needed to as well – he was Halifax through and through and always wanted them to win," said Wyer.

Eric Boothroyd said: "A lot of opposing riders didn't like Kenny. He was a cocky, little devil who would put people's backs up, but he was liked by his Halifax and Bradford team-mates. I never knew of any problems between Kenny and other riders in the team.

"He was good at geeing up the others if they needed a bit of a kick up the backside and I thought he was a good captain, easy to deal with. He never gave me any problems."

There were other occasions when Carter found time to think of others much less fortunate than himself. After Milton Keynes' Aussie teenager Brett Alderton was killed in the second half at King's Lynn on April 17, he said: "I know what it's like to have a tragedy in your family, because I've lost my mother and a brother. I'd like to say to Brett's parents that I'm willing to help in any way by riding for nothing – anywhere – in a benefit meeting in their son's name if it will contribute to some fund."

Jimmy Ross recalls how the Halifax favourite agreed to take time out from his hectic international schedule to appear at a special party they were having at the

Who said he was always too intense?

local school for autistic and disabled children. Ross said: "He looked a bit uncomfortable with it at first, sitting around all these young kids in wheelchairs. I think it reminded him a bit of his mother.

"But I knew the headmistress at the Lower Edge special needs school which is at Raistrick, near Halifax. She said the kids were all Kenny Carter mad and asked if I could get him to send some of his stickers for the kids. I told him we could do better than that, so I asked him to do me a favour by visiting for their special occasion.

"The kids loved it. Kenny stayed for a couple of hours – signing autographs, giving out stickers and free tickets to the next home meeting at The Shay and having his picture taken. He even ate jelly and ice cream with the children – they were all thrilled to see him and you could see it meant a lot to them.

"And at the next home meeting, Kenny made a point of going up to the kids in the crowd to see if they were enjoying themselves.

"People thought Kenny was nasty, unpleasant, a monster. But he did have a caring side that most people never knew," said Ross.

He certainly never cared much for the Americans . . .

Chapter 11

KENNY HATED DRUGS

KENNY **knew how to antagonise the Americans. He lit the blue touchpaper on the eve of the England v USA Test series in April 1982 with outspoken comments that did not go down well in the USA camp. Before the first Test at Wimbledon, he jibed: "They may be great when they're in front but they chuck the towel in when things start going wrong."**

The first Test at Wimbledon was badly affected by rain which made track conditions treacherous. Kenny's battle to shake off the effects of 'flu were not helped by the dip in temperature at Swindon, where he suffered a first race fall and exclusion after tussling with old rival Penhall.

But Carter admitted: "There was a bit of talk of Bruce knocking me off but it wasn't his fault. We were both racing for the same piece of track and I left him too much room on the corner."

While most of the England team favoured the new, wider Carlisle tyre, imported from the USA by Barry Briggs, Carter kept making consistently fast starts on the English Dunlop. It said something for his open-minded approach to pairings that he did not concern himself with who was alongside him at the starting gate, whether they were wearing the English lion or stars-and-stripes on their body colour.

In the course of the five-match series against the Americans, he rode with four different partners – Gordon Kennett (at Wimbledon), Steve Bastable (Swindon), Andy Grahame (Ipswich and Belle Vue) and John Davis at Poole, where he moved down the order to accommodate a new opening race pairing of Michael Lee and Malcolm Simmons.

Eric Boocock, who managed Carter with England in both 1982 and again in 1986, said: "If we had to juggle the team around, Kenny would never mind. If we asked who he wanted to ride with as his partner, he'd say: 'Anybody – who wants to ride with me?' because, whatever happened he was riding for himself. I'm not saying he wasn't aware of his partner but if his partner was in the way he wouldn't have cared if he knocked him off, because he wanted to pass whoever was in front as well. His attitude was 'stuff you' all the time and that's why he wasn't popular with the other riders.

"Now and then there was a bit of friction in the camp because of him, although it was rare. It would be a case of 'Kenny didn't look for me at the first corner' or 'we were on a 5-1 and he didn't look'. But what did they expect? That was Kenny.

"If we had a word with him about moving somebody over to get past he'd say: 'Well, they were in my way'. He'd complain his partners weren't going fast enough

Kenny always loved going wheel-to-wheel with Bruce Penhall. Action from the hostile 1982 series.

and that he wasn't going to slow down for them! That was the attitude he had and, when it comes down to it, what was wrong with it? The lad was a born winner. He'd set his stall out to make it and he would have made it, although we all know the tragic ending.

"In any case, what his team-mates thought of him didn't bother him at all – it wasn't his problem, it was somebody else's. He didn't have a problem with any of his team-mates – if there was a problem, in his eyes it was because they had a problem with him," said Booey.

Briefly giving up the No.1 England body colour in the fifth, and final, Test at Poole didn't faze Carter, though. He knew full well that he was by this stage the nation's one and only likely World Champion and at Poole he bounced back from a last first time out to win his next five rides on his second bike, including two defeats of Penhall.

Carter, the only Brit to reach double figures in a heavy 39-69 drubbing, recorded England's only heat advantage (with Davis) on a miserable night in front of a large Wimborne Road crowd. What fans did not know about was the growing hostility between the teams behind the scenes.

It had been generally accepted that the Californians brought over to England a casual approach to the use of what is known in polite circles as 'recreational drugs'. These were considered to be marijuana and cocaine and neither was considered to be a performance-enhancer by any of the riders any more than alcohol. The best such drugs could offer was a diminished concern for safety and survival.

But amphetamines, commonly known as 'speed', was very much a performance-

Getting the better of Penhall during the '82 Test series.

enhancer. True to its name, the drug speeded reaction times as well as giving the user a feeling of euphoria.

There was a feeling of suspicion among the top English riders that some of the Americans were using this drug which caused ill feeling. Never one to keep his opinions to himself, Kenny was very vocal both to and about the Americans he believed were using these drugs, and he was by no means alone in his opinions.

Of course, making wild accusations was one thing but at that time producing proof was something else. It was during this series that things came to a head and the England riders considered refusing to race against America at Poole. Given an assurance something would be done about the situation, the riders took part in the meeting but most paid lip service to the racing.

Kenny Carter wasn't that kind of rider. He happily mouthed off to anyone who cared to listen about the "cheating bastards" being on drugs, but he took them on anyway and put on a tremendous show in what was otherwise a very one-sided match.

As a consequence of the representations from the English team during and after that series, random drug testing was introduced into British speedway.

Kenny was not a drinker. A couple of halves of lager with his best mates and fellow riders at the Prospect pub, situated on the hillside at Boothtown with speedway pictures decorating its walls, would satisfy his alcoholic requirements following a night's racing at the Shay. But he abhorred drug-taking. For all that has been said and written about his dislike of Americans, it was perhaps this issue that caused the greatest animosity between some of them and Carter.

Carter admitted the USA deserved their 3-2 series win but he did nothing to endear himself to his fellow countryman when he wrote in *Speedway Star*: "I don't think the English lads talked to each other much during the meeting – there seemed to be no team spirit or any interest in team riding. The Yanks, by contrast, rose to the occasion and we got well licked."

For the World Pairs, Boocock and Berry brought northern rivals Collins and Carter together for the semi-final in Prague. PC dropped a point to Hungary's Zoltan Adorjan before the decisive last race in which he and Carter led from the gate to win the meeting and inflict the only defeat on defending champions USA, represented by Bruce Penhall and Dennis Sigalos. In sweltering heat, Carter was unbeaten by an opponent on his way to 16 (paid 18) points. With Collins contributing 13, they finished three clear of the US duo.

It said everything about Carter's pride and enthusiasm for representing England that, despite being an established No.1 for club and country at senior level, he also rode in four Tests for a Young England side against the National League on second division tracks. He flew in from the Pairs semi in the Czech Republic to score an 18-point maximum at Exeter that same night, followed by further unbeaten scores of 18 at Middlesbrough, Newcastle and Edinburgh, while also collecting a couple of track records along the way.

But a brilliant 12-point maximum by Kenny could not save England from a disastrous exit from the World Team Cup at the semi-final in Vojens, where the USA and Denmark qualified for the final. It was another remarkably defiant performance by Carter who ignored doctors' advice to rest for four weeks for fear of infection and, ultimately amputation, having ripped the nail from the fourth finger of his left hand in a second half spill at Wimbledon the previous week. He missed practice in Denmark but, aided by four pain-killers, insisted on taking his place in the meeting. "I've got a job to do and a bit of pain won't stop me," he told *Speedway Star's* Richard Clark 24 hours before the WTC round.

Phil Hollingworth revealed that the night before Carter crashed at Plough Lane, he and Kenny had been up late drinking cheap Russian champagne that he had brought back with him from one of his recent trips to Eastern Europe. "Kenny wasn't used to drinking much and he was spewing up in the van all the way down to Wimbledon!" his mechanic recalled.

Despite Carter's heroics in front of 9,500 Danish fans, England were eliminated in third place. The result was a disaster for the BSPA who had to stage the World Cup Final at White City in August without the host country to draw a crowd worthy of the occasion.

Kenny did not concern himself with the problems of the British promoters. The afternoon after scoring his WTC maximum in Denmark, he went to Germany and won the prestigious Golden Key of Bremen event. Attention then returned to the individual World Championship trail, with 10 qualifiers set to progress from the Overseas Final at White City on American Independence Day.

Despite beating eventual winner Dave Jessup, Carter dropped three points in his first two rides on an abysmally slick track that was widely condemned as a gater's paradise. It was Kenny's swift starting that got him through and at least he managed

A rare moment of empathy between Penhall and Carter before the 1982 Overseas Final . . . but the smile soon disappeared from Bruce's face after the White City crowd turned against him.

Showing his back wheel to Dennis Sigalos and Ole Olsen at Vetlanda, 1982.

to avoid being caught up in the kind of controversy that marred this qualifier a year earlier. The same, though, could not be said for Penhall. If Kenny had been miffed by all the adulation 'Juicy Brucie' and his fellow Americans had previously received from the British public, he would see his main rival's popularity nosedive in the space of just 72 seconds at the Wood Lane track.

In sacrificing overall victory and the £1,000 winner's cheque to allow three of his compatriots to finish in front of him in heat 19, Penhall badly misjudged the changing mood of the fans. While Sigalos and the Moran brothers sailed off into the distance, Penhall poodled around at the back while pulling wheelies. He even admitted he threw the race in a pits interview for ITV.

But the majority of the crowd was far from entertained by his complicity. Disgusted by his blatant act of patriotism, they hurled empty tin cans onto the track at the end of the race and then loudly jeered him onto the presentation rostrum. "The most vicious barrage of abuse I have ever heard from a British World Championship crowd," according to journalist Peter Oakes.

The published picture of the top three told its own stark story. Jessup and Carter, who finished a point behind DJ, were all smiles after an England one-two. A bewildered Penhall, who had been outwitted by Jessup, had a face like thunder. He was guilty, all right – of naivety as much as anything else.

In reality, Penhall had been a victim of his own transparency. He could easily have disguised his actions by making it look good, just as many riders who have helped out others in similar situations have done over many years of the old World Championship qualifying system. Or he could have simply laid his bike down on the first bend – no questions asked.

Instead, he completed four effortless laps, keeping well out of the way of his three

Pulling away from Bruce Penhall during the Inter-Continental Final at Vetlanda. It would get much uglier between them in their next World Championship showdown.

There was nothing like another trophy to put a smile on his face . . . this time it's the Golden Helmet.

Offering his hand to congratulate Shawn Moran after losing the Helmet to the American at Birmingham.

friends – all in the best interests of the promoters of the 1982 World Final who desperately needed as many Americans as possible through to their big night at the Los Angeles Coliseum. Harry Oxley, the most well known American track boss and a partner with Ivan Mauger and Barry Briggs in World Class Inc, the organisers of the World Final, was seen in the White City pits before the infamous race, deep in conference with Penhall and the three other American riders. Although it is understood they did not pre-determine the finishing order of heat 19 – Sigalos, Kelly and Shawn Moran genuinely raced for the crucial points – Penhall was really left with no choice but to play a submissive role in this all-American farce.

The fact that three Americans made it to the Inter-Continental Final – Shawn Moran was beaten by Les and Peter Collins in a run-off to clinch the last two qualifying places at White City – was small consolation to Mauger, who was among the six eliminated at the London track.

Unsurprisingly, Carter showed the embattled Penhall no sympathy whatsoever and said that the criticism his big rival received from the public and press was self-inflicted. He said: "Personally, I wouldn't have done it. I've done favours in the past but when it comes to the World Championship I reckon the best thing is to ride for yourself and put the people out who are likely to be your main rivals.

"It's all right being friends, but I wonder how Bruce would feel if Dennis Sigalos wins the World Championship? I bet he would be pretty sick if that happened."

Kenny had never been to Sweden before competing in the Inter-Continental Final – effectively the semi-final of the World Championship. The Vetlanda Motorstadium is 360 kilometres from the capital of Stockholm – or on this occasion, a little over six minutes from Los Angeles in racing terms.

That's roughly how long it took Carter to amass the 11 points that earned him second place in the ICF behind surprise packet Les Collins, who won with a point more on the wide, sweeping circuit. Carter was denied the chance of a run-off for the title with Collins when beaten from the back by a desperate Andy Grahame in his last ride.

There were one or two lingering question marks surrounding Carter's choice of tyres. It was suggested afterwards in the press that he could have won his first major World Championship event but for his continued loyalty to the English Dunlop tyre – he also tried the Italian Pirelli in Sweden. Gundersen was the only other rider who did not start the ICF on the new Carlisle tyre, although he later switched to the American rubber in a futile bid to qualify.

It was at the start of '82 that Barry Briggs became the UK importer for the Carlisle, a larger configuration tyre designed to provide increased traction between the rubber and the track surface. It was more expensive at around £28, compared to the Dunlop priced at £19.50 and the Pirelli costing £18. The BSPA tried unsuccessfully to ban its use in Britain on the grounds that it increased costs – regardless of the Carlisle's durability, riders tended to throw them away after two meetings and put on a new one. They were also blamed for an alarming increase in serious crashes.

The Carlisle debate intensified during July when Reading's quiet American Denny Pyeatt crashed and died at Hackney. He picked up an unexpected surge of uncontrollable drive, catapulted through the wire fence and into a steel lamppost. But Briggo and others, including Mauger, urged the British authorities to pay closer attention to safety standards and track preparation, not the controversial Carlisle tyre.

Mauger would have plenty more to say about tyres – and Carter's preferred choice – before long.

The build up to the World Final in California appeared to be going well for Kenny. He was not best pleased to see Bruce Penhall pip him to top spot in the Yorkshire TV Trophy meeting at Sheffield, especially as only a fall stopped him from retaining the title, but it was really no big deal. It was another welcome opportunity to test machinery without the pressures associated with the more cut-throat world title race.

He had to settle for second place again, this time behind Bo Petersen, when 3,000-plus turned out to see a world class line-up assemble at Milton Keynes for the Brett Alderton Memorial event. This emotional occasion was definitely all about taking part, not winning.

But Kenny took a great deal of satisfaction from victory in the annual Golden Hammer classic at Cradley Heath – the same West Midlands track that threatened to ban him from future open meetings there after he missed a BL match at Dudley

Wood the previous year. Even the Penhall-worshippers now had to concede a grudging respect for the little tyke who roared to a faultless 15 points, with the home track American way down the field on seven having missed his first ride and fallen while chasing Carter in another. Penhall would never win his track's most coveted individual prize.

Ipswich favourite Dennis Sigalos was another faller at Cradley, breaking his ankle in a first bend clash with Carter and his fellow American, Reading's Bobby Schwartz.

Kenny relished the chance to silence his critics at Cradley – and so did his dad. Phil Hollingworth said: "There were one or two occasions when I had to act as Kenny's minder at Cradley. The fans there hated him – so much so, he used to keep a metal baseball bat hidden in his van in case they ever tried to tear him apart!

"I remember Mal causing a commotion there once. A big Scottish guy was stood on the terraces in front of the bar on the first/second turn and he was bad-mouthing Kenny, calling him a 'dirty little bastard'. Kenny was hard but he wasn't dirty and he didn't deliberately go out to hurt anybody.

"Mal Carter, who had been a bit of a hard boy in his time, heard the fan and went outside the bar to have a word with him.

"Mal said: 'That's my son you're talking about'.

"The fan said: 'I don't give a f*** who he is'.

"Mal had been smoking a cigar and he just removed it from his mouth and stubbed it out on the fan's forehead – and then he butted him. It kicked off big-style then!"

The old-fashioned 'Glasgow Kiss' became a trademark of the Carters over the years, Kenny included.

Phil added: "Mal told Kenny and me what had happened earlier with the Cradley fan when we met up with him in the bar after the meeting. Kenny would rarely go in to the bar after racing unless his dad was there.

"Kenny and his dad didn't see eye to eye. Mal was a very hard man in his time and I suppose you could have likened him to a bare-knuckle gypsy fighter. He showed no visible sign of compassion or emotion, not even when Kenny's mum died.

"Mal has gone through a lot of tragedy himself and maybe that's what made him such a hard person.

"He did a lot for Halifax Speedway, though, and at one time sponsored the whole team for a new bike and a car each.

"I last spoke to him about two years ago. I was out riding my bike and he asked me what I'd been up to. He warned me to be careful on the bike and I thought: 'You've changed your tune'. He said he'd had triple heart bypass surgery and he did look a lot thinner in the face. He seemed to have mellowed.

"I like Mal. He's had a lot of money – he was in to all sorts – and has blown much of it on sponsoring the likes of Ron Haslam. But for all his bravado and hard-nosed image, he is a very generous person at heart and would give you his last penny.

"After he gave up sponsoring the Halifax riders, he once told me: 'I bought them bikes and cars and do you know what? Not one of them even said 'thank you'. He had given them a lot of backing and deserved more thanks in return."

The Scottish Heathens fan irritated Mal Carter more than he did Kenny, who said:

"The Cradley crowd can have a go at me if they like. It doesn't bother me."

A 17-point haul at home to Swindon, followed by 16 at Poole, did not prevent Halifax from suffering consecutive league defeats but the results did no harm to Kenny's lofty position at the top of the BL tree.

Leading the national averages, through to his second World Final, wife Pam expecting their first child and a lovely new home they were about to move into. . . life surely felt very good to Kenny Carter.

But then he went to Ipswich and met Preben Eriksen. . .

Los Angeles seemed a million miles away as Kenny lay in agony, barely able to breath, in the intensive care unit at Ipswich Hospital on the night of Thursday, August 5.

The World Final was only 23 days away but with tubes sticking out of his mouth and pain etched all over his face, there seemed little hope of him making it to America to fulfil his dream of winning the sport's biggest prize.

A furious Kenny was in no doubt . . . it was all Preben Eriksen's fault.

Ipswich's Dane was fast developing a dubious reputation as an aggressive, fearless rider and he was clearly pumped up to beat Carter. But even people within the Ipswich camp had to agree that his antics on the first corner of heat 20 of the individual Star of Anglia meeting were stupid and unnecessarily dangerous.

Dictating his *Speedway Star* column from his hospital bed, Carter pointed an accusing finger at the man whose reckless first bend antics threatened to leave his world title dreams in tatters.

"I'm blazing mad about the crash and you can say that Preben Eriksen doesn't number among my best mates at the moment," he said. "It's thanks to him that I'm here in hospital. He wrote in the local papers about how he was in front and didn't see where I came from, and how he got his arm caught up in mine.

"That's not the way I remember it. I needed to win the race to retain the Star of Anglia trophy. Eriksen realised he had a chance to win the meeting himself and it would have been one of the greatest achievements of his career. But I think he tried to ride above himself."

Eriksen, whose uncompromising style also angered seasoned England internationals Dave Jessup and Malcolm Simmons during the same period, argued that the blame for his crash with Carter should have been apportioned "50-50."

But Carter countered: "As far as I'm concerned, he T-boned me right into the boards. I was in front, so he should have knocked off. I've got the pictures here to prove it.

"Eriksen came in to see me that day but I didn't want to talk to him.

"I'm lucky to be alive," he added, before vowing to again ignore doctors' advice and ride in his second successive World Final.

One visitor Carter was happy to see at his bedside was his England manager and Ipswich promoter John Berry. Recalling now the conversations he had with Carter at that time, Berry said: "I learned more about Kenny from the few hours of chats we had, when he was stuck in the intensive care unit at Ipswich Hospital with broken ribs and a punctured lung, than at any other time.

"A mixture of the pain and medication had slowed him down from his usual warp speed to something much nearer my own level.

I was able to better understand the characteristics of the man.

I have never known anyone so driven to be a success before or since. The confidence in his own abilities was also clear.

"What had been washed away by the drugs were the bullshit and bluster that normally pushed the determination and confidence into theatrical arrogance. All that was missing.

"It was clear there was also, tucked deep away, some self-doubt not normally seen. There is little doubt to me, the overly aggressive side of Kenny was entirely a product of his upbringing."

Just nine days after arriving by ambulance at Ipswich Hospital, a battered and bruised Carter discharged himself, ignoring medical staff who told him he should remain in there for at least another week, and that he would be stupid to even think of riding in the World Final.

Since when did Kenny heed the advice of doctors who tried to stop him from doing what he did best? He was up and soon on his way back to Yorkshire to prepare for another big battle in the USA . . .

Chapter 12

PENHALL v CARTER – Part 2

IVAN Mauger's elimination from the 1982 World Championship had a silver lining in that he would be able to give Kenny his full and undivided attention in helping him to try and win the first World Final ever to be staged in America. Mauger had hoped to make another slice of history himself but, at the age of 41, he had to finally accept that it was time to hand over the baton to the younger brigade.

Meticulous as ever in his preparation, Mauger took advantage of Carter's injury lay-off to whisk him off to the States two days ahead of the official party that included most of the other European-based World Finalists, their mechanics and all their racing equipment.

Ivan and Kenny set up base at Mauger's Garden Grove condominium, some 20-odd miles away from the $69-a-night University Hilton where most of the other finalists stayed.

"I wanted him to be in the States early, to continue his physiotherapy there and to feel comfortable in a relaxed environment," Ivan explained. "I wanted him to have a couple of days of sun and time in the Jacuzzi before practice. He wasn't riding in England because of the injuries he suffered at Ipswich, so he was better off flying out with me," added Mauger.

It was arranged that Pam, along with other members of her and Kenny's families, would take a later flight to California.

Two weeks before he and Carter touched down in LA, Mauger acted as a guinea pig for his protégé by testing the new £25-a-piece Dunlop 'DART' tyre in an open meeting at Kempton, Germany, which he won in the fastest times of the day. At that stage he did not seem concerned that Carter remained one of the very few world class riders yet to jump on the Carlisle bandwagon.

Mauger said: "I wanted to try out the Dunlop to give Kenny a valuation, especially as he hasn't been able to ride for a few weeks.

"He wants to stay British. He's got that bulldog spirit and all his equipment is British-made – from Weslake engines, to Comet frames, Kangol helmets, Talon wheels and NEB clutches."

He did ask for some 'foreign' assistance, however. Apart from having the Kiwi Mauger in his corner of the pits, Carter also paid for Graham McKeon, the respected engine tuner he knew well from his previous visits to Perth, to be on hand to help his regular mechanic Richard Pickering at the LA Coliseum.

Before leaving Yorkshire, Kenny did not mince his words when he boasted to journalist Richard Bott how he was going to win at the Los Angeles Memorial Coliseum. Speaking from the farmhouse where his in-laws lived, while renovations to the marital home just up the road were being finished, he said: "At the moment, with a week to go, I feel pretty lousy. If I don't take pain-killers I'm in agony. But there's nowt I can do about it except rest and hope I'll be a good bit better by the time I get to Los Angeles.

"I've got to push myself against the pain when the time comes.

"I feel the World Championship should be mine. I want to win it more than anything and, apart from the injury, I feel the time is right. I was dead keen to win last season at Wembley and pig sick when I didn't. I thought I was good enough to win but my set-up wasn't as good as it is this year.

"If I'd won at Wembley it might have come too early. This year it would be right. And it's not that I think I am the best rider in the world . . . I KNOW I AM! If you think you're the best, why say owt else?"

Carter regretted the fact that he had not been able to ride or practice in the three-week gap between his crash with Preben Eriksen at Ipswich and the World Final, but he took some positives from the enforced lay-off. "I hadn't been riding 100 per cent, apart from in a couple of meetings, before Ipswich. Maybe I'd been doing a bit too much, lost my edge – I hadn't been my normal self.

"Now I'm hoping this break will bring the sharpness back. I'm not bothered about any psychological effects of the crash. I've been riding and falling off motor bikes all my life and I came back okay last year after breaking my jaw."

Carter was convinced he would make an ideal World Champion, someone who would project a strong image for the sport and attract a lot of publicity. No-one could argue with him on that point.

He added: "If I can't win it, I hope one of the other English lads does. But I've got to say that quite a few riders in the final haven't got the right image to be a good World Champion.

"There's been plenty of rivalry between Bruce Penhall and me but he's been a good World Champion," Carter admitted. "He's got the right image for the sport. The trouble is, he's been no use to England!

"We need our own World Champion."

Carter said, diplomatically, that up to 10 of the 16 finalists were capable of winning on the night but he added that he reckoned no more than two or three had a realistic chance. He singled out two riders who could possibly stand between him and the fulfilment of his ultimate dream – Dennis Sigalos and Bruce Penhall.

A YEAR **earlier most people were happy to acknowledge Bruce Penhall as a fine World Champion, a superb ambassador for the sport and a media man's dream. There had been good looking speedway riders before but he also had the skill, drive and dedication to match his charisma.**

However, in the weeks leading up to the defence of his crown, his popularity had seriously dwindled. This was due in part to his role in the White City shenanigans but much more to do with his imminent plans to start a new career outside speedway.

For Penhall had stunned his adoring Cradley Heath fans and the sport as a whole by finally confirming persistent rumours that he would soon be quitting the British

Looking very sharp in practice at the Los Angeles Coliseum.

League to pursue a new career in acting. He was all set for a lead part in the American TV cop show *CHiPS* and with film opportunities also on the horizon he did not have the time to compete in Britain, although he claimed he would race occasionally in California and also in European open invitation meetings. He also pledged that he would see out his contracted commitments until the end of the '82 season.

His mind was made up, though. He craved Hollywood, not Dudley Wood.

The last thing British speedway needed was an occasional bit-part player – albeit a supremely talented one – who would flit in and out of the country when it suited him, cherry-picking his meetings and turning his back on the bread and butter league programme. What the sport in Britain badly needed was a fully active crowd-pulling superstar who could help arrest the continuing slide in attendance figures at tracks everywhere. The fans needed someone to love and, yes, even someone to hate.

Someone like Kenny Carter.

After a long and typically colourful pre-meeting parade full of razzmatazz had ended and a disappointingly low 30,000 crowd had settled into their seats, Kenny's opening race in the 1982 World Final went perfectly to plan. He took early command of heat 2 from the outside gate and there was no way the unfancied trio of Edward Jancarz, Vaclav Verner and Jan Andersson could catch him once he moved across and hugged the white line around turn one.

Showing no sign of nerves or the effects of his Ipswich crash, he netted another vital though hard-fought three points in heat 8 when he went wheel-to-wheel with Dennis Sigalos around the first bend, before powering around the tall and talented

Team Carter before the 1982 World Final. Graham McKeon (left) and Richard Pickering are the mechanics.

American. With Jiri Stancl relegating lone Dane Hans Nielsen to last place, this was a very significant win for Carter.

On paper, heat 11 was expected to be the easiest of Kenny's five rides, and so it proved. He scorched clear from the tapes, leaving Georg Hack, Kai Niemi and Mikhail Starostin trailing.

By the interval stage, after the finalists had all taken three rides each, Carter was in the driving seat as the only unbeaten man on nine points. The good news for him was that Penhall had already dropped a point in heat 4 to the mercurial Les Collins, proving that his Inter-Continental Final victory in Vetlanda had not been a fluke. But then the Leicester trier undid all the brilliant skill and hard work he had put in to outwit Penhall by taking just one point from his third ride, behind also-rans Stancl and Andersson and ahead of his elder brother Peter.

Only much later in that long evening would Les realise the full impact of those two dropped points.

After they had all taken three rides, the leading scorers looked like this: Carter 9, Penhall 8, L. Collins 7, Sigalos 7.

Just as everyone knew it would, heat 14 was ultimately going to decide the 1982 World Championship.

Centre green announcer Bruce Flanders did his best to whip the crowd up into a frenzy as the Coliseum drew its collective breath. "The biggie," he called it with more than just a hint of melodrama.

Carter, wearing the No.8 body colour and lining up in gate three, versus Penhall,

Watching his title dreams disappear in LA.

with '13' on the back of his stars-and-stripes race jacket, alongside him in grid two.

Would it be lucky 13 for Bruce?

Supposedly making up the numbers were former World Champion Peter Collins, who had mustered just one point by that stage, and Australian, Phil Crump, faring little better with three to his name. PC and Crumpie were yesterday's heroes – first and third respectively in the 1976 World Final at Katowice – and knew that all eyes would be on the other two.

With nerves jangling as the USA fans hollered for their hero, Carter pushed the tapes and then Collins, on the inside, let his clutch out so far that his front wheel came to a stop on the other side of the tapes! PC deftly held down the bottom tape with his right boot as he slowly wheeled his bike backwards . . . and as he did so, Penhall turned away from the gate and rode back towards the pit gate on turn four to make more last-second adjustments. Under current rules, Carter, Collins and Penhall would all have to be excluded but back then this was all just part of the psychological warfare that preceded vital World Final races.

And then, amid a deafening roar from the crowd, they were finally ready to go.

Collins had spent most of his career 'missing' the start but this time – determined to pull out all the stops to help brother Les – he shot away first, inches ahead of Penhall. Carter was a yard behind the American, with Crump nowhere as all four roared towards the first bend . . . . and a place in World Final folklore.

O f all the many verbal and written accounts of this incident-packed race, one of the most bruising encounters in speedway history, four times World Champion Barry Briggs described it as well as anyone, so let's relive the drama and bitter controversy of heat 14 once again through Briggo's eyes . . .

"Bruce Penhall knew that if Kenny got in front of him he was finished," Briggo told *Speedway Star*.

"Coming out of the start Bruce just kept going straight and wouldn't let Kenny turn. That allowed Peter Collins to get clear." (Crump also nipped through the huge gap left by Penhall and Carter on the inside. By the exit of the fourth bend, both Penhall and then Carter went surging past the Aussie as he then drifted wide.)

"Coming off the last turn on lap two, Kenny banged Bruce, who would have finished up in the 15th row if he had just been sitting on his bike and not ready for trouble. The two of them battled down the straight but at the end of it Kenny was a length-and-a-half clear.

"That was when he lost the championship, in my opinion."

"If he had got down on the line, Penhall would have had no chance. But he drifted wide and gave Bruce another opening, which Bruce took with a brilliant corner.

"It's a difficult thing to explain to people who don't ride. Halfway round a corner the angles suddenly become very different. Kenny had two choices – either to shut off or to go on. He went on . . . and ran out of track."

It has to be said also that when Carter and Penhall locked horns along the main straight, it was a six-of-one and half-a-dozen-of-the-other scenario – Bruce leaned over to his left to try and block Kenny's move past him on the inside, while Kenny

Wheel-to-wheel between Kenny and Bruce Penhall seconds before the moment that decided it all.

Penhall stops to see his main rival down on the other side of the safety fence –
or "by the hot dog stand," as Bruce facetiously described it.

Barry Briggs (left) and Richard Pickering help a shaken and bewildered Kenny back to the LA pits. Would love to know what Richard found to laugh about!

gave him a hefty wallop. If Penhall, who was on the more vulnerable outside at that point, had gone down then, Kittilsen would almost certainly have excluded Carter. It said a lot for the skill of both riders, though, that they both managed to stay upright under extreme physical pressure.

Although Carter barged his way past Penhall and had moved into second place as they went into the first turn on the third lap, his momentum took him too far into the corner. He had allowed Penhall too much room on his inside . . . and the American took it, turning quicker than Kenny and running him wider and wider as they exited the second turn.

Then, crash! Carter, with the safety fence looming large, ran out of room as Penhall edged ahead of him and went down in a heap, disappearing under the fence like the last skittle in a strike at the bowling alley.

The Coliseum crowd held its breath again.

Was it maybe a pang of guilt or genuine concern for Carter's well being that caused Penhall to pull to a halt on the track, just a few yards from where staff were trying to retrieve the fallen Englishman from beyond the other side of the fence? Or, as Penhall would mischievously later describe his rival's landing position, "by the hot dog stand."

Penhall rode back to the pits, waiting anxiously for the referee's decision.

It was an angry, disbelieving Carter who finally got to his feet and saw his white exclusion light illuminating the Los Angeles night sky.

Norwegian referee Tore Kittilsen had stopped the race and awarded a rerun without the shell-shocked meeting pacesetter. "Oh, they can't exclude me for that," Carter was heard to say as he walked back into the pits, searching desperately for the telephone.

A crestfallen Carter picked up the phone and made an impassioned plea to Kittilsen to reinstate him.

In one of the most memorable speedway scenes ever captured for television, the cameras of ITV and US network CBS zoomed in on Carter, eavesdropping on his every word to the official in charge. We can imagine what the nervy Norwegian must have been saying in reply to him at the other end of the line, but this, unedited and word for word, is what Carter said to him:

"I absolutely can't believe it.

"I had turned in the corner and Bruce just took my legs and both of my wheels from under me. He just ran me straight through the fence coming out. I was on the outside, in front, and he just took my legs straight underneath me.

"I'm not kidding, referee, I just hadn't chance. I've been injured as it is. He just stuffed me straight in. He took my leg and everything. I had no chance.

"Excuse me, ref, how can I cause the stoppage of the race when he just took my legs straight from under me? Unfair riding, obviously.

"I mean, I passed him on the pit corner and he bloody turned right – I mean he turned left. I went from the start and he turned right from the start and went straight across the front of me.

"And then when I came past him on the inside, he went straight across and hooked

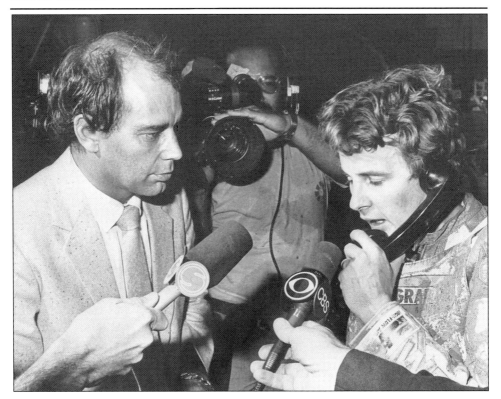

"REFEREE – I had Noooooooooo chance . . . "

up on to me. He was elbowing me and I was trying to get off him, because my handlebars were stuck on him, and he just went straight into that corner and took my leg straight from under me.

"You can ask Barry Briggs, Ivan Mauger, ask anybody. That's disgusting."

Carter listened to Kittilsen's response and then, his angry voice growing more desperate by the second, he pleaded with the stubborn referee again:

"Can't you speak to somebody . . . that's just robbed me of the world title, has that, do you know that?"

A few more words from Kittilsen and then Carter resumed:

"No, will you have a look at it NOW! You come down from your box. That's gonna cost me the World Championship. Ivan Mauger and Barry Briggs is here. You . . . you come down from your box and have a look on the video, and have a look on the telly down here with the promoters and that. That's gonna rob me of the world title. I want you to come down and have a look at it . . . that's not fair."

An enraged Mauger, standing by Carter's side, was like a volcano about to erupt.

He shouted down the line at Kittilsen: "They've got the replay down here, Tore, and if you don't come down that's bloody criminal. The whole World Championship is gonna rest on your very bad decision. They've got it down here and you can see it in black and white, Tore.

"Christ almighty, you're a responsible man. You've come all the way round the world to make this decision. You can't just sit up there like a bloody god and say I'm not going to do anything about it."

Kenny interrupted: "Ivan, he took a minute-and-a-half to put my red . . . er, I mean

An irate Kenny calls for his bike to be brought back to the start line before the rerun of heat 14.

my colour on."

Ivan slammed the phone down, looked at Carter and the TV interviewers who had gathered tightly around them, pointed down towards the receiver and blasted Kittilsen again, telling the reporters: "I wanna tell you, that's not the first time he's made such a bad decision. That's the FIM for you, that's the establishment."

Kenny picked up the phone and said to Mauger: "We've gotta get him down here."

Mauger turned to the media men again and added: "We bring that man halfway round the world to make a decision like that."

American CBS reporter, bearded Dave Despain, poured more fuel onto the fire raging within an incandescent Mauger when he asked innocently: "You've had this problem before, Ivan?"

Mauger took the bait, hook line and sinker, replying: "I've had the same problem with him before . . . 1968 at Wembley . . . he did the same thing to me, left me lying on the track when I got knocked off. Wouldn't stop anything."

Despain asked him: "What do you think the outcome will be?"

Mauger: "The outcome is this . . . the World Championship is not going to go to Kenny Carter, on that one man's decision."

Amid pandemonium in the pits, it was easy to forget that Mauger was not supposed to be there solely to look after Carter's interests, but also as a member of the three-man promoting consortium, along with colleagues Harry Oxley and Barry Briggs. Despite the high drama unfolding on and off the track, the $750,000 showpiece event proved a costly exercise – America never applied to host the individual World Final ever again.

It's all over now . . . Richard Pickering, Ivan Mauger and LA security finally persuade Kenny to leave the track.

English reporter Bob Radford witnessed the chaotic scenes from close quarters and said: "It was mayhem in the pits, almost out of control, and even Ivan and Barry had words. At one stage Briggo asked Ivan, 'are you the meeting co-promoter or a rider's manager?'

"I have never seen Ivan so heated, especially as coolness was his greatest mental asset as a rider.

"The protests went on so long, there were times when I wondered if we would ever move on to the rerun!"

Carter simply could not accept Kittilsen's hugely controversial decision to exclude him as the prime cause of the stoppage. He walked back on to the track and stood, angry and forlorn alongside the starting gate, looking up at the official's glass-fronted box high up in the main stand, as Penhall, Collins and Crump reappeared for the rerun.

As Kenny threw up both of his arms in despair, mechanic Richard Pickering wheeled his bike towards gate two, before being ordered by track staff to divert to the centre green

In the end, it took a gargantuan yellow-shirted 'heavy' from stadium security, with the physique of a man who might otherwise have been engaged at the same Coliseum bowl as a member of the Oakland Raiders NFL gridiron team which moved there that year, to 'persuade' Carter to leave the track before the rerun could go ahead. There was a more familiar hefty-looking character in the thick of it all down by the starting gate area – a balding man with long, brown sideburns. It was Mal Carter.

After the rerun of heat 14, centre green presenter Margo King walked over to

Carter and handed the infield microphone to him. His next outburst angered Penhall's fans but won him the respect of Speedway Star's Eric Linden, who wrote: "No matter what he said I think Carter handled the crowd magnificently. And, in view of the pent up emotion that must still have been choking him, the message was clear, concise and coherent.

"He said what he wanted to say. He reviled nobody. He silenced the loud mouths long enough to get in his killer blow – that he intended to sue the referee. And he had the sense then to hand back the mike when he reckoned he wasn't going to quieten them a second time.

"For me he came out of that situation (on the centre green with the freedom of the mike) with a great deal of honour.

"Whoever decided to put him out there was either the world's best gambler or the nearest thing to a loony in the place."

ITV's roving mike man in the pits, Dick Barrie, grabbed Carter for an interview immediately after the re-staging of heat 14. Barrie, a DJ on Radio Forth back home in Scotland, loved the limelight but his work had for the most part been previously confined to Berwick and Glasgow, speedway backwaters compared to a World Final. Now he was at the heart of the biggest row in World Final history – and revelling in it.

Barrie approached Carter and asked: "Kenny, we've heard your end of the story, what did the referee say to you?"

He replied: "Somebody said to me he put my light on a minute-and-a-half after the decision. Bruce Penhall took my leg. I couldn't even turn.

"I've been injured once in hospital in intensive care. I'm not gonna fall off on purpose. All me bike and me leg and everything went under the fence . . . I had noooooo chance." The 'no chance' comment became almost an unwanted catch-phrase for Kenny.

With all the world-weariness of a broken man on Death Row who had been denied his last plea for clemency, he sighed: " . . . And the referee won't come and have a look at it on the video."

US reporter Dave Despain turned to Penhall for his side of the story. Bruce said: "We had about three or four tussles earlier in the night, you know. I mean, what am I supposed to do, shut off and let him go by?

"I didn't do it deliberately. He was on the outside of me and I didn't even see him after I got by him. And then I just felt a little bit and . . . it was him."

Given the magnitude of the decision, the physical pain and mental anguish Carter must have been suffering in those moments following what was his second heavy fall inside three weeks, it was astonishing that he remained as calm as he did in his vain efforts to persuade Kittilsen to reverse his decision. When you consider how today's prima donna footballers routinely harangue the referee and his assistants using the most obscene language imaginable if as much as a throw-in is given against their team, it was to Carter's remarkable credit that he did not fire even one mild expletive Kittilsen's way.

However, for his personal verbal assault on the Norwegian, Mauger was later heavily fined and censured by the FIM. It was what he said when he returned to the

Brave or just plain crazy? Margo King hands the microphone to a very unhappy young man.

pit phone to vent his anger on Kittilsen after another incident that did most to land him in hot water with the sport's world governing body.

After the Czech, Vaclav Verner, was excluded from heat 16 for causing Germany's Georg Hack to fall on the same part of the track in not too dissimilar circumstances to the earlier incident, Mauger questioned Kittilsen's professional and personal integrity when he shouted at him: "The guy rubbed the guy's leg in an everyday type race, how can you be such a hypocrite? What a hypocrite you are!

"Five minutes ago you would not disqualify Penhall because he's here, in front of his American fans. He completely bundled Kenny Carter into the fence. Vaclav Verner just rubbed Georg Hack's leg and you disqualify him! What a hypocrite!

"I ask you, would you have disqualified Vaclav Verner if he'd had stars-and-stripes on – if he was American? How can you do that!"

Of course, what happened in that race between Penhall and Carter in Los Angeles is a matter of opinion, not fact.

The official video/DVD of the '82 World Final is a must-have souvenir for any serious speedway fan or connoisseur with a sense of history. Do yourself a favour and buy it. It shows replays of that race from numerous different angles, so you can continue to argue the rights and wrongs of it until your heart's content. Did he fall or was he pushed? Well, it often depends who you ask.

What few could understand, though, is why Kittilsen did not take the opportunity to at least review a television replay of the dramatic incident before reaching his conclusion. It was, after all is said and done, the moment that decided the 1982 World Championship.

Or, as Kenny Carter's fans will still tell you, the decision that cost their hero the world title he deserved.

Penhall, of course, saw it all very differently and still insists to this day that Kittilsen called it correctly. Speaking from his California home in 2007, he said: "CBS covered the meeting for American TV but MGM, who were filming my last meeting as part of my introduction to the *CHiPS* show, had 25 cameras around the stadium. The one they had positioned high up at the back of the stand, overlooking turn three, showed that there was a lot of daylight between my back wheel and Kenny's front wheel. Well, three or four inches anyway!

"What was I supposed to do? Put my blinker on and move over to let him past?"

Penhall admits, however, that until he saw Carter's exclusion light come on he genuinely feared the referee might throw him out of the rerun and leave his title defence in tatters. "Sure I did. In any incident of this kind you always wonder what the ref has seen and whether it was really what had actually happened. I just hoped he would call it correctly – which he did.

"I'm absolutely sure that I didn't hit Kenny when he went down. We know when we have hit another rider – you feel it happen. I admit that I didn't leave him any room but he just ran out of track and ended up by the hot dog stand!"

Penhall admits he was 'looking for Carter' from the start of the race. "I made a mistake by concentrating more on Kenny than I did on PC and Crumpie, who both checked out on us. Kenny was fast at that time and I was going to do all I could to block him – not fence him. I knew Kenny was the man to beat every time I met him.

"After we left the start, he had his elbow under my chin and we were fighting on the track. It was ugly and not the first time I'd encountered this with him.

"Into turn three, he was on the outside and I went up the inside and completely slammed the door on him.

"Obviously, the racetrack was starting to tighten up a little bit and he's got to know that when one rider is in front of the other, the man in front has the right of way. I could slam the door on him as much as I wanted to and he knew he had to shut the throttle off and go to Plan B, and try to get me in the next turn or the next lap or so.

"But I know for a fact that I did not hit Kenny Carter. He absolutely ran out of racetrack. It doesn't mean I didn't hit him and he didn't hit me prior to that incident."

This last comment by Penhall raises the intriguing possibility that Kittilsen could have taken the unprecedented decision to exclude BOTH Penhall and Carter for their over-aggressive riding before Carter fell on the third lap – which, as it transpired, would effectively have handed the title to Les Collins on a plate. Or, alternatively, he could have stopped the race after Kenny fell and ordered a rerun with all four back. Both options would have required the brave hand of a single-minded official on the button, but Tore Kittilsen was not known for his courage under pressure – especially if a home rider or team was involved and there was a softer option available.

To be fair to Kittilsen, on the night he allowed the ITV cameras and commentator Dave Lanning into his box to offer his interpretation of events in heat 14. Most referees would have kept their own counsel but then, having ruled in favour of the home favourite, he had little to fear by way of retribution from the crowd. Kittilsen, who was not impressed with ludicrous talk of being sued by Carter, maintained that as Penhall 'had the line' and was slightly ahead coming out of the second bend, he had 'right of way'. It was, he said, Carter's choice to either shut off or face the consequences.

Five years later Kittilsen gave an interview to the quarterly *Vintage Speedway Magazine*, by which time he had retired from refereeing and become the FIM's treasurer . His view of what he saw that night had not changed. He said: "I'll never forget what happened in Los Angeles. That was really something.

"The first person to ring me up about it was, very surprisingly, Ove Fundin. He said he had seen what happened and he told me, 'I fully support you'.

"A month later, of course, we could see from the tape of the meeting that I was vindicated. People were saying that Kenny Carter was pushed out by Bruce Penhall. He wasn't. Bruce never touched Kenny. We could see that later on.

"The pressure on me at the time was incredible. I coped with it because I have a strong heart – and I survived. But I was 100 per cent sure that I was right."

Maybe Kittilsen unwittingly let slip how that high pressure situation may have influenced his decision, though. He told VSM: "Don't forget we were in the United States, dealing with journalists from America. They are really special journalists. It was something new for me.

"But I excluded Kenny Carter because he was the cause of the race being stopped. I had to exclude him."

Kittilsen agreed that the two protagonists had been "fighting" earlier in the race but evidently not violently enough to give him cause to bring a halt before Carter disappeared in a cloud of dust.

He said: "The whole thing started on the opposite side from me. They were fighting as they went past me. But something inside of me was also saying, 'but this is a World Final, so we know it will be hard'."

Barry Briggs agreed with Kittilsen's view. The World Final co-promoter, among those trying to calm Carter by the starting gate as he tried to prevent the rerun of heat 14, said: "I'm a great fan of the kid. I think he's great. I like his attitude and his confidence. But I thought on the night, as I do now, that the referee was right."

A few weeks after the final, Mauger said that if video replay technology could not be permissible, then the referee needed more on the spot human assistance. He explained: "For years I have campaigned at the FIM for linesmen to be placed on each corner and Tore has been one of those opposing it. It would have been easier to accept a decision from a man literally on the spot rather than one over 100 yards away who was watching four riders.

"I have sympathy for a World Final referee and feel that too much pressure is placed on him on the night and with nobody to help. That could be changed and TV could become a part of the future."

Experienced journalist Peter Oakes, who has covered many thousands of meetings and written more words on speedway than any journalist still covering the sport, was in no doubt afterwards who should have been excluded. Oakes, now team manager at Coventry and also the England Under-21 boss, said it then and he sticks by his belief today: "I believe that Kenny Carter would have been World Champion had he not been knocked off. And I also believe that Kittilsen made a grave error of judgement in excluding Carter."

Carter was not the only one sickened by Kittilsen's decision. As the Carter-Penhall debate continues to rage 25 years later, it is often overlooked that the defining moment of the meeting also denied Les Collins a chance of a run-off for the title with Penhall. In the original attempt to stage heat 14, while Carter and Penhall were engaged in their own version of kick-boxing and what might also have served as a decent audition for the World Wresting Federation, Peter Collins was quick to point out that he held a clear lead when the red stop lights came on.

PC agreed with Kittilsen's decision to exclude Carter but he would much rather the race had not been stopped at all. He told Brian Burford for *Backtrack* magazine: "Les was the one who was robbed by that incident. I was already 50 yards in front and there was no way they were going to pass me. If they wanted to fight it out together, that was their mistake – not mine, as I had already cleared off.

"It was all about Les," continued PC. "He had dropped only a point and I'd had a couple of duff races. Les faced Jan Andersson and Jiri Stancl. It was our third ride, so I told him that I wasn't going to get in his way and I'd let him get away at the start. But Andersson and Stancl got away from him. He got third place and I was last.

"Maybe when he dropped those vital points, I had given Les a false sense of security by saying that I was going to stay out of his way.

"But if I had beaten Bruce and Kenny in heat 14, then Les would have been back in the driving seat. I made the start and was about 50 yards in front, going like hell trying to win this race for Les – it would have put him in a run-off with Bruce if they had both won their last rides, which they did.

"I looked back and when I saw Crumpie behind me, I thought: 'Even better, now Les won't need a run-off', I kept looking back and I could see Bruce and Carter giving it elbows. Of course, we all know what happened next and the referee stopped the race.

"As Kenny wasn't in the rerun, Bruce was not concentrating on him any more. He was concentrating on me and Crumpie – and he beat us both."

Collins shares Penhall's view that Carter was the architect of his own downfall. PC said: "What a lot of people don't seem to realise is that the straights were very narrow and the bends were dead wide. If you were out wide you had to get back in because the fence was coming up on you. It went from being 16 metres wide on the bends to around 10m on the straights. During practice we had all been riding narrow coming out of the corners, because we knew that the fence sneaked up on you and the track funnelled out on the bends. ALL the riders knew that.

"I think Kenny elbowed Bruce first. He got his elbow under Bruce's arm and lifted his arm up, which was naughty. Then they got themselves sorted out and Bruce came under Kenny. He was ahead of him and he couldn't see him any more. When you're ahead of someone you can't see where they are.

"Kenny was on the outside but Bruce wouldn't have known that because he couldn't see him. All you get is a buzz in your ear and Bruce may have thought that Kenny was coming up on his inside, but he wouldn't have been sure. Every now and again you hear the other rider's engine when he's close, but you can't see where he is coming from.

"When they were exiting the straight, Bruce was in mid-track but the track was getting narrow. Kenny was coming around the outside and he just kept coming. What he should have done was shut off and dropped behind Bruce's back wheel, or cut back earlier and come inside him. But to keep coming down that outside when you know you're coming into a funnel…big mistake!

"Bruce didn't see him, Kenny kept coming, kept the throttle on and he just ran out of track. He put it down and went under the kickboard. Basically, the bottom of the fence wasn't fastened down like it should have been. There is no way in the world that you should go under the kickboard. Kenny was fortunate he didn't get wrapped around the post behind it and was able to walk away.

"At the end of the day, the throttle works both ways. The pair of them were both riding hard and I think the referee got it dead right by thinking that Kenny should have knocked it off. You can't keep going when you run out of track – and he knew what was coming. He knew – like me and everybody else did – that the track was narrow coming out of the corners.

"I don't think Bruce touched him. I think Kenny realised he was running out of track, so he leaned it over and fell across Bruce's back wheel."

And with an unfortunate choice of words, Collins added: "It was a suicidal move."

PC continued: "But when you're racing someone like that and you're running out track, you've got to make plans sooner than Kenny did. He wasn't on the bike when he went under the fence. It happened gradually, because the pair of them were going wider and wider.

"But Bruce left him an option all the time – he hadn't taken his leg away. What Bruce did wasn't blatant. He rode his line and left Kenny to make his own judgement."

"Everyone has their own view of that incident but all I will say is that it cost Les the chance of being World Champion.

"The thing is, Kenny had gone out and under the kickboard, so the ref should have let the race run. It was the third lap – and it would have been absolute justice if Bruce had come third in heat 14," said PC, offering another perspective on how Kittilsen might have handled a very difficult situation.

And now a word from the man who many have said must have had the best view in the house – back-marker Phil Crump. The Australian legend said: "Penhall was pretty well on fire then and I suppose Kenny Carter was the only one capable of beating him, although I never thought Carter was the same quality rider as Penhall.

"It was crazy, because I was enjoying watching those two race instead of racing myself!"

Penhall's view that Carter should have eased off the gas and attempted to pass him later in the race – they were already on lap three – is not shared by Crumpie, who believes the Englishman was in a do-or-die situation at that stage of the race.

The likeable Aussie continued: "They both gave each other a hard time, it was one hell of a race, and it got to the stage where Penhall gave Carter the option to either shut off or fall off. But Kenny was in the desperate position where he had to take a chance – either to try and pass and risk falling off, or shut off and Penhall would be gone anyway."

But ask Phil if he thinks Tore Kittilsen got it right and he remains as indecisive as many other observers still are to this day. "I think the referee got it right . . . but then again, maybe he didn't," he said.

"If he had excluded Penhall, then Bruce would have felt bloody hard done by, that's for sure. To be honest, it could have gone either way.

"Les Collins was unbelievable that night but, at the end of the day, Penhall deserved to win it. Carter got himself in a position that gave the referee no alternative but to exclude him.

"But the debate will go on forever," added Crump.

Even if Kittilsen had excluded Penhall, we will still never know whether Peter Collins would have beaten Carter in the re-run. Or whether Les Collins would have kept his nerve to beat Carter in heat 17 . . . and then possibly defeated either him or Penhall in a run-off for the championship. There are a few very big ifs in those last two sentences.

With all due respect to nice guy Les Collins, he was a shock merchant riding above himself, albeit at the peak of his career. He had won the BLRC in 1980 and showed his class again a few weeks before LA by winning the Inter-Continental Final round in Sweden. He was an established No.1 for Leicester Lions.

But he was not a genuine World Champion – never in the same league as Penhall and Carter.

Somehow, Kenny managed to summon the energy to climb aboard his Weslake for one last ride – what proved, for him, to be a meaningless heat 17. A win would have earned him a run-off with Sigalos for the bronze medal but, totally de-tuned and his head spinning with persecuted thoughts of what might have been, it was some achievement for him to even finish third – behind Les Collins and Moran but ahead of Dave Jessup.

A bronze medal would have meant nothing to Carter.

Barely 10 minutes later, Penhall easily won heat 19 to clinch his second world title, a point ahead of the younger Collins. The producers of CHiPS filmed the final scenes of the meeting to use subsequently in their show – Penhall played the part of Bruce Nelson in the series shown both in the States and in Britain – and they could not have scripted it better. America's golden boy was back on top of the podium, World Champion again.

And then, as the fireworks rocketed skywards, the final explosive act was played out. Having shattered Carter's title hopes for the second year in succession, a jubilant Bruce waved to the LA crowd and unashamedly announced to all that he had, in fact, ridden his last competitive race. Not only had he quit the British League, but he would not race speedway competitively again – anywhere in the world.

He was heading for Tinseltown but none of the TV shows and movies he featured in after he left the sport compared to the drama he starred in at LA in '82 – a speedway epic to rival any half-decent Hollywood blockbuster.

Penhall admits now, though: "Obviously, what happened in that race with Kenny took a little bit of the shine off it for me."

Penhall had retained the title with a large slice of good fortune but he did not leave speedway on a high. Without warning, the sport had lost one of its biggest drawcards – by then Carter was pure box office and certainly as big in the sport as Penhall, even without a world title to his name. There had been talk of Penhall hanging up his leathers as far back as the previous January, when he let slip to a TV audience in Sydney that he would be quitting speedway at the end of the 1982 season. But this had been quickly denied by his management team.

In the final weeks of his racing career, Bruce had let down a number of people – the Cradley Heath management, headed by Peter Adams, in particular, and also his loyal Heathens fans and others who put him up on a pedestal. He never rode again for the Black Country club after the World Final and as a result of his absence they lost the BL title to Belle Vue and the opportunity to complete the league and KO Cup double.

He admits: "The 1982 World Final raises so much controversy still because I left speedway that night. A lot of people want to point fingers at me and say I left the sport in a shambles, and how I shouldn't have won in LA."

After examining the evidence, and hearing all the conflicting views in minute detail, perhaps there was no true winner of the 1982 World Championship. The record books will always credit it to Bruce Penhall but he retired on the spot and never cashed in on his second successive world title. His comments in the previous few paragraphs suggest that he felt his victory had a hollow, somewhat tainted ring to it and that it will continue to provoke endless debate. Did he truly deserve it, as he undoubtedly did at Wembley in 1981, or did he just get lucky at the hands of a referee who many believe lacked the bottle to exclude the all-American hero in front of American fans in, er . . . America?

Carter said later: "I couldn't possibly win because it was in America. If I'd knocked Bruce off, they would have excluded me. And when he knocked me off, they blamed me anyway." You can see his point.

It could even be said that Bruce enjoyed a major slice of good fortune twice that night. As well as winning Kittilsen's hotly disputed call, Penhall also benefited from the rerun that gained him the extra point he needed to avoid a run-off for the title against Les Collins, who had already beaten him in their first ride.

Not surprisingly, Kenny's Halifax boss Eric Boothroyd remains firmly in the Carter camp.

"I think he would have been World Champion in 1982. That was his best chance – in LA. He should have won that night and didn't deserve to be excluded in that race with Penhall. The referee took the easy way out.

"He thought to himself: 'Oh, I'd better not exclude the home favourite and defending champion here in America', so he took the easy option and excluded

The saddest picture from LA, 1982.

Kenny instead."

As I suggest, treat yourself to the video or DVD and relive it all again for yourself. For me, the most memorable image from more than two hours of footage from the final is a haunting image of Carter in the pits once he knew his big chance had gone. Looking utterly sad and completely helpless, the tears were welling up in his eyes but somehow he fought them back – he couldn't bear for others to see him cry. Watching him rest his chin on his hand and staring into oblivion, you wonder if he was replaying all the tragedies and setbacks of his troubled past in a mind that must have been spinning at one hundred miles per hour. It's an incredibly sad picture of a broken man who must have been thinking that he had the world against him.

If only Kenny had won that night, it could have all turned out so differently.

Eric Boothroyd wonders what might have been, too. He said:"I know this much . . . if he'd become World Champion that night, British speedway would have gone in completely the opposite direction – upwards. He would have been a great champion, he was big box office and the fans came from everywhere to see him race, because he was a true entertainer."

Carter's England manager John Berry said: "We all have our own views on THAT race in California. It was one of those times when you wouldn't want to be the ref. For what it's worth, I believe the dice were loaded far too heavily in one direction. I have my own opinion but I think each camp will see it how they want. It would have needed a little green man from Mars, dropped into the ref's chair at the start of the race, to come up with a decision devoid of outside influences and not involving personalities, location, or politics."

British speedway lost out badly because the sport was deprived of another authentic superstar once Penhall quit on the rostrum – the first time the reigning World Champion would not been seen on English tracks.

Les Collins was a loser who, had the cards fallen differently, could have finished the night as gloriously as it began for him with that breathtaking wheel-to-wheel victory over the eventual champion. Although instead of cursing Kittilsen's decision, he should still be kicking himself for messing up in his easiest ride.

Kenny Carter was undoubtedly the biggest loser of all on that momentous night – and, if John Berry is right, not only in terms of being robbed of the world title he so desperately wanted.

Berry provides further food for thought with this final incisive comment: "I am convinced that had Kenny been crowned World Champion on that day in Los Angeles, or even at Bradford (in 1985), his life and attitudes would have changed, and those tragic, horrific, nightmarish events which haunt us all would not have taken place."

Chapter 13

TYRED OUT

IVAN Mauger has had a quarter-of-a-century to ponder what went wrong for Kenny Carter on that fateful night in Los Angeles and the deep-thinking Kiwi still has strong views on just why he believes the title slipped away from his protégé.

He blames Kenny's choice of the Dunlop tyre, as opposed to the more popular Carlisle, as the primary reason why he lost the 1982 world title to Bruce Penhall.

And for choosing what he still maintains was the wrong tyre on the night, Ivan points an accusing finger at Kenny's overbearing father, Mal.

These two factors, insists Mauger, cost Kenny the 1982 World Championship.

He says that the true Brit's anti-American agenda also proved his undoing when it came to speedway's biggest night of all.

Ivan resigned as Carter's manager at the end of 1982 – but he says now that he more or less made up his mind to terminate their written agreement halfway through the practice for the LA World Final. That is when he believes Kenny effectively lost his chance of winning the big prize.

He explained: "In those days the Carlisle tyre was far superior to the English Dunlop. But his father came into the pits with an armful of tyres, dumped them beside the bikes and said words to the effect of: "Yanks can't make f*****g tyres, put these Dunlops on . . . I've just got them from the factory'. He said Dunlop had made them especially for Kenny to use in the World Final.

"The Dunlop was only 100mm wide, but the Carlisle was 110mm in width and had a tread depth of 14mm. They were like big tractor tyres by comparison and Kenny was going like a rocket on them in the first three-quarters of the practice.

"But when his father arrived with his entourage – there were always two or three hangers-on – and he came barging into the pits, Kenny meekly allowed them to switch the Carlisles for Dunlops.

"This was totally against the agreement I had made with both Kenny and his father in my office in Woodford, when they first came over to discuss me becoming Kenny's manager.

"At that first meeting I told both of them that I was interested in looking after a good, young English rider who had talent and ambition, but only if I had control of all aspects of the racing – such as bikes, physical and mental training and all that was required to win the World Championship.

"I made that stipulation because I did not trust Kenny's dad not to interfere. He had been involved with road-racing but knew nothing about speedway.

"They both agreed to that stipulation then, so we drew up a formal contract.

"But once Kenny's father entered the scene during the practice, I had no further

Ivan Mauger and Barry Briggs – World Final co-promoters at LA – try to get the show moving again.

say – Kenny only took notice of him.

"There is no question about it. He was by far the best rider in practice, doing everything right. And he had all the guts needed to do it on World Final night as well, despite the pain he was in. He wasn't the type who was going to crumble at the start line. He was ready to win it.

"On the morning of the final we had Kenny's bikes in my garage and I urged him again to choose the Carlisle before the start of the meeting. But he used Dunlop instead – he wouldn't go against his father."

When it was pointed out to Ivan that Kenny had in fact won his first three races at LA in convincing style, and was the only rider still undefeated at the interval stage, he had his response ready: "My opinion is that if Kenny had been using a Carlisle, he would have been out of trouble. You have only to ask any of the riders around at that time what a huge disadvantage Dunlops were compared to the Carlisle.

"Kenny's father, or maybe it was one of his crew, then came down and started to blame Penhall. But I said to them: 'You can't blame Penhall. If you hadn't brought those effin tyres here, Kenny would have been 30 yards in front of Bruce – so you are just as much to blame as anybody else' I gave him a short shrift and was definitely on the outer with Kenny's dad and his entourage.

"Anyway, I had words with his father after practice and again after the final itself. I also had words with Kenny after the meeting, which was a bit difficult because he was still going to be staying back at my house in Orange County."

Despite publicly fighting Carter's corner in the bitter row surrounding the heat 14 incident with Penhall, Mauger says he had already made his mind up to stop managing Kenny.

He recalled: "We had a long talk in the spa at my house the day after the final. We went over the accident and how and why it happened. I gave him my opinion as to why it happened.

"He realised that I was right in what I had said. I explained to him that he was a very good, fast starter but, on the Dunlop tyre, he had been giving everybody a 10-yard start in the first half-a-lap.

"I said also to him: 'If your father's going to interfere in the way he has been doing, it's not going to work. It's detrimental to you. It's great being English – I appreciate all that stuff – but' . . ."

And 25 years on from the most talked about World Final in history, Mauger still insists: "If his father had not gone to LA, Kenny would have won that World Championship."

But Phil Pratt, the respected Weslake engine tuner Mauger introduced to Carter in 1981, said: "Ivan shouldn't have backed down on that issue. Kenny was paying him to help him win the World Championship and give him all the knowledge he'd built up over many years.

"If Ivan was cute enough to see the difference in Kenny's performance between using the Dunlop and then the Carlisle in practice, then Kenny surely had to listen to him.

"Ivan should have got hold of Kenny on the day of the World Final, when his old man wasn't allowed in the pits, and told him to 'get those bloody tyres off!'

"If Kenny had won the world title in Los Angeles, nobody would have said a word about him using all-British equipment bar an American-made tyre," said Phil.

Mauger believes that Carter's fierce patriotism, allied to his dislike of most things American, was another big contributory factor in his failure to win the world title.

He said: "That was one of Kenny's faults – he was British to the core. He would love to have won the world title using everything English-made, the whole lot. He had a Comet frame that was made in Yorkshire, a Weslake engine and, from my sponsors, I got for him Talon wheels, Venhill cables, NEB clutches, Renthal bars, Renold chains. etc…everything was English-made and he was English through and through.

"Kenny's favourite saying was: 'I hate those bloody Yanks'. I said to him: 'Kenny, they're good guys, really nice people, Bruce has been around me in New Zealand

Mal Carter enters the centre green melee, alongside Richard Pickering and Ivan.

and other places around the world since he was 17 or 18. He wants to win the World Championship just as much as you do and you can't hate him or the other Americans for wanting to win the same things as you'.

"I'd known Dennis Sigalos and the other American guys since they were kids and they were all nice guys. Hard riders to beat, but that's life. You have to beat hard riders to get to the top.

"But being the Yorkshireman that he was, Kenny didn't like them at all. When sitting together in my spa a week and 10 days before the '82' final, I said to him on several occasions: 'Just forget about them, just go and race them this time'.

"And he'd say: 'Oh, I wanna do this to them and I wanna do that to 'em'. I said: 'OK, if that's what you absolutely want to do, then do it next week – in a league match, not the World Final. Just go out to race everybody at the Coliseum'."

For Ivan it was all or nothing where Kenny was concerned. He could not tolerate any outside interference. He said: "That was the beginning of the end for us. I don't know whether Kenny told his father about our conversation but I didn't trust that situation not to happen again.

"I was so disappointed the way Kenny's dad had come into the pits at practice and demanded Kenny change everything we had worked so hard for. I couldn't accept the thought that he could completely ruin things that he knew nothing about.

"I told Kenny the day after the World Final that when we got back to England I wanted to exercise one of my rights in our contract to terminate it on December 31st."

Carter's friend and mechanic Phil Hollingworth claims that Kenny had also privately expressed to him his concerns about Mauger's handling of one or two of his sponsors and that, ultimately, the split of rider and manager was a mutual one. Phil recalls a heated argument between Kenny and Ivan in a hotel restaurant in Sweden after Kenny had confronted him about his concerns.

But asked about a possible dispute with Kenny, Ivan denied it and said: "I never had anything to do with his sponsors except to limit any demands in the build-up to important meetings, at practice sessions and at the actual meetings. He had some sponsors that gave him only product but thought they owned him and didn't know when to keep their noses out.

"Kenny's sponsors were very much down the order of priority for me, and that included his dad. My involvement was purely and simply to help him win the World Championship and he could have done that without any sponsors. Kenny was very well aware of this.

"I also told him that if he got to be World Champion, I'd several big-paying sponsors for him. As politely as I could, I told some of his small sponsors, who wanted to keep getting in the way, to piss off out of the pits."

Carter did not agree with his manager's strongly-held beliefs on the Dunlop-Carlisle dilemma. In his first column for *Speedway Star* following the '82 World Final, Kenny wrote: "I've heard it said that I won't win anything big in speedway until I stop using Dunlop tyres. But that's a load of rubbish in my book.

"The rest can use what they like – I'm sticking to Dunlops.

"There wasn't a lot wrong in my first three rides in Los Angeles or in the Golden Hammer at Cradley, where I cleaned up."

Carter remained utterly convinced that he had been unfairly denied the world title he believed was his. He went on: "Nearly every person I've spoken to since the World Final has told me I was 'robbed' by the referee and that Bruce Penhall knocked me off.

"You'd be amazed how many people, including non-speedway supporters, have come up to me after watching the final on TV and said how disgusted they were at the decision. And I'm talking about people from all over the country, not just Yorkshire.

"A few idiots have said I reacted stupidly on the mike when I was excluded. And Bobby Schwartz annoyed me with his column last week.

"He wrote that I made a fool of myself by having a go at the referee and wondered if I would be regretting it by now. He must be joking! If the same thing had happened to him when he looked like winning the World Final, he'd have gone mad.

"I'll tell you, and him, something. I'm amazed I stayed so calm. If I had been feeling 100 per cent fit I'd have gone mental. It was only because I was off colour and so shocked by the decision that stopped me from going completely berserk.

"I've no regrets – except that I cannot turn the clock back."

Back in 1982, Mauger commented a few weeks after the final that he remained convinced that Carter could still become World Champion – but he added provisos.

"I still believe Kenny can become World Champion but he must change his attitude drastically over several points before he will do it. At this moment in time he's a long way from being champion. He has finished second, third or fourth in so many individual meetings but it cannot always be bad luck that he hasn't won the ones that matter."

Mauger claimed that Carter put too much emphasis on his league form, and suggested that the 21-year-old's public outbursts did him no favours either on track or with the public at large. He said: "I've made plenty of statements in my time but they were usually about things I thought should be done in speedway. I never made predictions about winning meetings.

"It's part of Kenny's character. He is a brash, young Yorkshireman. But he only makes it harder for himself.

"But at the same time he is British and he is honest. He says what he thinks. What I cannot understand is why he hasn't a larger following among the British public.

"To understand Kenny you have to understand that he has exceptional ambitions. That is one of the things that attracted me to him in the first place.

"Surely the British fans realise that England only has Kenny and possibly one or two other riders who can become World Champion in the next five years. British speedway desperately needs a British World Champion and Kenny would make a good World Champion," Mauger added.

In 2007, knowing how Kenny's career panned out between the events of LA and his death in 1986, Ivan seems less convinced now that the rider he managed for the best part of 18 months would have been an ideal No.1 for the sport.

He said: "Would he have been a good World Champion? It's difficult to say because he never won it. But he was British to the core – so was his dad – and ultimately that cost him the World Championship.

"Britain needed a new World Champion, especially after Michael (Lee). Kenny most certainly was drug-free, and he tried to win every race. He would have been a huge asset to any British World Cup or Test team and was the only British rider who could have given Erik (Gundersen) and Hans (Nielsen) a bit of a hurry-up for a few years."

Chapter 14

MORE AGGRO WITH THE AMERICANS

AWEEK after the most controversial World Final in history, 11 points earned Kenny Carter only fourth place in the first Embassy British Open on yet another ultra-slick White City track. Dennis Sigalos beat Hans Nielsen in a run-off to win speedway's richest prize of £5,000 but the event never lived up to the pre-meeting hype.

Carter did not blame track conditions for his disappointing performance. He admitted: "I rode like an old woman! I was tired out."

Kenny could sometimes make you laugh even when he did not intend to. His biggest gripe about the British Open was not the slick conditions that became the unacceptable norm at a White City track with a reputation for processional, boring racing, but a dispute with stadium officials that nearly saw him thrown out of the West London venue before the event had even begun.

The rumpus centred around his van and the position he had parked it. Ever the opportunist when it came to giving his sponsors good mileage, he had deliberately parked his vehicle in a spot where he knew the ITV cameras would pick it up in the background while panning round the third/fourth bend!

But on this occasion Kenny was ordered by stadium staff to park his van elsewhere. Clearly disgruntled that his attempt at free advertising on national television had been foiled by a White City jobsworth, he took the opportunity to have another pop at his fellow English riders, criticising them for not projecting themselves to would-be sponsors. "They win titles," he said, "but people outside the sport, ordinary Joe Public, have never heard of them.

"I make sure they've heard of me!"

Carter's condemnation of his fellow Brits probably explained why none of them spoke up in support of him over the Los Angeles affair.

In the next breath, he ended his hard-hitting column for Speedway Star by plugging his three newest sponsors. Nike? Barclaycard? Or perhaps a tobacco or fuel giant? Nope.

"I've just signed three more deals," he wrote . . . "with Macdee Kitchens, Wamster Ovens and Spencer Trousers."

Eric Boothroyd appreciated the efforts Carter made to maximise exposure for his backers, regardless of their value. He said: "Kenny was a wheeler-dealer, just like his father, and wasn't backwards in coming forward.

"He was very good at getting sponsors for himself. Always very well presented, he went about business in a professional manner – he didn't turn up for meetings with would-be sponsors dressed in scruffy, old jeans, as a lot of riders did.

"He always worked very hard to do his best for his sponsors and it was through

Picking up drive during the ill-fated 1982 British Open at White City, just a week after the World Final.

Kenny that the Hams, Bobby and Allan, got involved with the Dukes – initially in our last season at The Shay and then when we had to move the team to Bradford."

The much-vaunted Embassy British Open represented another defining moment in speedway's decline from the start of the 80s. With World Champion Bruce Penhall nowhere to be seen, the attendance figure at White City was dismally low and there was even a bizarre call from Len Silver for the FIM to strip Penhall of his world title and hand it to his fellow countryman Sigalos, as reward for 'Siggy's' British Open victory. There was about as much chance of that happening as Bruce appearing in a re-make of Gone With The Wind. Len didn't mention how Les Collins might feel if the FIM mandarins in Zurich had taken his hasty advice!

There was briefly talk of the BSPA suing Penhall for breaking his contract with Cradley Heath and his agreement to ride in the British Open but no legal action was ever taken against him.

A report in the *Sunday Mirror* claimed that there could be a 'showdown' between Penhall and Carter in Las Vegas. Kenny welcomed the idea but it never got off the ground.

Speedway had to accept that it would have to get used to life without Bruce Penhall. And so would Kenny Carter. Their rivalry had been a focal point of the

England v USA Test series, World Team Cup meetings and all the individual and team events where their clashes were always very eagerly anticipated. Simply, no rivalry of this intensity between two top riders has existed in the sport since Penhall left.

The 1982 season had been a difficult one for Eric Boothroyd, who later revealed that the average attendance at The Shay had fallen to 2,700 per meeting - – 300 people a week short of the track's break-even figure.

From a Halifax perspective, the one downside to Carter's acceleration to world class status was that he had become in increasingly constant demand for England and of course progress in the World Championship also caused him to miss a number of domestic meetings. The fact that Saturday was the Dukes' regular race night, the same day a number of other BL clubs also ran at home, only exacerbated the problem, with Kenny invariably riding in internationals on many weekends of the season.

In a diminishing British League that had lost one club every year since 1978, Halifax slumped to a final position of 13th in a league of 15 – the lowest in the BL's history to that point.

Use of the rider replacement or guest facility rarely provided adequate cover for their No.1 rider, especially as other members of the team were struggling for form. Apart from the wrist injuries that forced Merv Janke to return home to Australia early, and which presented chances for Martin Dixon, their loanee from Middlesbrough, and young Swede Mats Olsson, Ian Cartwright had found the pressure of the club captaincy a burden during his testimonial year. In September, he handed the responsibility to Carter who wanted to be skipper almost as much as he relished being Halifax No.1. Kenny had helped his partners wherever possible before, not only on the track but also with the loan of his bikes.

He was not into doing any favours for Americans, though.

After riding for England in an ill-conceived international four team tournament staged on four BL tracks, won by new world champions USA and also featuring Denmark and Sweden, there was only one more meeting for him worth winning as the 1982 season reached its climax.

Just how determined Carter was to retain the British League Riders' Championship was made abundantly clear in a ruthless heat 9 – the race that brought an otherwise drab meeting to life. As the in-form Dennis Sigalos tried to pass Carter on the outside around the pits bend, the defending champion moved wider and wider, slammed the door shut on 'Siggy' who hit the fence and landed in a heap on the heavy, rain-soaked track. This time there was no Tore Kittilsen for Carter to worry about, and referee John Miller had no hesitation in excluding the lanky American.

The chorus of boos that greeted Carter's win in the rerun did not bother him one iota. He had already taken care of the main challengers in his first ride, won from Shawn Moran, Chris Morton and Les Collins, and despite some blatantly robust attempts by Bobby Schwartz to exact revenge for Carter's treatment of his fellow American Sigalos, 'Boogaloo' just could not quite pull it off.

Summing up the ill feeling that had built up between Carter and a number of the

After retaining the BLRC, with Shawn Moran and Hans Nielsen the runners-up.

Americans, Schwartz was quoted afterwards as admitting that he deliberately set out to 'do' the England No.1 when they clashed in heat 16.

Schwartz, who was typical of sensitive Americans hurt by criticism or loss of popularity, subsequently phoned the Speedway Star office to deny he had begun a vendetta against Carter. He claimed: "Kenny Carter didn't knock Dennis Sigalos off at the BLRC but he left him nowhere to go. I was prepared to do the same thing to him. But it is ridiculous to say that the American riders are going to get Kenny."

Sigalos was adamant that Carter left him no room and protested that it was the Halifax rider's fault when he hit the fence. But Carter shrugged it all off and completed a 15-point maximum to round the British season off in typically controversial style – on the bonnet of a Rolls Royce that carried him around the Hyde Road track.

Naturally, Carter had his say on his so-called feud with the Yanks. Somewhat unconvincingly, he said: "Let's get one thing straight. I'm not having a running battle with every American rider and I'm not looking for one."

He pointed out: "I get on great with Kelly and Shawn Moran and most of the others." Before he added: "The only three I have had trouble with are Bruce Penhall, Dennis Sigalos and Bobby Schwartz."

With even more inflammatory zeal, he went on: "I'm sick of Schwartz sounding off about incidents that have nothing to do with him. He must have the biggest mouth in speedway at the moment and I think Sigalos is trying to step into Penhall's shoes when he is just not big enough.

"It has been suggested that Sigalos' mechanic had a go at me in the pits but that isn't true. None of them said a word during the meeting. But they said plenty afterwards.

"It was easy for them to call me a cry baby in Los Angeles but who was doing the crying this time?

"I'm not happy with the stuff they were coming out with and some of the remarks attributed to Bobby Schwartz disgusted me. I think the BSPA or the Control Board should fine Schwartz for some of his remarks. I know his personality and I'm not surprised he tried to have a go at me later in the meeting. But I was smart enough to keep out of his way.

"When speedway is a family sport, it's not nice to read about so-called vendettas and threats.

"I won the BLRC fair and square and got the luck I had been missing in so many big ones. My victory shut up a few people who had been harping on about how I had won nothing this season."

Carter travelled alone to Australia, stopping over at Perth for a few days before making his way to New South Wales where the 1982 World Pairs Final would be held at the Liverpool Raceway, near Sydney, on December 11 – the first motorcycle world championship event ever staged in Australia.

He had ridden the Liverpool track the previous winter, scoring an 18-point maximum, but this time he would be up against 12 class opponents.

A number of people questioned the decision to partner Peter Collins, the 28-year-old Belle Vue star, with the new England No.1. On the previous August Bank Holiday, the two Northern rivals had clashed on track during a league match at Halifax. Carter fell but Collins protested against the ref's decision to exclude him and the riders exchanged angry words at the time of the incident.

Carter said: "Peter Collins and myself exchanged a few words at Halifax and it's been suggested that there's been a bit of ill feeling between us and we would hardly be the ideal pairing for England in the World Pairs Final. But whatever feelings he's got it's not likely to affect our riding if we are picked for the Pairs. And I still think we go well together."

Collins also tried to play down their fall out before leaving for Australia, saying: "We both made our points about how we felt at the time and said what we thought of each other. It probably did us some good at the time and that was the end of it. It's all in the past now."

But it was never forgotten by either rider and their relationship continued to deteriorate, albeit gradually at first. With Bruce Penhall out of the way, Carter had made a new enemy, although his gently simmering feud with PC would take another couple of years to come to the boil.

Even if Carter and Collins had been bosom buddies, it is unlikely they could have lived with the brilliant American pair of Bobby Schwartz and Dennis Sigalos who entertained a capacity Liverpool crowd on their way to maximum points. England

Kenny and Peter Collins tussling during a Halifax v Belle Vue match The Shay in 1982, when they clashed before becoming World Pairs partners. Doug Wyer is the rider with the ringside seat.

finished a distant second, eight points adrift of the Americans, and though Collins sparkled with a superb 15 he received poor support from Carter, who had been caught out by the grippy track conditions and managed only seven (paid 10) from his six rides.

It was largely thanks to the mechanical efforts of Martin Hignett, Mike Lee's former spanner man and a regular visitor to Australia, that Carter got going at all in the latter stages of the meeting. He followed Collins home for 5-1s against Denmark and Czechoslovakia to ensure England pipped Danes Ole Olsen and Hans Nielsen to the silver medal.

Speaking in 2007, Collins said: "Kenny and I met up for the first time in Australia that year when he just turned up at the practice. He had been in Perth beforehand and I seem to remember him having problems while he was there. He had apparently brought a Mercedes car over for somebody and I think there was a load of aggro that he left behind him when he flew from Perth to Sydney.

"I had been staying with Martin Hignett, who worked for me in the year I was World Champion, before moving on to become Michael Lee's mechanic, so we go back a long way. Martin's brother, Robert, worked for me right until the end of my career.

"I wasn't happy that Kenny had given me all that crap beforehand, saying in the press how angry he was that I'd been chosen as his partner. I saw it written somewhere that he wanted to be with someone who was more capable of winning the Pairs rather than someone who, like me, who had been around a long time.

"What he didn't take into account is the massive experienced I'd got. I'd spent most of my career racing in Australia during the British winter and I'd previously ridden at the Liverpool track loads of times.

"I had a cracker of a meeting, setting a new track record and beating the home favourites. But Kenny was struggling. I sacrificed the best gate against the

Americans for him, because it was the only chance we had of getting a 5-1 against them. But he totally squandered it by coming last. Looking back, I should never have done that."

An honest but very much down in the dumps Carter admitted afterwards that he felt he had let Collins and England down, while acknowledging that America were deserved winners of the Pairs title for the second successive year.

He said: "I'm sorry about the Pairs. I feel I let England down although I tried 200 per cent. The track was slick in practice and I was flying. But when it came to the meeting the track had changed completely. It was very grippy and I just wasn't fast enough.

Taking it easy on international duty.

"It was very disappointing because PC rode so well," added Kenny.

Not that Carter took all the blame for England's latest defeat to the Americans. He highlighted the BSPA's half-baked attitude towards international competition. British promoters had been conspicuous by their absence from the individual World Final in LA, where the expenses could not even be found for team manager Eric Boocock to be on hand in the pits for the benefit of the four English riders – John Berry had resigned midway through the season to concentrate on running Ipswich. Knowing also that the BSPA would not pay for him to be with PC and Carter in Australia, Booey then quit in dismay, so the Lions duo in Liverpool were also lacking support.

After the Pairs final, Carter praised the efforts of Martin Hignett but then added: "I'm not making excuses, because the Americans were both fantastic, and we'd have had to be at our very best to beat them. But PC and myself were a bit upset that Howard Cole, who was supposed to be team manager, didn't even turn up for the meeting. We both feel that Eric Boocock should have had his return air fair paid to Australia."

As it turned out, Eric's brother, Sydney-based Nigel Boocock, who had offered to do the England job, helped the Americans to win the Pairs. "England really deserved what they got," added Carter.

Collins echoed his partner's criticism of the BSPA, adding: "Kenny had problems with his equipment in Australia but there was nobody to help him sort out the aggro. How do you think we felt standing in the pits at practice looking around for the man

Gordon Kennett doesn't look over-keen on Eric Boocock's decision to partner him with Kenny.

who was supposed to be our manager? Martin Hignett, who was once my mechanic and now manager of Jim Airey's shop, assisted us.

"He did what he could but Kenny and I were very disappointed that we didn't have a manager. How can people take speedway seriously when things like that are allowed to happen?"

Chapter 15

HIGH ROLLER TO WORLD CHAMPION

THE year began on a high for Kenny with the wonderful news, in January, that Pam had given birth to their first child, daughter Kelly Marie – named after Kenny's favourite American rider, Kelly Moran! There were initial concerns when the otherwise healthy baby suffered an aneurism but the scare soon passed and the family settled into their finally fully renovated farmhouse.

The converted stone-built property was set back a couple of hundred yards off Taylor Lane in approximately two acres of land that provided wonderful open views towards Halifax, just five miles to the south.

The property included sealed double-glazing, an oak-fitted kitchen, stone fireplace, lounge with stone-built bar, dining room, three bedrooms, luxury bathroom with whirlpool bath and gold plated fittings, and shower room with adjacent sauna. Alongside the gravel drive was a patio area with a barbecue.

To the side were two large green-painted Nissen huts that Kenny had fitted out as workshops. He kept all his bikes and other racing equipment in one and, later, the other was used by his brother, Alan, and his mechanic, Howard.

To deter would-be burglars, Kenny stationed his Alsatian bitch guard dog, Gypsy, outside the farmhouse, tethered on a chain. He had rescued the dog from a scrap metal yard where it had been badly ill-treated. Although for a while it terrified any visitors to the farm who came near it, Gypsy became a loveable pet. The Carters also owned a whippet called Tiger who seemed to go everywhere with Kenny.

After fitting out their new home to his and Pam's taste, Kenny set about plans to build his own moto-cross circuit within the grounds.

Phil Hollingworth enjoyed many fun hours at the home-made track with his friend and said: "It looked just like a proper moto-cross circuit.

"Eric Boothroyd gave Kenny an old starting gate from The Shay and we'd race each other on 250cc Honda ATC three-wheel trikes.

"We went at it hammer and tongs, doing all sorts of stunts. Once, for a laugh, I jumped over Kenny's head!

"We laid a concrete square for the start area. The electric starting gate was powered by a wagon battery. Kenny reckoned the gate, with proper elastic tapes, was good for improving his starting reflexes.

"Once the tapes went up, we'd race down a steep hill and then over other big jumps that had been carved out of the ground with a digger.

"Worn out tyres were placed around the edge to add a further touch of realism."

England line up before facing the USA in the first Test of 1983 at Wimbledon. Left to right: Kenny, Peter Collins, Malcolm Simmons, Wally Mawdsley, Michael Lee, Les Collins. Front: Dave Jessup, Chris Morton and John Davis.

Before the start of the '83 season Kenny signed a new sponsorship deal with the Land Rover Centre of Huddersfield, where founding director Peter Garside handed him the keys to a personalised V8 Land Rover.

It was around this time that Kenny bought his first Rolls-Royce and declared that he wanted to be a millionaire by the time he was 30. The cream and brown Silver Cloud, registered in 1973 and valued at £10,000, was specially acquired so that he could chauffeur his mechanic Phil Hollingworth to the church for his wedding to Debbie Kaney at Sowerby Bridge.

Phil said: "Because Kenny married Pam when they were still both so young, he kept badgering me to get married too. He said: 'If you get married, I'll buy you a Rolls-Royce'.

"It wasn't his sort of car – he was more into XR3s and Mazda X7s – but he was looking for an excuse to buy a Roller and that's what he did for my wedding. Afterwards, he let me use it all the time.

"One day I came in and told him that Debbie was pregnant. About three weeks later he said to me: 'Guess what? Pam's pregnant!' That was him all over, he didn't like to be outdone."

Carter's face was becoming an increasingly familiar sight. BBC TV invited him to their Manchester studios to appear on *A Question of Sport*. He was even featured in the *Sunday Times* colour supplement, whose writer, clearly unfamiliar with the shale sport, re-christened him 'The Cinder Track Super Brat!'

No half measures . . . driving hard under Bobby Schwartz during the final Test of the '83 series at Sheffield.

This time Halifax had no difficulty reaching agreement with Carter to lead a side that Eric Boothroyd hoped would have a more youthful look to it following the reluctant £5,000 transfer of second heat leader John Louis to King's Lynn.

But mechanical gremlins severely hampered Carter's form in the early part of the season. In the first two Test matches against the USA at Wimbledon and Swindon, he contributed only nine points. And much to Kenny's annoyance, he was even dropped after his second ride by new manager Wally Mawdsley, who brought in 37-year-old reserve Malcolm Simmons as a replacement.

An embarrassed Carter said: "Wally Mawdsley dropped me after I came last in my second ride. But I'd had a paid win with Chris Morton in my first, so why did he drop *me?*

"I know I had another bad meeting but I was the one who carried England in the series last year. Now *I'm* being pulled out!"

Carter's four-letter outburst in response to being left out of one race saw him led away by Mawdsley towards the privacy of the Blunsdon dressing rooms where they had a clear-the-air chat behind closed doors.

"My pride has been hurt. I like to think I'm England's No.1 but that means I've got to ride like a No.1," said a despondent Carter, who again blamed his misfiring Weslakes. "This must be my worst ever start to a season," he added.

But Kenny resolved his motor problems in time to inspire England to a series victory over the Americans. Spearheading his country with 16 points in the Lions' 63-45 third Test victory at Poole, he top-scored again with 13 in the 66-42 defeat at

Kenny and Neil Collins about to surge through the gap left by Dennis Sigalos in the deciding Test at Sheffield.

Ipswich, where he took home favourite Sigalos from the back.

Carter never needed any extra motivation to win at anything, least of all a race against the Americans. But perhaps even he was a little more fired up than usual to score points at Ipswich that night after being handed a poison pen letter in the pits from a female supporter.

Colin Gear, who succeeded George Barclay as secretary of the Speedway Riders' Association at the start of 1983, became a witness to the anti-Carter brigade whose unhealthy hatred of him had been fuelled by previous friction between the England star and the top Americans at the end of 1982.

Gear recalled: "I saw a young woman call Kenny towards her when she was stood at the side of the pits. She handed him a letter and then walked away. Kenny read it quickly but then just threw it on the floor and walked off.

"I went over to pick up the letter and was surprised to read words to the effect of, 'if you're not careful, you're gonna get your comeuppance'. It clearly didn't bother him in the least and he went out and rode brilliantly."

The role of SRA secretary was always a frustratingly thankless one because this toothless association has forever been undermined by its own members who can't agree or stick together on any of the major issues that have affected them. Gear said: "Kenny never turned up for any of our AGMs while I was doing the job but he did have more time for me, and he became quite friendly with my partner Marilyn and I, after I managed to do him a favour once.

"He had won an individual meeting sponsored by the *Sunday Mirror* but they still owed him his £1,000 prize money weeks after the meeting. Kenny had tried to get a cheque out of the Mirror Group himself but when he had no luck, he asked me to help him. I'd never spoken to him before but he phoned me at home one night and, with typical brashness, said: "You do f*** all for the money we pay you, so get off you're arse and get my money for me!'

"I had to admire his front and, I'm pleased to say, John Lewsey, promotions manager at The Mirror, did eventually pay Kenny the thousand pounds they owed him.

"After that, he would always come over and say 'hello' to me and Mal if he saw us at a track, and one night after a meeting at Halifax in '83 he spent a long time chatting and enjoying a quiet drink with us at the bar."

A 7,000 crowd, Owlerton's highest post-war attendance, saw England win the decisive fifth test, 58-50, to clinch a 3-2 series success. Kenny rode side-by-side with Neil Collins for the first lap and was content to sit behind the Leicester rider as they rode to a 5-1 in heat 17, before PC and Michael Lee stretched the winning margin in the final heat.

Two wins by newcomer Simon Wigg saw England scrape through the UK qualifier of the World Team Cup at Reading, where they had trailed New Zealand by eight points at one stage, with the Americans comfortable winners. Kenny scored eight, though he was surprised to be beaten by his 43-year-old former manager first time out!

For the World Pairs semi-final at Bremen, Carter was an automatic choice to partner Peter Collins after recapturing his best form at the end of the Test series against America. Although Dennis Sigalos and Bobby Schwartz began their defence of the title with a win, 15 points by Carter and 10 from Collins was enough to see England comfortably through in second place. And Kenny's confidence was further boosted by the fact that he was the only rider to beat the Californian duo.

Carter and Sigalos started the new season as long-term favourites for the 1983 world title, which would reach its climax in Germany. A strong finish at Leicester saw Kenny ease through the British semi-final with 11 points but his hopes of winning the British Championship at the third attempt were dashed at Coventry, where Chris Morton won the title despite winning only two of his five rides.

Morton admitted afterwards that he had a point to prove after being overlooked for the World Pairs. But no-one had a bigger point to prove in the World Pairs Final than Carter.

As the first of the year's three World Championship finals approached, there were more questions being asked of Kenny Carter. Although he was fully justified in boasting to be England's No.1, he still had not won a major title to support his claim.

And while Americans Sigalos and Schwartz were slight favourites to retain the World Pairs crown in Gothenburg, where the Yanks were going for a pairs hat-trick, there was increasing pressure on Carter and Peter Collins to bring back the silverware that England had not won since 1980.

PC and Kenny – the body language says it all.

Above: World Final or not, Kenny finds time for a nap in the Gothenburg pits.

Right: Making a point to referee Sam Bass while Hans Nielsen awaits his turn on the phone.

Below: A 5-1 with PC against the German pair, Karl Maier and Egon Müller.

Wally Mawdsley ignored the form of new British Champion Chris Morton and kept faith with the duo who had been beaten out of sight by Sigalos and Schwartz in the 1982 final in Australia the previous December. And the England manager's faith in them was handsomely rewarded as his duo temporarily put their northern rivalry on hold to combine effectively as a partnership.

Maximum points in their opening two rides, against Germany and hosts Sweden, got PC and Kenny off to a flier before the anticipated much tougher challenge of Denmark in heat 10, a race that ultimately proved the most important and controversial.

Needless to say, Kenny was in the thick of it. He and old adversary Hans Nielsen involved themselves in what looked like a spot of psychological warfare as the two of them rubbed elbows at the starting gate and neither would budge an inch. Referee Sam Bass, a policeman from Australia, summoned both Carter and Nielsen to the pits phone to warn them about their conduct but the shenanigans continued.

As Kenny, off the inside, and Nielsen continued to delay the start, the Dane actually fell from his machine in a desperate attempt to stop it from careering through the tapes. Bass ruled that, although the tapes did not break, the Birmingham rider's rear axle had in fact crossed the start line, so he was rightly excluded.

In the second rerun, England got the second major slice of good luck they needed and, some would argue, they earned, when Nielsen's partner Erik Gundersen suffered an engine blow-up while well ahead at the end of lap three. Carter punched the sunlit Swedish air in delight as he rode by the disconsolate Dane.

With America unable to recover from a dismal start, the resulting 5-0 over the unfortunate Danes virtually gifted England the title, although not before they had shared the points with their other main rivals, Australia.

The classy Billy Sanders, who along with Nielsen was the best rider on view, won heat 15 by a mile but Collins and Carter rode a tactically sound race to keep the other Aussie, Gary Guglielmi a distant fourth. Australia could still regain the lead in the meeting if they won their next race but, in looking for his partner on the first bend, Sanders locked up and fell to tarnish an otherwise brilliant performance.

Denmark ended Australia's fading hopes when Nielsen, unable to catch Sanders, relegated the battling Guglielmi to third place. It left England needing four points from their last ride to clinch victory and they duly completed the task with Carter easing round Mauger on the first turn and Collins staying comfortably ahead of Larry Ross.

PC admits that his victory with his good mate Chris Morton a year later meant much more to him than this victory shard with Carter. He said: "We were riding in the Pairs but not riding as a pair, if you know what I mean? And there was no social side to our partnership whatsoever.

"What I found with Kenny in our World Pairs meetings was that he never seemed to know what was going on when it came to team tactics. He was always saying what a big England man he was but he was such an individualist and his head always seemed to be somewhere else. I was on the ball regarding how many points we needed in certain situations but he never seemed to know what we needed to do and

Referee Sam Bass lays down the law to the England pair and manager Wally Mawdsley.

who we needed to beat.

"Even before our last race in Gothenburg, Kenny didn't even know what we required to win the trophy. The plan was that Kenny would take care of Ivan while I had to beat Larry Ross, but he wasn't aware of the efforts I was making to beat Larry."

Surely, though, it was team manager Wally Mawdsley's job to ensure both riders were fully kept in the picture about what was required from them at every stage of the meeting?

PC replied: "Yeah, but it still didn't seem to register with Kenny. He knew what he was doing but he didn't know what else was happening around him. I just felt I was doing quite a lot of work and he didn't quite understand it, because he simply wasn't interested.

"You can understand somebody being selfish in individual meetings – you have to be. But when it comes to the Pairs, that's a totally different animal."

In common with too many major meetings at Gothenburg, the 1983 World Pairs Final was not much of a spectacle. There was a distinct lack of genuine racing on a hard, slick surface that left 6,240 fans in the impressive Ullevi Stadium with little to remember it by.

Pam Carter was at the stadium but she spent most of the evening rocking five-month-old Kelly Marie to sleep in a van in the car park, although mother and daughter were present in the pits in time to see the new World Pairs champions presented with their medals.

The partnership was not brilliant but it had been efficiently effective on the night. Carter scored 15 (paid 16) points to Collins' 10 (plus 4). It was PC's third success in the competition following his victories with Malcolm Simmons in 1977 and Dave

Partners who became arch enemies . . . PC (10) and Kenny on their way to glory in the World Pairs Final at a near empty Ullevi Stadium in 1983. Below: Handshakes all round after their title-clinching win over the Kiwis.

Jessup three years later.

On the flight home from Sweden, in a rare moment of introspection, Carter told *Speedway Star's* Peter Oakes: "I needed to win something. I've not been as keen on winning this year as I should be. I know it but I cannot explain why. I've always known my ability but I must admit I was beginning to wonder whether something was always going to go wrong when it mattered."

Having apparently laid to rest the World Championship ghosts that had haunted

The top three in the 1983 World Pairs Final with Sam Bass. PC and Kenny are joined by fellow riders Gary Guglielmi, Billy Sanders, Hans Nielsen and Erik Gundersen. Below: Pam and Kelly Marie in the pits.

him at Wembley in 1981 and Los Angeles a year later, Carter was again being considered as a certain future World No.1. It was surely only a matter of time before he would lift the big one.

In the meantime, he had at last become a World Champion. It was not enough, though, to satisfy him. The gold medal from the FIM was nice but he knew the glory of winning in Sweden was a joint effort, one he had to be share with Peter Collins who, under normal circumstances, he would regard as one of his biggest rivals.

Kenny's insatiable desire for personal glory was heightened by the success his brother, Alan, was enjoying as a prominent member of the Kenny Roberts-backed Yamaha team in the World Motorcycling Grand Prix. Teamed with Wayne Rainey, the 18-year-old made history when he won the French GP at Le Mans in 1983 to become the youngest-ever GP round winner. He finished 12th overall that season and was the highest placed Brit again in 1984 (ninth) and 1985 (seventh).

The friendly rivalry between the brothers proved a great motivating force for them both and nothing would have pleased Kenny more than for him and 'Our Nipper' to have won the World Championship in their respective chosen sports. Kenny made this point when the Carters appeared together on Yorkshire TV's *Calendar* show the weekend after what proved to be Alan's finest achievement.

The thing about Kenny was that because he divided opinion like no other rider of his generation, there were always plenty of people – outside Halifax -– who came to see him lose rather than win. Bruce Penhall had long since departed the speedway scene but they have long memories in the Black Country. One imaginative Cradley Heath fan displayed a home-made banner on the White City terraces bearing the words: 'Erik (Gundersen) eats three Shredded Wheat – Kenny's still on Rusks!'

Hans Nielsen, who added the Inter-Continental crown to his previous wins in the Danish and Nordic finals, was very much the man in form, with Gundersen and Michael Lee – who grabbed second spot in the London qualifier – among the prime contenders for the world title. The Ipswich pair of Dennis Sigalos and Billy Sanders were also showing more consistent form than Carter as the big day in Germany beckoned. Even Ole Olsen, through to his ninth World Final, could not be completely discounted after he turned back the years to glide through the ICF.

The prospect of Denmark filling the top three positions on the World Final rostrum at Norden, the unlikely countryside venue for the big occasion, gathered momentum after the World Team Cup Final at Vojens. Despite the best efforts of Lee and Carter to keep England level with the Danes and only one point adrift of the USA, it was Olsen's highly motivated and well drilled Vikings who romped to a victory that heralded a new era of Danish domination.

Not that Denmark, who won by eight points from England despite the absence of the injured Tommy Knudsen, had much competition in the way of professionalism at Vojens. All five Denmark team members had two bikes each, with another three spares ready in a van.

By comparison, England had seven bikes between five riders, with only Carter and reserve Peter Collins taking two bikes each to the final of speedway's most important team event. Lee, who top-scored and dropped his only point to

Gundersen, had to lend his machine to Dave Jessup after DJ's expensive new GM engine blew in his first race, while Chris Morton had problems with his only bike.

Many had written off Lee after he had fallen foul of the authorities with increasing regularity but as the '83 season neared its climax he had regained the tag of England No.1. He did not shout it from the rooftops nor, as Carter did, have the proud boast emblazoned in words along both sides of his van. But his move to Poole appeared to give him a new lease of life and saw him recapture something close to peak form at just the right time.

Lee was certainly a very serious threat to Carter's title hopes at Norden, especially after the 1980 World No.1 beat his compatriot,

2-0, in the first leg of their Golden Helmet match-race at Poole . . . and then absolutely crushed him in the return at Halifax. Lee turned up at The Shay with a 'special' engine that he was trying out for the World Final. Not only did he embarrass Carter by whipping him, 2-0, on his home patch, he knocked almost a second off Kenny's track record in the first race (down to 61.6) and then beat the old previous best time (62.5) again in the second.

To rub salt into Carter's wounds, Lee then defeated the Halifax kingpin again when they met again in the subsequent best pairs event. "He beat me easily, I couldn't get near him," admitted a bewildered Carter who was seething inside. He hated being made to look a mug, especially in front of his home fans, but that is just what Lee did to him that night.

There were some in the Halifax corner of the Shay pits who wondered whether Lee's 'rocket machine' was within the legal 500cc limit, but they chose to keep their suspicions to themselves, believing that an official protest would have been ridiculed as sour grapes.

Phil Pratt, who had tuned Carter's Weslake engines since 1981, recalls receiving a phone call from an unhappy Kenny around this time. He said: "The only time he got on the phone and was feeling a bit miffed with me was when he rode against Michael Lee at Poole for the Golden Helmet. At that time I was doing Michael's engines as well.

"Kenny couldn't even get the bike off the start – he stalled it on the line – and he told me, 'the engine is no good anyway'. I told him to come back to my place and we'd look at it later that night.

"He couldn't believe it – all he'd done was oil up a plug. He just needed to change it and he'd have been away. But that's knowledge he didn't have."

At least Carter regained his self-esteem by winning the Elf Golden Gauntlets at Leicester ahead of a field enhanced by eight other world finalists, including Lee, Nielsen, Sanders, Olsen and Morton. Apart from the Daily Mirror/Weslake 16-lap marathon race at Ipswich, the Blackbird Road classic was the only domestic individual title of note he would win all year.

The one he really wanted, of course, was the world title in Germany – and there was trouble there before Kenny had even reached the track.

Chapter 16

DRIVING OLE CRAZY!

AFTER his high profile clashes with the Americans the previous year, Kenny adopted a less confrontational attitude to speedway in 1983. Journalist Richard Bott, who got to know Carter better than any other speedway scribe, detected an uncharacteristically subdued mood in him when they spoke just prior to the 1983 World Final at Norden.

Perhaps mindful of all the hype that surrounded his dramatic showdown with Bruce Penhall the previous year, a low-key Carter told Bott: "I just want to keep myself to myself this year in the build up to the final."

He betrayed no signs of a lack of inner-belief, however. When interviewed by BBC Grandstand's Tony Millard before the meeting in Germany, Carter did not care to dwell on his recent emphatic Golden Helmet defeats by Lee or single out any other riders as being a particular threat to his title chances. He said: "I've just come here today to beat 15 riders. I don't care who's in the race, I just want to beat everybody."

The main difference for Kenny in the build up to his third World Final compared to the previous two was the absence from his corner of Ivan Mauger. Having cut his business ties with Carter following the Los Angeles final, Mauger provided a little help, albeit in a much less visible way, to one or two other world finalists in the days immediately prior to Norden. He attended private practice sessions with Chris Morton at Belle Vue and also had words of advice for his fellow Kiwi, Mitch Shirra.

Being involved with Carter had cost Mauger financially, although it could have been far worse. The FIM took a very dim view of his infamous telephone rant at referee Tore Kittilsen in LA and at one stage they suspended his racing licence for a year. It was not until March '83 that Mauger finally won his appeal against the governing body's ruling. Instead of losing his licence, he was fined 3000 Swiss francs for verbally blasting Kittilsen. Mauger rarely lost a battle with the sport's hierarchy and so it proved again on this occasion. The fine – roughly the equivalent of £1,000 – was peanuts compared to the tens of thousands of pounds he stood to lose had he not had a licence to compete on the lucrative continental scene and resume his beloved pursuit of the World Longtrack Championship.

Despite his split from Carter, Mauger knew that in the most open – or should that be weakest? – World Final for years, Carter was very much a main contender for the crown vacated by Penhall's retirement. He said at the time: "Even if he is not going as well as last year, Kenny on half form is still better than 90 per cent of the others on top form."

Kenny turned to his former Halifax team-mate and veteran England international, John Louis, for moral support in Germany. Louis, one of England's leading stars of

Studying the changing track conditions at Norden with John Louis.

the 70s and the World No.3 in 1975, had left the Dukes and moved back to East Anglia to join King's Lynn at the start of '83 but he was flattered, if admittedly somewhat bemused, by the invitation to help. Now promoter at Ipswich, the track where he made his name, Louis remembers receiving a phone call from Carter, but he said: "Kenny didn't need any advice from me – he was totally single-minded."

As well as calling up Louis for what he might be able to offer by way of speedway advice, Kenny once again also paid for Graham McKeon to fly over from Australia to work alongside his regular UK mechanic, Richard Pickering. A third mechanic, Phil Hollingworth, was due to be in the Carter pit corner, too, but withdrew at the eleventh hour. He explained: "I didn't go after we'd had a big fallout over who was going to travel out to Germany with Kenny in the van. Originally, it was agreed that Kenny, Pam, my missus, Debbie, and me would go together, while Mal, Alan and the others would travel out there in separate vehicles.

"But then, for some reason or other, right at the last minute, Kenny said Debbie couldn't go with us in the van. She didn't attend that many speedway meetings but she had been really looking forward to seeing Kenny ride in the final. So I told him that if she wasn't going, then neither was I. Instead, I stayed at home and watched the meeting on TV."

Although Phil and Kenny had been very good friends since Carter started in speedway, they had their fall-outs along the way and Ollie never allowed the younger man to push him around.

He said: "Richard would bow and scrape to him but I remember the first time I worked for Kenny at The Shay on my own. When the time came for him to leave the pits and get changed on the other side of the stadium, where the dressing rooms used to be, Kenny said to me: 'Right, bring my bag' and started walking off in the direction of the changing rooms.

"I said to him: 'Get your own f****** bag, you lazy bastard! I'm your mechanic, not your dogsbody'.

"He didn't like that. But when he was in his pomp and things were going well, it wasn't like working for somebody. It just felt like two lads going round together.

"I could be honest with him. There were times when I'd tell him to his face: 'You rode like a w****r' and he'd say 'yeah'. Or then he would say: 'But if we did this and we did that . . .' He'd try and react constructively rather than just come back in and kick the bike. To be fair, he didn't have many bad races anyway."

Ollie confirmed that Kenny was also prepared to get his hands dirty on occasions if necessary. "If he had been riding at Halifax on a Saturday, I'd usually clean his bikes on a Sunday morning. But if we were particularly busy and had another meeting to get ready for that night, Kenny would help to clean them too – he liked to tinker with his bikes. And he wasn't averse to cleaning his own leathers either if we had to be off early somewhere the next day."

Phil knew how to get inside Kenny's head when it came to speedway and the psychological ploys a mechanic might use to get the best from his rider. He recalled: "At the British Final once he came back in after winning a race by about 80 yards and complained that the bike was 'shit' and saying how he wanted to ride another one in his next race. I tried to tell him that the bike he'd just used was the best for the track conditions at that time but he wasn't having it and thought he knew best. 'Don't f****** argue with me, I want to ride that one,' he told me in no uncertain terms.

"Anyway, Kenny then disappeared from view, presumably to watch the next heat, and while he was out of sight I simply switched the cover from the bike he'd just ridden to the bike he said he wanted to use in his next race.

"He won his next race easily and when he came back into the pits, I asked him: 'So what do you think, then?'

"He said: 'Fifty times better.'

"I said: 'Well, it's the same f****** bike you rode before – and I haven't done a thing to it!'

"Kenny was gobsmacked and, pointing at the machine he thought he'd been on, said: 'You bastard! I wanted to ride that bike!'

"This was typical of speedway riders – it's all up here in their heads. I think they're the most fickle bunch of motorcyclists of all."

What those mind games in the Coventry pits taught Kenny was that he could trust Phil Hollingworth's judgement better than he would trust any other mechanic who ever worked for him on a regular basis.

Ollie said: "He trusted me with everything. If I needed to go over to Eric Boocock's shop in Wakefield to pick up some Weslake parts, Kenny would send me over their with his cheque book, with a blank cheque pre-signed by him, to collect whatever he needed for the next meeting.

"Once, Booey's wife, Diane, couldn't let me have any stuff because Kenny owed them money from way back, but it was soon sorted out. Sometimes, I even forged his signature on the cheque if a bill needed paying there and then!

"There were times when Kenny would even let me decide for him what gearing to pull and, if Halifax won the toss for gate positions, the best starting position to take in the first race. He'd let me walk the track to look at the conditions while he sat in the pits or his van.

"I remember before the first race of one match, Neil Evitts went up to Kenny and asked him what gate positions they were going to take. 'Ask Ollie,' he said, 'he knows what gearing I've got on and the track conditions.' He trusted me enough to decide for him what gear he should pull.

"At the old Belle Vue, because he was so light on the bike, he used to pull a gearing that was two teeth less than the nearest gearing pulled by anybody else. He just rode the Hyde Road track absolutely flat stick all the way round and never knocked it off, which is why he could pull such a high gear and produced so much speed round the outside."

"We just clicked so well and most of the time I knew what he was thinking. It was as if we'd been mates since our earliest schooldays."

That is not to say that Carter was disorganised. Phil said: "Kenny kept a log detailing the gearing he pulled at every meeting, the name of the referee and how long each one held the riders at the gate before releasing the tapes. Before every away meeting, he'd have a quick flick through his book to check what set-up he had used the last time he visited that track."

People often regarded Kenny as a selfish loner. This doesn't explain why he financed a convoy of six car loads of people to travel by ferry with him for the final in Norden.

Controversy and disaster were never far behind the Carters and the ferry trip over was no exception. It seems Kenny's brother, Alan, was flirting with the croupier in the ferry's casino. Her boyfriend took offence and threatened the jockey-sized road-racer, who promptly launched himself at the man and a full scale riot commenced.

When the ferry docked the next day, the police were waiting to interview all those who took part. There was some doubt expressed by the police when the injured party picked out the diminutive Alan as being the culprit, but the group were detained for some four hours.

Graham McKeon, concerned this was not the ideal preparation for a World Final, managed to get Kenny to use his silver tongue in settling matters and the convoy were finally allowed to leave the port. Hardly the way to proceed to a World Final showdown but typical of the trials and tribulations of everyday life for Kenny Carter.

Given these unnecessary distractions, no wonder he arrived in Germany prepared for what he called a "muck and nettles" job, which was not an inappropriate way to describe what lay ahead at this much-maligned track in a rural northern outpost of West Germany – a millions miles away from the grandeur of Wembley and the colour scenes at the Los Angeles Coliseum.

Winning his second ride in Germany from American Lance King and Czech Tony Kasper.

This very basic German venue in a field was not a patch on Katowice or Gothenburg either – and that was after this uncovered 55,000 stadium, with its wooden benches and terracing, had received a £1m facelift. It was, at the time, the worst venue ever chosen to stage the individual World Final and no wonder no more than around 30,000 ventured out of their homes to endure the traffic jams along the single lane route that led to the only stadium entrance.

I know of only one person who still looks back on the 1983 World Final with much affection and that is the man who won it – Egon Müller. A superstar in all forms of German tracksport, most notably on grass and long-track, for one day he 'Mullered' the best speedway riders in the world in conditions tailor-made for him.

A cabaret and pop artist from Munich and showman supreme, Müller stamped his authority all over the final from the outset. His first ride, in heat 3, was against Carter, who missed the start from gate one. By the time Kenny recovered from being pinned on the kerb by Zenon Plech and eased his way past the Pole, the German favourite was half a straight ahead.

They might as well have given Müller the trophy there and then. For the other 15, it was a hopeless cause.

Carter, wearing the No.10 jacket, won heat 6, his easiest ride, all the way from tapes to flag and kept alive his rostrum hopes by winning his third ride in even more impressive style. Heat 12 was always going to be his toughest test but he trapped sharply from gate three to lead all the way from Hans Nielsen and Ole Olsen, with Michael Lee disappointingly shut out at the back after his fast first race win.

Müller, riding a slightly wider line to everybody else on this typically flat, sweeping continental circuit with long straights and wide corners, was the only unbeaten rider at the interval stage. But Carter and Billy Sanders were just a point behind on eight each – and they met in a vital heat 15.

On the way to the second of his two wins, he leads Danes Hans Nielsen and Ole Olsen in heat 12.

Over-watering by staff during the interval had left the surface heavier than before and after impatiently pushing the tapes twice, Carter collected a face-full of wet shale when he found himself last off the grid and having to battle his way around Mitch Shirra on the first turn. Erik Gundersen quickly built up an unassailable lead but Carter and Sanders were both desperate to grab second place and their bruising battle provided one of the few talking points of an otherwise largely uneventful damp squib.

Australian ace Sanders needed to call on all his prowess as a promising amateur schoolboy boxer to hold Carter's repeated thrusts at bay – how they avoided a nasty collision on the back straight remains a mystery – and 'Billy the Kid's' second place here effectively secured him the silver medal.

"I got wiped out on the first bend, I couldn't see a thing," Carter complained. "I wasn't trying to shift Billy out of the way. I didn't know he was there!" he claimed.

Carter could still have joined Müller and Sanders on the rostrum had he fared better than third place in his last ride. But, disappointed with himself and track conditions, he made another bad start, took most of the first lap to pass Chris Morton on the inside and could make no impression on Karl Maier and Dennis Sigalos, who contested a thriller at the front.

Little did any of us watching know that we had just witnessed Kenny Carter's last World Final race. Lee won his fifth ride to end Carter's fading hopes of the bronze medal.

After Hans Nielsen's last heat chain break had denied him a certain rostrum place, the unstoppable Müller became the first World Final maximum man since Olsen triumphed with 15 points in 1975.

Then came the predictable gripes from the losers and British fans too ignorant to appreciate Müller's genuine talent. They tried to denigrate his impressive victory by saying the grippy track conditions and shape suited 34-year-old Müller's fabled long-track technique. They complained too that no other riders could live with the sheer speed of the German's super-fast GM engine and that he was given more practice time than anybody else.

But the inescapable truth is that Müller was by far the best rider on the day. Even the most experienced man in the field, Ole Olsen, in his farewell final at 37-years-old, could not contain the wafer-thin German for long.

Carter's criticisms after the meeting had a hollow ring to them, although they were echoed by many of his rivals: "I came to win and got eight points from my first three rides – then they made a mess of the track. I feel it was watered to suit Müller. The riders weren't asked about watering.

"Even so, Müller surprised me with his speed. He went like a rocket," said Kenny, who did take a new Italian-made GM with him to Germany but decided to keep faith with his Weslakes.

Bruce Penhall took time out from his Hollywood schedule to be at Norden to hand over his World Championship trophy. His presence only reinforced the reality that, for the second consecutive season, the reigning World No.1 would not be active in the British League. Not that Penhall gave a damn. To show he had got over all the hullabaloo that surrounded his win in LA, he breezed through the spacious Norden pits wearing a rosette . . . with Kenny Carter's face on it!

If Penhall could afford to joke, Carter certainly could not. With all due respect to John Louis, was Kenny missing Mauger's hands-on approach to management and attention to detail? Ivan would certainly not have allowed Kenny to become embroiled in the farcical ferry incident that were a needless distraction. Would Carter have been hoodwinked into believing the World Final track would be much slicker than it was had the Kiwi maestro been looking after his interests?

Even Phil Hollingworth, who admits he sulked at home and watched the '83 final on the telly instead, said: "I couldn't believe that Kenny had been caught out by how the track had changed so much between practice and the meeting itself. It was as slick as hell in practice but then the Germans piled on the dirt for Müller on race day – and they all should have seen it coming.

"If I'd been there, I would have made sure I went down to the track to see for my own eyes what they were doing to it after practice, even if it would have meant sneaking into the stadium late at night. When he got back from Germany, I told Kenny he was a bloody idiot – and he agreed."

Phil reveals that Carter, forever wrapped up in himself and his own speedway career, had hardly heard of Egon Müller before he had been trounced by the charismatic German at Norden.

He said: "They were talking at the Golden Key meeting in Bremen, not long before Egon won the '83 final, and Müller was telling Kenny how he should perhaps consider having a go at long-track racing himself, because, as Egon explained, there could be a lot of money in it for him.

"While Kenny was clearly interested in what Egon had to say, he was thrown a bit by the fact that the German didn't ride in the British League. He asked him things like: 'Have you got a proper job, then?' and 'what do you do for a living?'

"Kenny didn't have a clue that apart from being probably the greatest-ever German speedway, long-track and grass-track rider, Müller was also just as well known where he came from for his starring roles as a cabaret drag artist, chart-topping pop singer and whatever else he got up to away from the track!

"Kenny could be naive about some things, but not money matters," said Ollie.

Within days of the Norden debacle, Carter beat Sigalos to win the 'World Final Revenge' meeting in Amsterdam (Müller was fourth) and then won the Ole Olsen farewell event at Vojens. He was particularly delighted to win the Danish meeting – and a brand new Toyota car that came as first prize. Before the night was over, though, the Danish sponsors and Olsen himself would soon regret that the car was not won by any of the other 15 riders in the world class field.

Due to the international nature of the line-up, standard practice at Vojens was for the sponsor – in this case Toyota – to pay the prize-winner in cash to the value of the car or thereabouts, as agreed. Riders usually much preferred collecting the money instead of the car anyway, and by accepting payment in this way it would also save the sponsors the hassle of arranging for a foreign car to be transported to Britain.

Toyota and Olsen reckoned without a very stubborn and demanding Kenny Carter.

Phil Hollingworth recalls the story that said much about Kenny's intransigence when he was determined to get his way. He said: "I was in Ole Olsen's office after the meeting and Kenny kept insisting that he wanted to keep the car. Not only that, he wanted Ole to have it converted to right-hand drive and then delivered to him in England – at Ole's UK farewell meeting which was going to be held at Coventry just before the end of the season.

"Kenny told Olsen: 'I've won that car and I want it delivering to me at your farewell meeting at Coventry'.

"Ole politely pointed out that he didn't think Toyota could agree to that, but Kenny just wouldn't let it go. He said: 'I don't give a shit. I don't want the money – I've won that car and I want it delivering to me in the same colours as it is now, gold and black'.

"He got his wish in the end. I suppose the people at Denmark Toyota must have spoken to their colleagues at Toyota in England and the car was eventually delivered to him."

The exasperated Olsen was too long in the tooth by then to lock swords with a young upstart like Carter, but he had to take his hat off to the bolshy kid from Halifax. Not only did Kenny take delivery of the Toyota at Brandon, as he had insisted all along, but he snatched the glory at Olsen's farewell meeting by winning the Brandonapolis!

A crowd of around 20,000 packed into the Midlands track to say 'goodbye' to the Coventry Bees skipper at the end of his 17th season in the BL. This time Carter showed Müller and several other world finalists the way home – and, significantly, he did it aboard a brand new Godden GR500 engine he was riding competitively for the first time.

Spoiling Ole's night . . . the Brandonapolis winner had a new car to drive home.

After the meeting, Colin Gear saw the victorious Carter struggling to join the traffic queues leaving Brandon. He recalled: "Kenny drove by in his new car, he was obviously struggling to get used to the clutch as he kept crunching the gears. I asked him if the car was fully taxed and insured for him to drive, but he didn't seem at all bothered as he disappeared off."

Hollingworth said: "Kenny didn't sell the car on afterwards – he kept it. In fact, Pam drove around in it for a long while. That Toyota he won at Vojens was one of the first four-wheel drive cars on the market at the time and Kenny and the road-racer Mick Grant drove it up and down the hills of the moto-cross track at Kenny's place – in the snow!"

Even Wally Mawdsley was taking more of a shine to Kenny. Their early season bust-up at Swindon now water under the bridge, Mawdsley raised a few eyebrows by handing Carter the England captaincy for the first time when the BSPA dreamed up a tinpot end-of-season three team tournament in which the Lions met world champions Denmark and the Rest of the World (USA could not raise a full team) at Cradley Heath, King's Lynn and Birmingham. Well, pretty meaningless to all but a proud Kenny that is.

He said: "I was just about to write the season off as the worst I've ever had when I was appointed England captain. Fantastic – it's one of the best things that have ever happened to me in speedway. And just what I needed after the big let down at Norden."

Mawdsley, though, clearly did not have the measure of Carter's fragile temperament. Displaying a clear pride and passion lacking in many of his international team-mates, an unhappy Kenny said: "I was looking forward to carrying on in charge but when we got to King's Lynn for the second match Wally Mawdsley gave the captaincy back to Peter Collins, who missed the Cradley meeting.

"I've nothing against PC but I was really upset. I felt I had done a good job and that I should have kept the captaincy. I think it is time England started building for the future and brought in a few new faces.

"I'm sick of people rubbishing England and saying how good the Danes or the Americans are going.

"It's time England got back on top where they belong. And I'd love to be captain next season, because I think I can do the job.

"There are plenty of jokes about me being England's number one because it says so on my van. But that's what I want to be – number one.

"Bruce Penhall always rode number one for America but I've been messed around. I'd like to be number one and captain – and not just because it would be good for Kenny Carter. I want England to be the best."

This was typical of his serious approach to every meeting he rode in. Whether it was the World Final or a knockabout fixture-filler in the rain on a bleak night at the end of October, he treated them all with the same respect – and the same cannot be said of many of his rivals then, or the stars of today.

Although winning for the good of himself was always his priority, as it is for many top riders, he also wanted Halifax to be much more competitive than they ever were in his day, especially away from The Shay. They did slightly improve in terms of league position in '83 – up two places from the previous season to 11th – but they still ended up with the same points overall total and this time they did not manage a single away win. Kenny's BL and cup average had dipped by around two-thirds of a point a match, to 10.28, mainly due to mechanical problems, but he was still left to carry the Pennine Radio Dukes single-handedly on far too many occasions.

After one particularly bad run of defeats, team manager Dennis Gavros, who rode for the Dukes in the mid-60s, called all his riders to The Shay one Monday morning for private practice to try and resolve the problems. Kenny rode every other team member's bike and they all had a turn at riding his.

But Carter blamed the Dukes' problems on poor attitude, not sluggish machinery. He said: "I don't think the bikes have been the problem. I'm more bothered about the general attitude. I don't think some of the lads care enough or try hard enough in the away matches – that's what we've got to sort out."

Although Gavros had monitored Carter's meteoric progress since his earliest speedway rides at the Ellesmere Port practice sessions in 1978, he and Carter did not always see eye to eye. In fact, the team manager caused some consternation with his promoter after he dared to criticise the Dukes' skipper following their draw at Sheffield. 'Gavvy' was reported to have said that if Kenny "couldn't show more team spirit, he should start looking for another club."

Eric Boothroyd was unimpressed and suggested his team manager had overstepped his authority when he responded tersely: "Dennis had no real right to make a statement like that. There is no way that Carter will be released by Halifax."

If Kenny needed any reassurance in his own mind that he was bigger than the club itself, then the show of public support from Boothroyd was a resounding endorsement of his power. Perhaps not surprisingly, during the winter Gavros quit his team managing duties with Halifax to concentrate on his local garage business.

Reflecting ruefully on the 1983 season, Carter admitted: "It's been a disappointing year because I've had problems with my bikes and maybe I have been so involved building my own business interests that I've not given 100 per cent to speedway.

"But that's all going to change, believe me. Norden was obviously a let down. I was 'conned' along with the rest by the track. It was so different on the day from what it had been in practice. My bikes weren't set up right. Norden taught me a hell of a lot."

Hopes that he would end the season with a hat-trick of BLRC victories were spoiled by Erik Gundersen, a deserving winner of another wet meeting at Belle Vue where Kenny finished fourth.

Even so, victory at Coventry on the Godden and the brief taste of the England captaincy had boosted Carter's appetite for the following season and he said: "I intend to make it a big year for me. I'm going to stay at home this winter and get myself fully prepared for 1984."

He announced that his new main sponsor, Peter Garside, of Land Rover Centre main dealers in Huddersfield, would become his new manager and that he was keen to enjoy a slice of the lucrative long-track pie in 1984. A holiday in Florida, where

Showing he could be a good sport, too. Kenny congratulating Erik Gundersen after the Dane had denied him a hat-trick of BLRC wins at Belle Vue in 1983. Erik was the Danish rival Kenny liked most.

he met up with his old friend, wealthy Ripponden-based Ron Oldham, a helicopter pilot who had business interests in the States, proved another end of year tonic.

Kenny was upbeat again – he even believed that more and more people outside West Yorkshire were growing to like him!

He said: "Now I've quietened down a bit, I think my own popularity is increasing," he claimed. "Take my visits to Cradley Heath. When Penhall was there they used to boo and chuck rubbish at me – I needed a police escort to get out of the place. Now they cheer me.

"My official fan club is doing good business, too. They sold 3,500 T-shirts before the World Final."

Kenny Carter, quietened down? Calm before the next storm, more like.

Chapter 17

NO MORE MR NICE GUY

IT is probably fair to say that Kenny Carter was in a minority of one among riders who believed he should be handed the England captaincy when he was awarded the honour by new national manager and fellow Yorkshireman, Carl Glover, at the start of the 1984 season.

Glover knew he was making a risky move by taking the captaincy away from Peter Collins – Wally Mawdsley's first choice – and handing it to his big northern rival on a more permanent basis, but quite how far reaching those repercussions would be did not become clear until midway through the season.

The 31-year-old Sheffield co-promoter Glover, the only other contender for the manager's job when he beat Mawdsley to it by a vote of 9-6 at the promoters' annual winter conference, could hardly ignore Carter's loud claims for the role of skipper.

Emboldened by his £1,000 victory in the individual indoor event at Birmingham's National Exhibition Centre at the end of January, Kenny seized the moments immediately following his Midlands success to unleash his first verbal outburst of the year.

He was always 'good copy' for journalists, who lapped up his every utterance with eager delight, never more so than after this, his most lucrative win to date. Carter held court at the NEC and told the assembled hacks: "I feel as though I'm the only person England can pick for captain. It's not anything bad against Chris Morton, Peter Collins or Michael Lee. I just feel nobody wants England to win more than I do.

"I'm sure I can keep my job as England captain because I'm the best for the job.

"Anyone riding for England in 1984 who turns up with only one bike should, as far as I'm concerned, never ride for England again all year. Dave Jessup in Vojens cost England the World Team Cup. Okay, he borrowed a bike, but that's no good.

"I'm so cheesed off at the rubbish England have to take. The public tonight were booing me at first but they were shouting for me in the end and when England are on the up again there will be twice as many people going to speedway."

Most riders invited to take part in these close season indoor meetings at Wembley Arena and the NEC treated them for what they were – a bit of fun to help plug the vacuum during the off-season and not to be taken too seriously. Jan Andersson, the dour Swede who even perfected his technique on frozen lakes near his home in winter, was the most notable exception to the rule. If the FIM had given out gold medals for winning indoor meetings, dead-pan Jan would now have more than Ivan Mauger and Tony Rickardsson put together.

But not even the so-serious Reading star could contain a determined Carter this time.

The day before his individual win on the concrete, he had ridden poorly as skipper of an England team beaten by Europe, and he admitted: "I was disgusted with myself. I didn't go to bed until 5.30 in the morning. I had a few drinks and because I don't drink much, it affected me.

"But I was so determined when I woke up this morning that tonight was going to be my night.

"For me this is the launch. If I'd lost I'd have gone home in tears."

It was hard to believe that he was talking in such serious tones about an indoor meeting that would soon be forgotten by most of those present once the new conventional season got underway.

Carter went on to insist that he had abandoned his car and van sales business and would be putting all his efforts – "my whole life" – into speedway for 1984. He made it his business, though, to organise probably the most professionally run fan club in the sport, offering members a range of merchandise in the red, white and blue of his club and country. Supporters paid £1.50 each to join and Kenny claimed they got £2's worth of goodies back in return. "It's not a money-making thing," he insisted, perhaps trying to quell accusations that he was simply cashing in on his growing fame.

Carter used his personalised and re-painted red, white and blue Land Rover to pull a trailer which doubled as a souvenir kiosk that he would park up at the top of the terraces at The Shay on racenights. Well before Jason Crump capitalised on his success as Speedway Grand Prix champion with his own merchandise outlet at Belle Vue, Carter was exploiting on his popularity at Halifax, where Eric Boothroyd pretty much gave him carte blanche to do as he pleased – the Dukes boss would get the track ready for Kenny to practice on at the drop of a flat cap.

Kenny was fond of wearing the padded satin-style jacket, with the logo and words 'Kenny Carter Racing' on both the front and back, over his leathers before racing. Many fans bought the KC Racing jackets, making them highly visible accessories on The Shay terraces. He passed the responsibility of running his souvenir sales franchise to Heather Lund, Pam's closest sister who still attends Sheffield Speedway today.

Not all Halifax fans loved him, though. There were some who did not approve of his cocky arrogance and relentless self-promotion.

Carter admitted that he did not ride purely for the love or the thrill of it. He loved winning and being the best but he was never in love with speedway per se. "I always said speedway was OK but I didn't really like it," he admitted. "I almost packed speedway in last year. But I'm enjoying my speedway now and I'm just going to prove to all my critics they were wrong."

He dismissed new speculation that a £50,000 deal might tempt him to switch to road-racing, where his brother, Alan, was still the top Brit in the 250cc class, and could not resist a dig at Bruce Penhall in the process. "And when I do win it (the world title), I won't 'do a Bruce Penhall' and retire on the spot. I intend to be around speedway for another three years at least.

Don't think Dennis Sigalos would have been tempted to buy one of Kenny's new fan club jackets.

"Last year I was the Kenny Carter that wasn't," he continued. "In 1982 I was me. Last year I was told I had to be Mr Nice Guy, so I decided I would be. I'd say I might win and I might not win.

"It just messed me up so bad. I felt as though I went 10 years backwards. Now I'm going to be Kenny Carter. If they love me, okay. If they hate me, tough luck!"

The 1982 version of Kenny Carter – love him or hate him – had returned with a vengeance.

However, journalist Peter Oakes pointed out: "His after-meeting speech (at Birmingham's NEC) was nowhere near as arrogant, bombastic or downright conceited as you will probably think as you read it. He has an engaging character and one big plus as far as speedway is concerned, the inborn ability to become England's biggest personality."

Carter no doubt delivered his calculated comments to send a timely message to Carl Glover, who began his new role by managing the England team at the NEC and

Aiming to shoot down the Americans in this publicity shot at the start of 1984.

who would shortly be naming his captain for the conventional outdoor season. Glover also considered the credentials of the much more experienced Dave Jessup but, in the end, he put his head on the block for Carter.

Announcing the controversial appointment of the youngest-ever regular England captain at a speedway writers' luncheon in Manchester, Glover said: "My final decision was reached after the NEC meeting.

"The thing that was worrying me about Kenny was that he had so many outside business interests, so when he told me he had sold them to concentrate on speedway he became the logical choice. I have got a great deal of admiration for Dave Jessup and it was a hard decision between the two of them. Kenny's

On his only appearance for England in 1984 – in the first Test against the USA at Swindon.

enthusiasm for the job and his youth, and at the same time his experience at international level, eventually swung it.

"If he does the job according to what he can do he's got it for the year. But if there are any serious problems during the American Test series, I could change it.

"But I look upon him being the England captain for a long time to come."

Glover praised outgoing skipper Peter Collins for the dignified manner in which he accepted his decision – although still a force, PC was not an automatic choice for all tracks. Speaking more recently, Glover said: "I felt Peter had lost a bit of ambition. I didn't really know Kenny that well then but he was the new kid on the block and I thought he'd shake a few up. I was prepared to give him a go and see how it worked out.

"But I was determined that Peter would be the first to hear the news and I managed to keep it to myself, and out of the papers, until I spoke to him on his return from Australia.

"Peter told me that he knew all along that I'd be making Kenny captain. He was as good as gold, gave me 100 per cent every time he rode and we became good friends.

"Dave Jessup was still a very classy rider and good at communicating, but the distance between us – him down in Kent and me up here in Sheffield – would have made it hard.

"When I broke the news to Kenny that he was captain, he had to be tied down like a balloon that was about to take off."

A proud Carter said: "The England captaincy is the best thing that has ever happened to me in speedway and the 22 years I've been alive."

It was Kenny who urged Glover to smarten up England's image and re-adopt the

Leading by example on and off the track at the start of 1984.

The Dukes of 1984. Left to right: Eric Boothroyd, Craig Pendlebury, Steve Finch, Kenny, Steve Baker, Eric Monaghan, Doug Wyer and Neil Evitts. But their captain wouldn't be with them for much more of the season.

blazer, tie and slacks attire that Ian Thomas and Eric Boocock had introduced at the start of the grand slam year of 1980. He wanted to see England riders fined if they arrived for meetings not wearing their 'uniform'.

The image-conscious Carter jumped at a second invitation to appear on BBC TV's popular A Question of Sport quiz show, in front of 11.5m viewers.

Carter cooked up a lucrative new sponsorship deal with Ham Construction, a Bradford-based company run by brothers Bobby and Allan Ham, who were new to speedway but had a good footballing pedigree in Yorkshire. They ensured Carter would be the most visible speedway rider on the motorways of Britain by providing him with a £35,000 mobile home. It was 28ft long, had a cocktail lounge, a microwave oven, a shower and could sleep up to eight people.

It was the early forerunner to the state-of-the-art motorhomes the top Grand Prix riders and their teams of mechanics use today. Beneath the front windscreen was a sign bearing the word 'BRAVE', an apt description of its owner in view of events that were about to unfold.

Phil Hollingworth said: "The Winnebago had a seven litre petrol engine and did about six miles to the gallon. We drove up to Newcastle for an open meeting one night and it cost Kenny £120 in fuel – when petrol was 40p a gallon!"

Even then, the ever-resourceful, wheeler-dealer Carter solved the gas-guzzling problem by getting his juice sponsored by his local Jet filling station, through petrol wholesaler Townson Thornber.

"It was good to drive, though," continued 'Ollie'. "It was a left-hooker but it had power-assisted steering, cruise control and a 1600 Ford Cortina engine as a generator that slid out of the back . . . it was a right bloody tool!"

On the track, Carter was given a major boost by his first works sponsorship deal with Kent-based Don Godden to ride his GR500 machine,

The only niggle – for Godden almost as much as Kenny – was the stubborn stance of the Speedway Control Board who declined his application to be included among Britain's nine representatives in the World Long-track Championship. Carter had set his heart on cashing in on this bigger version of speedway – most commonly staged on 1,000-metre tracks in Germany on Sunday afternoons – but the SCB would not support his application on the grounds that he had not competed in the necessary number of grass-track meetings to make him eligible for an ACU grass-track licence. It was not so much another example of speedway bureaucracy gone mad, but a cynical way for the ACU to insure top named riders would front up for the rounds of the national grass-track titles, which did not interest Kenny in the slightest.

This was the most specific case of where the ACU governance of grass-track and speedway was bad. Of course, if you were a grass-track man your attitude would be, why should these speedway riders with no interest in grass-track 'steal' our places? It begs the question, is long-track racing speedway or grass-track?

But before long Kenny had much more serious issues to upset him.

Carter's pride was dented when his first official Test match on shale under Glover ended in a 58-50 defeat to the USA in the opening match of the series at Swindon on the afternoon of Saturday, April 14. Carter, accompanied by Phil Hollingworth and manager Peter Garside, had driven the new motorhome down to Wiltshire early and slept in the Abbey Stadium car park overnight to ensure the new England skipper was there bright and early on race day.

If only England had been as outstanding as the Cartermobile. When Kenny, who went on to score 10 (paid 11) in the No.1 race jacket, and Simon Wigg opened with a 4-2 over the otherwise immaculate Dennis Sigalos in the first race, it was the only time the hosts led in the match. A hotly contested tapes exclusion, which presented his reserve replacement Kelvin Tatum with his England debut, did not help Carter's cause.

But then the mental pain Kenny felt at losing the opening Test to America was nothing compared to the agony he endured a week later, when Halifax visited Cradley Heath on Easter Saturday. Kenny was chasing hard after the Heathens' Lance King in the opening heat of the League Cup clash when he lost control and fell on the first bend of the second lap.

He was just getting to his feet when team-mate, Craig Pendlebury, unable to take evasive action, smashed into him. Pendlebury's footrest inflicted the blow to the shin that left Carter with four breaks to his right leg.

It was not Carter's first crash of the season – he had taken a couple of tumbles and blamed these mishaps on the new tyre regulations. The thinner, shallower tread Barum tyre – brought in to try and slow the riders down, save money and improve safety standards – had resulted in a spate of early season falls as riders struggled to adapt to them after the SCB had banned the wider Carlisle from domestic racing.

Carter was stretchered from the Dudley Wood track in obvious agony and rushed by ambulance to the nearby Corbett Hospital in Stourbridge.

Seconds away from disaster . . . Lance King leading at the first bend, with Kenny and Craig Pendlebury tucked in behind and King's Cradley partner Bill Barrett on the outside. Right: Kenny is wiped out by Pendlebury.

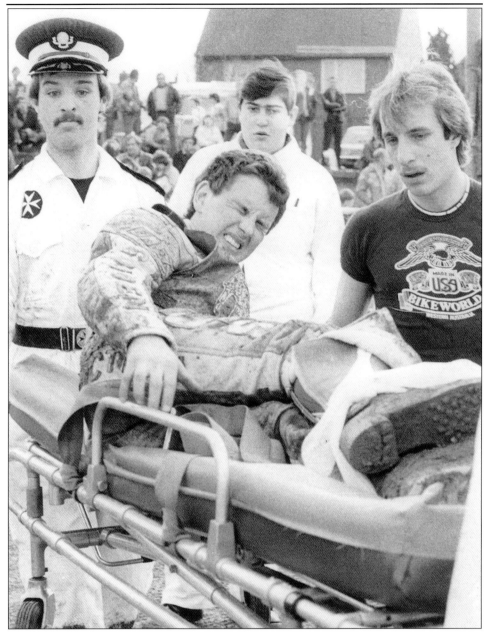

The look on mechanic Chris Fagan's face says it all as Kenny is removed from the Cradley track.

Carter sustained a clean break of the tibula and fibula and Eric Boothroyd explained: "The surgeon said that if Kenny had been anyone other than a speedway rider he would not have plated his leg. It's still terrible news for Halifax and England, though."

Carter said to journalist Richard Bott: "I told the specialist, 'just set my leg – I've got to ride in a World Championship meeting next month.'

"The next day I talked to Dad and said, 'I want the best specialist available to get me riding again for the British semi-final.' He rang around and then came back and told me that one of the best specialists in the country was already working at *this* hospital.

With Craig Pendlebury in happier times.

"On the Tuesday after the crash, Mr Cowie operated and put a steel plate into my leg. The plate was bigger than usual, because I had to be able to ride again quickly.

"He didn't think I was mad. He said he admired me for trying to have a go.

"I had the 'pot' off after three days so that I could start building up my leg muscles."

Speaking from Perth, Western Australia, where he and his wife emigrated to in 1997 after 17 years in Auckland, New Zealand, Craig Pendlebury said: "My recollection is not that detailed, although I can remember Kenny falling right in front of me. I had nowhere to go and I hit him.

"It was one of those unfortunate racing accidents – I didn't feel guilty or blame myself and I don't think Kenny blamed me either. Some of his mates did, though, and maybe a few supporters too – perhaps more than I knew at the time – but that's the way it is. He was the team hero, not me."

Pendlebury admits he did not visit Carter in hospital but another Halifax team-mate, Doug Wyer, was one who did. Wyer smiled when he recalled: "When I saw Kenny in hospital he said: 'That Craig Pendlebury . . . he swerved three times before he finally got me!' All things considered, Kenny took what had happened fairly well."

The initial medical diagnosis was that the injury would keep Carter out of the saddle for around three months. In other words, his 1984 World Championship trail had finished before it had even begun. Speedway riders have always defied medical logic and advice but Carter astonished even those who knew how tough he was by declaring that he would race again IN FIVE WEEKS!

His target was the British semi-final of the World Championship at Oxford on Friday, May 25. Nothing, not even a broken leg, was going to stop him from being there to race.

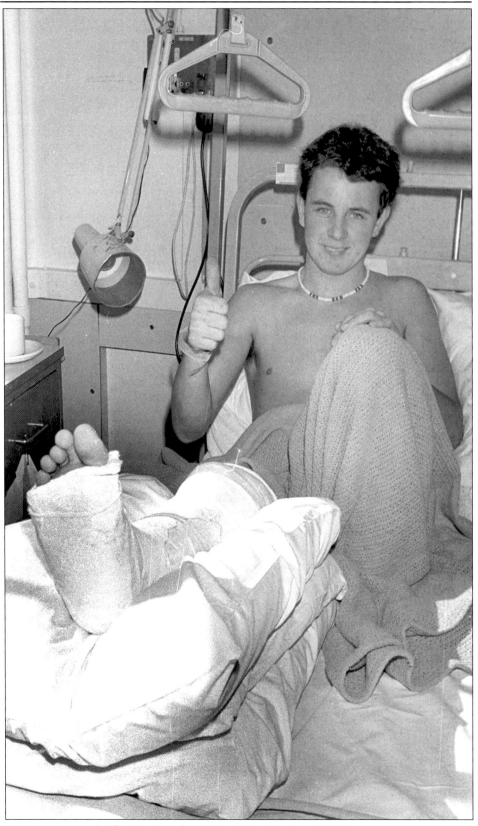

A defiant thumbs up from his hospital bed following the Cradley crash.

Chapter 18

NO STOPPING THE TYKE ON A BIKE

ALL eyes were on Kenny in the build up to the first stages of the 1984 World Championship. Even with his broken right leg in plaster, he kept himself in the spotlight with an appearance on TV-am, the daily breakfast show, where he hobbled on to the set with the aid of crutches to be interviewed by presenters Mike Morris and Anne Diamond.

He insisted that nothing was going to stop him from taking his place in the British semi-final at Oxford, even though he would have to be lifted onto and off his bike.

He had been sorely missed by England, who slumped to a 4-1 series defeat by the USA. After levelling the series in the second match at Sheffield, Carl Glover's men were beaten at Cradley Heath – where Kenny was there to watch – and Poole and smashed out of sight at Ipswich. It took a sparkling performance by the recalled 43-year-old veteran John Louis to ensure England followed the Americans through the UK World Team Cup qualifier at King's Lynn.

There were calls for the SCB to seed Carter direct to the British Final in June, and Kenny did write to them requesting a seeding. It would have been an unprecedented move by the governing body but they were right to refuse his request – even though Carter and Michael Lee were the only Brits good enough at the time to potentially go all the way and win the world title in Gothenburg that September. Where do you draw the line? The SCB had further justification for their decision when, within days of Carter's latest injury crisis, his fellow England international Simon Wigg broke his collarbone and, like Kenny, he too would have to go through the pain barrier to compete in the semi-final at Oxford. How could the Board excuse Carter the discomfort of riding under a severe handicap at Oxford and not Wigg? And what if another rider had become injured before the British Final itself?

Not surprisingly, a one-eyed Carter found it very hard to accept the Control Board's refusal to seed him direct to the Coventry round. Richard Bott visited Grey Horse Farm, braving the attention of Carter's Alsatian guard dog 'Gypsy' who was chained up and on patrol outside the house as usual, to hear the Halifax skipper sounding off in typically forthright fashion. Kenny told him: "I reckon I'm the best chance England has of having a World Champion – even with a broken leg!

"But I shouldn't have to ride at Oxford. I'm disgusted the way I've been treated. The Danes have seeded Peter Ravn (to the Nordic Final) and he's not even one of their top four riders. I'm the captain of England but nobody cares. Here we insist that rules are rules. Other countries bend the rules. Well, it doesn't surprise me that England doesn't win much at speedway. I've always been for England but the harder

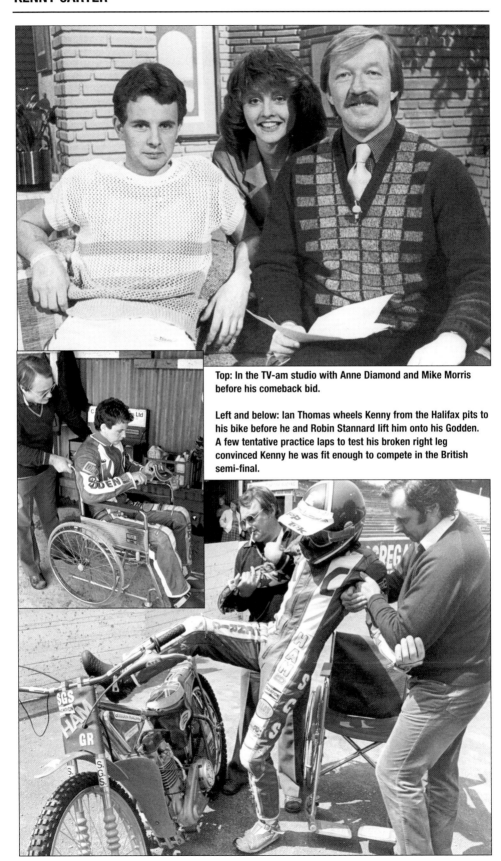

Top: In the TV-am studio with Anne Diamond and Mike Morris before his comeback bid.

Left and below: Ian Thomas wheels Kenny from the Halifax pits to his bike before he and Robin Stannard lift him onto his Godden. A few tentative practice laps to test his broken right leg convinced Kenny he was fit enough to compete in the British semi-final.

you try the more you get kicked in the teeth.

"I'm angry because I was sure the Control Board would seed me after the Test defeats by America. All they have done is cut their noses to spite themselves."

He had a dig at the BSPA, too, when he added somewhat wearily: "I didn't expect the promoters to support me, because they are only interested in their riders and the money going into their own pockets.

"But I've got a long memory. And I'll remember the people who kicked me when I was down."

As well as the highly visible presence of manager Peter Garside in the Oxford pits, Carter also called up former England manager and Newcastle boss Ian Thomas for help and advice in his World Championship campaign. Thomas knew the rulebook inside out and had earned a reputation as one of the sharpest managerial brains in the business whose motivational powers had served him well for club and country. While the burly Garside had the physique to lift Carter in and out of his motorhome, it was Thomas' job to fill in the programme and keep the injured hero updated with his progress throughout each championship round.

In his 2006 book, *Wheels and Deals*, Thomas said: "I thought he was nuts riding with a pot on his leg but if he was going to do it, then he needed all the help he could get. So we did a deal and I agreed to look after him.

"I was on board to make sure the arrangements ran smoothly, to keep any hassle away from him, and to ensure he knew exactly what he needed points-wise, race-by-race, to get through the qualifying rounds. That suited me, because I was experienced at reading situations and at pulling the odd stroke here or there when it needed pulling."

After safely coming through a private practice session at Halifax, where Garside and Thomas worked in tandem to lift the heroic Duke on and off his Godden bike, Carter declared himself ready to take his place among the 16 British semi-finalists at Oxford – a track he had not ridden at since he was with Newcastle in 1978.

Thomas was in his element. He phoned Oxford ahead of the meeting to ensure Carter had prime position in the pits, tucked away from his 15 rivals and where he had enough room to rest his leg on a fully opened sun lounger before and after each race.

His broken right leg, held together by four screws and a steel plate, was encased in a special oversized boot, reinforced with a steel panel for extra protection. He obviously could not put any weight on the leg, so he was transported to and from his motorhome in a wheelchair. Before each of his five rides, Garside and Thomas would carry Kenny to his bike.

It was pure theatre. And Carter was very much centre stage.

He eased his nerves by winning his first ride but the pressure was back on after he slid off at the pits turn in his second race while trying to thwart the outside challenge of Neil Collins. Three points lost but at least the minor spill had not done any further damage to his leg and, if anything, reassured him that his leg could take a slight jolt if not a heavy fall.

Second place, behind Peter Collins, in his third ride took his tally to five and he

Getting a lift to his bike by Peter Garside and Ian Thomas before his first ride in the British semi-final at Oxford.

Mechanic Phil Hollingworth and the champagne-popping Peter Garside greet Kenny after his last ride at Oxford.

was virtually sure of a qualifying place after victory over Andy Grahame in heat 15.

He needed at least a third place point from his final ride, heat 20, to be absolutely sure of reaching the British Final. The four who lined up in the final heat (with their cumulative points in brackets) were:

John Louis, King's Lynn (10)

Kenny Carter, Halifax (8)

Malcolm Simmons, Wimbledon (8)

Simon Wigg, Oxford (7)

Wigg, who was possibly hampered a little more by his heavily strapped left shoulder than Carter was by his leg, was the one who had it all to do. Although Louis had already qualified before the last heat, the other three were all aware that Peter Collins had already finished with nine points and would therefore eliminate one of them, depending on the finishing order of the crucial final race.

The finishing order (and final points) of heat 20 was:

Carter (11)

Simmons (10)

Wigg (8)

Louis (10)

Garside, dressed casually in baseball cap and spotless white trainers, was revelling in the spotlight as he popped the champagne cork and sprayed Kenny with bubbly even before he had re-entered the pits. While it was easy to appreciate the role of the canny and experienced Thomas in Carter's '84 World Championship campaign, Kenny's friends questioned what Garside brought to the table, apart from his sponsorship. He had a habit of turning up in celebratory pictures of Kenny and was never far from the TV cameras, too, at televised meetings in which Carter played a central role. Garside remains very successful in business, however, as chief executive of Land Rover Huddersfield, as well as running helicopter pleasure trips over the Yorkshire Dales.

Quite rightly, Carter's incredible raw courage dominated all the post-meeting coverage and overshadowed what was a fine overall victory for his Halifax team-mate Neil Evitts. Having joined the Dukes that season on loan from defunct Birmingham, he finished a point ahead of his more celebrated team-mate.

Within minutes of the finish, Carter was wheeled out of the pits and hoisted back into the comfort of his motorhome, where he held court with excited members of the press. He had given them another remarkable story to write about. "I was in agony. I cannot describe how bad the pain was. I was almost passing out after the meeting," Kenny said.

A few yards away Wigg cut a sad, inconsolable figure and was close to tears as he fell into the arms of his girlfriend beside his van after being cruelly eliminated, a point adrift of the qualifying cut-off.

According to Malcolm Simmons, whose second place effectively ended Wiggy's hopes on his home track, the outcome of heat 20 should have been different.

And he blamed Carter for the chaotic ending that sparked the biggest storm ever to hit British speedway.

In his controversial 2006 book, *Simmo: The Whole Truth*, he alleged that there was collusion among the riders to 'fix' the finishing order of that last race. Louis strongly denies any involvement and, it must be said, was subsequently completely exonerated by a Speedway Control Board inquiry into the Oxford affair some 10 months later. Of course Carter and Wigg, who sadly died of a brain tumour in November 2000 aged 40, cannot confirm or deny their part in the story all these years later.

What was undeniable is that *The People* newspaper, who claimed their undercover journalists gleaned the race-fixing scam from an unwitting Wigg, splashed the 'scandal' all over their back pages in September 1984. Their revelations prompted a full SCB inquiry at RAC headquarters in London, where it was decided that Wigg and Simmons were guilty of 'conduct prejudicial to the sport'. They were both banned from World Championship events for the whole of 1985, fined £1,000 each and ordered to pay a further £900 costs.

No charges were ever levied against Carter or his representatives.

Like the others implicated in the shenanigans, Simmons initially vehemently denied *The People's* allegations. But he has now confessed to his part in a pre-race arrangement with the other interested parties. He also revealed in his book that he received a £2,000 payment from Wigg and one of Simon's main sponsors to feign illness, to enable the Oxford racer to take his place in the British Final.

Simmo said: "Ironically, I would not have received a penny from Wiggy or anybody else if only Kenny Carter hadn't torn up our carefully planned script and won the vital heat 20 in question at Oxford. Wiggy had it all worked out in the pits before our last race. He knew exactly in which position Kenny, John Louis and myself needed to finish in our last ride to ensure we all got through to the British Final."

Whatever was or had not been agreed in hushed tones in the darkest corner of the Oxford pits, the mathematics of the situation dictated that even if Louis was to finish last, the possible permutations of the other three meant one of them would have to face PC in a run-off for the eighth, and last, qualifying place. Third place would be no good to Wigg, who needed to win to make totally sure of getting through. And if he won, whoever finished third out of Carter and Simmons would then meet Collins in an additional decider.

Simmons explained: "It was all going to plan until Kenny came charging past me and then Wiggy, who almost fell off. Kenny went on to win and Louis remained at the back. As John stood to lose the most for coming last, I thought the three of us chipped in to compensate his loss of earnings to the tune of £250. Wiggy and myself paid Carter . . . and I thought he paid the full amount to John. I think Kenny paying him by cheque, which, if it was the case, would have been a bit silly of him!

"Tragically, Wiggy and Kenny are not here to confirm or deny my version of events from all those years ago, but I phoned John recently, just to check my facts, and he remembers that night at Oxford completely differently to me. He insists he was not involved in that race-fixing in any way and received no payment whatsoever. He says that the reason he missed the start and was running last in that decisive heat was due to the fact that he had just started wearing glasses under his goggles. He says that they misted up badly on the start line in that race, caused him to miss the start and, on a track that was wet and mucky, there was no chance of him passing anyone.

"If that's how John remembers it, then so be it. In fairness to him, he was the only one of us who appeared before the tribunal who was completely cleared of any wrongdoing.

"After we came back into the pits and asked Kenny what the hell he was playing at, he just shrugged his shoulders and mumbled something about the track conditions getting worse and how he was worried about falling off again and risking further damage to his leg. He said he'd been getting in all sorts of trouble by riding too slowly at the back and so he had to get a move on.

"That was Kenny all over . . . he could lose the plot very easily," said Simmo.

Although Carter was never embroiled in the race-fixing controversy at Oxford in 1984, it did not mean that he would not be prepared to 'do a favour', as Simmo suggests many riders have done in individual rounds of the World Championship. Even long into their retirement, the great majority of ex-riders remain in denial that the buying and selling of points, or simple favours for team-mates, ever existed – in the same way they refuse to discuss the question of 'big' engines. Simmo has embarrassed and infuriated his former team-mates and rivals with his revelations but he should not be condemned for his honesty, even if his secrets have broken an unwritten law among riders.

Did Carter ever 'throw' points? Very unlikely, given his unquenchable thirst for winning even the most meaningless second half race. He can't answer that but what we do know is that he liked money and this revelation by Phil Hollingworth will raise eyebrows.

Ollie revealed that Kenny did once accept an illegal bribe of £7,000 from an international rival who needed a favour in a World Championship race. Libel laws will ensure the rider's continued anonymity but Ollie did say: "Although Kenny refused to let the other rider beat him in the race in question, he did agree not to spoil his chances by knocking him off!

"Kenny told me that he still received the full seven grand, as agreed, from the rider concerned!"

Former World No.2 Simmons had accepted that he was by then past his use-by date as a top rider. At 38, he no longer had world title aspirations, so he was happy to sell his British Final place to the fast emerging, 24-year-old Wigg, who was a genuine challenger. Simmons was an all round motorcycle purist, a stylist who always looked in control and rode comfortably within his ability. He and Carter were a generation apart.

Simmo said: "I rode with Kenny a little in my latter days with England, when he was the rising, self-proclaimed national No.1 and I was very much the old boy of the team. He was out for one thing and only one thing only – himself.

"He was probably the most single-minded speedway rider ever – certainly in my time – and he totally believed he would be the best in the world. Was he too obsessed? Can you be too driven? Ivan was also very driven, although he was obviously able to control it.

"You had to admire the way Kenny overcame bad injuries and still went out and won races, but he was also like a canon waiting to explode.

"Kenny couldn't control his emotions at all, and would let off at anyone and everyone around him when things were going against him. I think it was because he got badly hurt so many times, he didn't give a shit about crashing. If there was a gap, you could be sure that Kenny would go for it, even if he took you out in the process."

Michael Lee, for so long Carter's only rival for the title of England No.1, shared Simmo's concern for self-preservation when he found himself in opposition to Kenny. Lee said: "There was major rivalry between us and I used to hate riding against Kenny. He was like me in that neither of us wanted to be beaten.

"He would win the battle any way he could, whereas I wasn't willing to go to any lengths. He would rather we both lost the battle than allow me to win it.

"He'd even take himself out of it if it meant he stopped you from beating him. It was quite scary at times, because Kenny was full-on and you had to be quite smart when riding against him.

"I respected Bruce Penhall more than any of my other rivals but I didn't respect what Kenny tried to do on track. I wasn't scared of him but I was cautious and calculated whenever I rode against him. I made sure I had my act together because I knew how dangerous he was in every way. He was a hard rider, he did what he thought he had to do to win."

Bruce Penhall is even more scathing than Simmons and Lee in his recall of Carter's explosive on-track style. He said: "Was he a dangerous opponent? Absolutely, he was dangerous. You can be hard – and I was hard, I wouldn't take anything from the kid – but everybody knew that Kenny wasn't all there upstairs.

"He would do things that were totally out of his mind. I've seen him do things on the racetrack that were complete and utter craziness – and come out unscathed, when he should have ended up in hospital, and he did spend a lot of time injured.

"I knew that if there was one person he wanted to do in, it was me. I had to watch him for every second of every race."

Those who knew Kenny very well would argue against the opinions of Lee and Simmons. They say that Carter only knocked off opponents who he deliberately intended to take out, the ones he decided had it coming to them and whose names had been duly noted in his 'little black book'. His friends insist he didn't cause other riders to fall due to his own recklessness.

Penhall did not rate Carter as his most feared opponent ability-wise, though, He said: "If I made the start on Kenny I usually felt I'd win the race safely. He was fast, always a threat, but I would back myself against him.

"He was cocky but then so were a lot of riders who rode around that time. And I guess some people would say I was cocky, too.

"The rider I always had the hardest time beating was Michael Lee. I always knew that if I was leading him and there were still three feet between myself and the fence, Mike could come by me any time. When he was at his best, his most consistent, he was simply awesome. I'd say that Michael, Erik Gundersen and Kelly Moran were the most talented riders of my era."

Lee won back-to-back British Championships in 1977 and 1978 and the next Englishman to emulate his success was Carter.

"Yeah, he could ride a bike," agreed Lee. "You couldn't go as fast as Kenny did without being able to ride the bike – but I didn't like the way he went about things sometimes. No-one's going to win everything and sometimes you have to accept that you will lose the occasional race, or even quite a few races. But Kenny could never accept that."

Although Carter's bravery at Oxford paid off, he was not ready to resume for Halifax, who had to try and cover his absence with the use of guest riders or the rider replacement facility. Although Ian Thomas' Newcastle and Exeter, run by Peter Oakes and boosted by the return of Ivan Mauger for home matches only, had moved up from the National League to bolster the British League to 16 tracks, six of those clubs raced home matches on a Saturday. This gave the Dukes very limited choice in their search for suitable guests.

Even without Carter, fellow injury victims Wigg and Kelvin Tatum and the suspended Michael Lee, England recovered from their mauling by the USA to beat world champions Denmark in the Test series that began and ended in June '84. Carter was at The Shay to see the Lions beat the Danes and clinch the series, 2-1.

But Halifax and England had to get used to the idea of doing without their star man for long periods. His whole focus was firmly fixed on the British Final at Coventry on Wednesday, June 20 . . . and what turned out to be one of the stormiest nights in British speedway history.

No pain, no gain . . . British Champion at last, but the 1984 meeting at Coventry was clouded in controversy.

Chapter 19

BRITISH BULLDOG CHEWS 'EM UP

THE Halifaxapolis was a non-event in all but for the fact that not only did Kenny Carter ride in it, he ignored the pain to dominate the night with six straight wins and victory in the final! The World Championship qualifier at Coventry would be much, much tougher, of course, but as 'practice spins' go, this typified the bulldog spirit and competitive nature of the wee man with the huge heart.

Few are ever likely to remember that Halifaxapolis at The Shay.

Everyone who was at the 1984 British Final will recall the drama, excitement and bitter controversy of a meeting that almost erupted into a brawl involving two of England's top riders and would have significant repercussions for the national team.

The row revolved around the wet and slippery state of the Brandon track following afternoon rain in the area. The meeting started and the winners of the first three heats – Alan and Andy Grahame and Carter – seemed happy for the event to continue but they were very much in the minority. When referee Lew Stripp left his box to inspect the surface after the third race, several of the more senior riders argued strongly that conditions were too dangerous and the meeting should be abandoned.

John Louis, one of the most experienced on view, lost control and fell on the slimy outside of the track in his first ride and he was among the dissenting group who were all for calling a halt. Louis and Carter had become good friends during 'Tiger's' two years with Halifax but Kenny clearly lost some respect for the elder statesman over what happened at the '84 British Final. Mind you, at 43 and just four months short of his well-earned retirement, Louis was entitled to have a greater regard for life and limb. And there were 14 others who shared his concern.

Peter Collins, who had been ruled out of the sport for almost a year after suffering a serious shoulder injury in not too dissimilar conditions at the end of 1980, was also vocal in his condemnation of the Coventry track. As if the painful memory of that crash at Cradley was not enough to convince him that they should all pack away the bikes and try again another day, PC had also just seen his younger brother, Phil, fall in his first outing. Conditions were clearly taking their toll.

The arguments for and against a continuation raged on in the privacy of the dressing room but, thanks to one outspoken Yorkshireman, what went on inside there did not remain a secret for long.

It later emerged that PC and Carter very nearly came to blows as heated words were exchanged and the abuse became personal.

Scraping the muck to the outside before racing could resume at the '84 British Final.

Collins cannot recall the exact words used by either him or his former World Pairs partner Carter on that night but the memory of a miserable occasion for him and the other non-qualifiers has not left him.

Speaking from his Cheshire home in 2007, Collins said: "I must have been the spokesman and I had the other 14 behind me. In the changing rooms the majority of riders wanted the meeting off. But Kenny, because he was in such a bad way with his leg, and he could see that me and a lot of the others were down about the fact that we were going to have to try and race in those conditions, he capitalised on it.

"I probably called him some names. I can't remember exactly what was said, but it got a bit heated between us. Fifteen out of 16 wanted it off but he didn't stick together with the other lads.

"At the end of the day, it couldn't have got any worse for him. He was all psyched up to ride with his broken leg and he must have had the bike that was set up to do well, which it did. Of course, for him, it was the right decision to run the meeting. But for the rest of us, it wasn't.

"I never made another World Final after that. For various reasons, it all went sour for me."

England boss Carl Glover was summoned to the pits to try and de-fuse an explosive situation between his feuding star riders. "I'd heard something was going off in the pits and it was PC who called for me to come down to try and sort things out," recalled Glover.

"When it started raining and the riders were arguing, I thought it best to stay out of the way and let them sort it out between themselves. If eight wanted to ride and the other eight were against it, I didn't want to be caught in the crossfire.

Left: Peter Collins holding court with brothers Neil and Les (4), together with Mark Courtney (6) and Dave Jessup.
Right: A relaxed-looking Kenny and Neil Evitts can't understand what all the fuss is about.

"But when I heard that it was just one against the rest, I didn't need to ask who the one was.

"I went down to the pits – I think it was PC's mechanic who came to get me – and the majority of the riders asked me to have a word with Lew Stripp about calling it off.

"It was bedlam, I thought that trouble could flare up at any moment. PC and Kenny were having a go at each other and I told their respective mechanics to keep them apart.

"But Kenny was one of those people who would never let it drop. You'd get him into a corner, calm him down and just when you thought you'd dealt with the situation, he'd be up and at 'em again.

"Fifteen riders thought that if the majority didn't want to ride, then the meeting couldn't possibly go on.

"But when I looked at Lew's face, I could tell he was under tremendous pressure from the BSPA. That meeting was going on to the end no matter what. I told PC he was fighting a losing battle and that the meeting would never be cancelled.

"Kenny was on a mission that night and I thought to myself, I really don't need this', " said Glover, talking from the family bakery he runs in Sheffield.

Referee Stripp denies any suggestion that he was put under pressure either from the BSPA or ITV, who were covering the vital qualifier, to ensure the meeting ran its full course that night. The re-staging date would be the next day, Thursday . . . the same day the England riders' bikes would be transported to Sweden for the next round of the World Team Cup at Mariestad. Peter Collins, for one, believes that it was this ridiculous scheduling of major meetings in rapid succession that influenced Stripp's decision to proceed at Coventry.

He said: "Our bikes had to go off to Sweden so no matter how bad it became at Coventry, they couldn't call it off. And that, to me, was all wrong."

Colin Gear, the SRA secretary, was also dragged in to the row. He was summoned to Coventry promoter Charles Ochiltree's stadium office and revealed: "I'd never been invited into Charles' inner-sanctum before – it was a privilege given to few. He was most unhappy with the riders and asked me to go and have strong words with them to ensure the meeting continued – he pointed out that the TV cameras were present and a big crowd also wanted their money's worth.

"I asked the riders not to be too hasty in their decision not to ride, asking them to give the track staff time to get the surface into better condition – they were dragging wet shale from the inside to the outside of the track.

"But no matter what I had said to them, there was no way the riders were going to listen to me. Kenny and PC were at each other's throats and I don't think it helped the situation at all when the CO stormed into the dressing room and, in no uncertain terms, told all those who didn't want to ride that they were being unprofessional and, basically, a disgrace to speedway.

"Ian Thomas also told me that if I wasn't careful, me and the riders would end up killing British speedway!"

So, no pressure on the riders to carry on at Coventry, then!

Gear remembers that while 15 of the British finalists returned to their places in the pits, and the bikes had to be warmed up again, Carter retreated to his motorhome.

After a 45-minute delay while more remedial work was carried out on the sodden Brandon track, the dissenting voices had to accept that the meeting would continue. With the benefit of hindsight, Stripp – who had a reputation for not calling off meetings in bad conditions – can now argue that he was vindicated – the event was completed without injury to any rider and, as the circuit dried out, there was enough tense, hard-fought racing to keep a patient crowd entertained.

And, of course, nothing undermined those who wanted the meeting called off more than the amazing, courageous performance of the man most of the 10,000 crowd had come to see. With his gammy leg still encased in a protective boot and having to hop around the pits on crutches, surely the rider who stood to gain most from the meeting being called off was Carter himself? Under normal circumstances, yes. But Kenny Carter was not normal when it came to pushing the pain barrier to the limit.

Instead, he turned the adverse track conditions to his favour and displayed a steely resolve visibly lacking in some of his more experienced adversaries.

He backed the beleaguered Stripp all the way and made light of all the earlier protests and ill feeling to win three of his five races and clinch victory on 13 points with a brave last lap charge to pass both Peter and Les Collins in a cut-throat heat 20. Second place in that one left a despondent PC a point adrift of the top eight qualifying places. His Belle Vue team-mate, Chris Morton, also missed the boat, so both Aces would take no part in the next round on their home track.

It was a desperately disappointing situation for these lifelong pals, who had won the World Pairs title for England in Italy just three days earlier. They had allowed the poor conditions to affect their confidence and attitude. Collins said: "A lot of good lads went out of the World Championship at that point and I was one of them. With me, I wasn't the best trapper – more of a racer– and if I missed the start I needed a fair chance to be able to pass the other blokes. But Coventry on that night

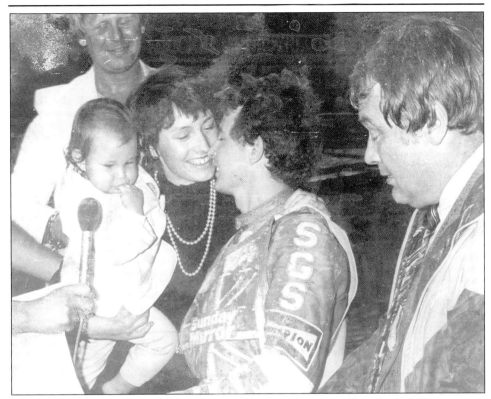

Pam and Kelly Marie greet the new British Champion, with Ian Thomas and Peter Garside looking on.

was just a lottery – wet and awful."

His England team manager Carl Glover, who rode for Boston, Sheffield and King's Lynn in the 70s, agreed with him. He said: "The British Final should not have taken place that night. It was a shocking meeting."

Today, though, even Peter Collins agrees that Carter deserved respect for an astonishingly brave effort. PC said: "To win that British Final with a broken leg was unbelievable stuff, a super-human effort, and you can't knock it."

Carter had ridden through the pain barrier again. But, unlike Oxford, this time he was the champion, the winner of the most prestigious individual meeting staged in the UK outside the World Final itself. Finally, he had silenced the doubters who, until then, had never stopped reminding him that he had never won a major round on the title trail.

And he had done it despite an enormous handicap.

Carter would go on to retain the British crown a year later, without any of the drama and rancour associated with this famous night at Coventry. Without doubt, this was the greatest achievement of Kenny Carter's remarkable career – possibly the most satisfying night of his life.

Even those who disliked or even hated him for whatever reason had to accept and acknowledge that Carter had produced probably the bravest winning performance ever witnessed on a British speedway track – ironically, Peter Collins himself had been no less heroic in finishing second to Ivan Mauger, in even worse track conditions than at Coventry, in the 1977 World Final in Sweden.

As Kenny's entourage all offered their congratulations to the deserved winner, there was also time for the new champion to enjoy a rare tender moment in public with his wife. Pam Carter rushed down from her seat in the main grandstand and, clutching daughter Kelly-Marie in her arms, she and Kenny briefly kissed and embraced in front of the press photographers.

At that moment, as Pam – who was pregnant with their second child – and Kenny gazed lovingly into each other's eyes, they appeared the happiest family in the world.

Even after the effects of his four pre-meeting painkillers had almost worn off and the strain of his night's efforts were beginning to take their toll, Kenny managed a joke at the expense of ITV's Head of Sport, Gary Newbon. He could have taught even Carter a thing of two about self-importance. It was a standing joke in the sport at the time that Newbon was the highest paid pits marshal in speedway for the arrogant way he would order track staff at the major televised meetings to 'hurry up' the riders before each race, in the interests of the broadcaster's time constraints.

But this time Kenny was too sharp for the interviewer when he informed Newbon, on air, that he and Pam would be naming their next baby after him.

"What, Gary?" asked a smug-looking Newbon as he held his microphone closer to the newly-crowned British Champion for confirmation.

"Nah, Wallie!" said a giggling Kenny, bringing Newbon down to size and an abrupt end to the interview! It is difficult to say whether it was Newbon or Carter, interviewer or sporting hero, who gained the most in terms of media profile from ITV's coverage of speedway in the early 80s. They enjoyed the kind of playful, good-natured banter that the BBC boxing commentator, Harry Carpenter, had with Ali and, later, Frank Bruno when the cameras were rolling.

After Kenny's mechanics had packed all the gear away, he again retreated to the luxury of his motorhome, parked right at the front of the Brandon car park, where he fed the press another plethora of juicy quotes for the morning tabloids as well as the weekly speedway publications. Revelling in the attention, he leaned back on a sofa, propped his right leg up, accepted all the deserved plaudits his admirers could possibly lavish on him . . . and then proceeded to let rip at his rivals.

Earlier in the meeting, Carter had made a point of revealing, on camera to Newbon, how he had waged a one-man dressing room crusade against his rivals. Now, with the title he craved safely in the bag, he was in full flow. The 'over the moon' rhetoric that he sometimes resorted to if he was not quite in the right mood to articulate his strong opinions had passed. Now he wanted to unburden himself of all the angst and emotion that had built up inside him throughout a stormy night.

He said: "I wasn't asking any favours at Coventry and certainly didn't get any. All I got was a load of stick from some of the other riders – including some of my so-called England team-mates.

"The things they said to me were disgusting and one in particular, whose name I'm not prepared to mention, threatened to punch me in the face after the meeting. I don't know whether it was jealousy or what."

Everybody knew Kenny was referring to Peter Collins.

He continued: "I thought the track was raceable and it turned out that way because we had some of the best racing there has ever been in a British Final."

And clever, calculating Kenny scored some useful PR points with the speedway public when he added: "Ten thousand people had come to the meeting and the TV cameras were there too. But the rider who threatened to hit me said: 'Stuff the crowd and the TV. What about us?'

"Well, if that's his attitude, I reckon he ought to retire. I feel the riders owe a hell of a lot to the public and the television.

"I couldn't really believe the way some of the riders ganged up on me. It's a pity the aggro had to spoil a fantastic night for me."

It was typical of Kenny Carter. Even in his happiest moments, there was inevitably an underlying problem just bubbling beneath the surface. It seemed that even his greatest successes, and this has to be the finest of all, had to be tarnished by controversy and ill feeling.

Carter may have made himself very unpopular with a number of his fellow riders during the ugly dressing room fracas between heat three and the long-delayed resumption, but it was his scathing post-meeting comments that most upset his England colleagues, Peter Collins and Morton. Perhaps some of Carter's anger was fuelled by Carl Glover's early, and logical, decision not to consider him for the defence of the World Pairs crown he and Collins had won the previous year, and to go with the Belle Vue duo at Lonigo instead.

In his 2005 book, *When The Can Ran Out*, Morton still maintained: "The track was not fit to ride on, let alone race on." But, believing that after reluctantly agreeing to 'give it a go' the meeting would be called off anyway, he also admitted: "On reflection, I entered into a really stupid mindset that I had never done before. I had made an enormous error of judgement and learned a valuable lesson to keep focused on racing."

Despite their World Pairs win at Gothenburg in 1983, the relationship between Peter Collins and Carter had been strained for some time. It plummeted to a new low after what happened at the '84 British Final, although it had yet to reach rock bottom. That was almost another two years further down the line.

But Morton, who was top of the BL averages at the time of the Coventry meeting, gave credit to Carter in his book. He wrote: "I have to take my hat off to him for firstly riding in his condition, recognising a way of enhancing his chances, then going out and winning the meeting. I handed over the British title without a challenge."

It was left to Carl Glover to try and repair the damage from the British Final rumpus. England would contest the Inter-Continental Final of the World Team Cup in Mariestad, Sweden just a few days later but four of the quintet had been eliminated from the individual World Championship at Coventry. It was therefore hardly surprising that the Lions trailed the USA and Denmark on a rain-soaked track.

For the second season in succession it meant England needed the reprieve of an extra Continental qualifier to reach the World Team Cup Final. By then, Glover found himself caught between a rock and a hard place. Carter's leg injury – OK to risk in pursuit of the golden individual prize but not yet up to the strain for either club or country at that point – had ruled him out of the qualifier in Sweden but he could possibly have ridden in the semi-final round at Pocking a few weeks later. Glover's dilemma was either to leave out Carter, who was an automatic choice if fit; or recall him to the team and upset the others who clearly did not want him to be part of the group?

It was obvious that England would not have the strength to beat holders Denmark and America at Leszno without a fired-up Carter. And then the question was asked: if the captaincy was taken away from Kenny, would he be prepared to ride for England again anyway?

Carter immediately answered that question himself by writing a letter to stand-in BSPA chairman Reg Fearman, on his patriotic red, white and blue Union Jack headed notepaper, confirming his continuing desire to ride for England – "anytime, anywhere." He also made it clear to Fearman that he bore no grudge against Glover.

But after discussing the problem with the five riders he took to Sweden, Glover confirmed that Carter would be replaced as skipper by Chris Morton. The national manager had bowed to the majority but it was not hard to share his view that he had been put in an impossible position after Carter had provoked a war of words with some of his England colleagues at Coventry. He justified his decision to choose Morton when he said: "I couldn't have a rider leading the team who was neither liked nor respected by any of his team-mates."

Glover continued: "I might have had more aggravation if Kenny had been fit but I would just have had to get hold of him and Peter Collins by the scruff of their necks and told them to get on with the job.

"I spoke to Kenny and Peter about what went on at Coventry. The problem was that although Peter kept quiet about the trouble behind the scenes, Kenny didn't. PC knew he had done wrong but it was Kenny who aggravated the situation by making it public when it was something that happened between them in the dressing room. That is what upset PC most."

There was also a feeling among some of Carter's England colleagues that the team would do better without him, on the grounds that his outspoken anti-foreign propaganda only served to bring the very best out of the Americans and the Danes. The usually ebullient Californians hardly needed much motivation but knowing that the England No.1 was selling 'I Hate Americans' stickers through his fan club and sales outlet at Halifax simply fired them up even more.

Bruce Penhall spoke for his compatriots of that era when he said: "I suppose we could've taken offence to the stickers Kenny had made up but it didn't bother us in the slightest – we knew what he was all about. We wanted to go out and win against England anyway but, without a doubt, those things he said about us just made us want to beat him, in particular, even more."

Carter claimed he was misunderstood over his stickers. "The Yanks used to wear 'I Hate Kenny Carter' badges," he said. "So, when I took over the souvenir shop at Halifax, I had 'I Hate the Yanks' badges made.

"It was a joke, a laugh, that's all. But it was taken the wrong way."

Bobby Schwartz, who succeeded Penhall as American captain at the end of 1982, seemed to see the funny side after a while. He said: "I still have the 'I Hate

Kenny is Best Man at the wedding of Americans Eddie and Christina Ingels. Others pictured with the happy couple are Newcastle co-promoters Ian Thomas and Robin Stannard and team boss Dave Younghusband.

Americans' badge on my wall. Kenny and me didn't really have a problem. We talked, and he may have disliked me because I was an American, but I wasn't a threat to him because I wasn't nearly as good as Bruce."

Eddie Ingels, another American who raced in the BL, must also have had time for Carter. Kenny appeared as Best Man at the wedding of Newcastle's US rider. After the ceremony, bizarrely held on the track at Brough Park where Kenny had begun his racing career, he joked: "I don't hate Americans and surely that proves it!"

He definitely won himself a few new admirers among English supporters during 1984. He boasted how his fearless riding with a broken leg at Oxford and Coventry had won him a whole new army of fans who once hated him but who had now learned to respect him for the courageous rider he undoubtedly was.

In between putting his feet up and riding in the next round of the individual Overseas Final of the World Championship at Belle Vue, Kenny made the short journey to Bradford's Odsal Stadium to attend a press conference to announce plans for a £1.5m makeover for the old venue that would become the new home of British

Elbow-to-elbow with Shawn Moran at the start during the Overseas Final at Belle Vue.

speedway's major international meetings following the much lamented loss of Wembley. Odsal, the home of Bradford Northern rugby league club, had been chosen by the SCB to stage the 1985 World Final and Carter had already set his sights on becoming the local hero come good that day.

First, he had much tougher tests to face before he could reach the '84 final in Gothenburg. His preparations for the Overseas Final – ironically to be held at Belle Vue but without Collins and Morton – were not helped by an infection in his broken leg caused by one of the 10 screws having worked itself loose. There were plenty in speedway who already believed that Kenny had a screw loose before his injury!

To try and relieve the pain he had physio treatment from Alan Sutton, the Halifax Town FC masseur, but doctors said another operation was not advised at that stage because his skin would not have been up to undergoing further surgery. They were wasting their time telling Kenny that he should not have even been thinking about riding again for at least another three months.

Belle Vue was never going to be an easy hurdle to negotiate but, weighed against that was the fact that Carter was a renowned Hyde Road specialist. Seven points from his first three rides meant that just one more from his last two outings would be enough to see him through in seventh place. But with five of the six non-qualifiers all English, it left only Carter, Alan Grahame and Simon Wigg – making the most of his earlier reprieve facilitated by Malcolm Simmons – to keep the home flag flying in Manchester, where American Lance King was unbeaten.

Afterwards, Carter slumped back on a chair in his motorhome and the pain was written all over his face. "It's really bad and my leg feels worse now than it did when I rode at Oxford," he grimaced. Having ruled out more surgery before the Inter-

Continental Final, the last round on the road to the World Final in Sweden, he simply had to soldier on.

But as each qualifying stage came and went, the going got increasingly tougher. And the ICF at Vojens would prove a step too far.

Instead of flying out with the other riders, which would have involved uncomfortable airport delays, Kenny travelled to Denmark by road and ferry in his motorhome along with his mechanics and other minders. Apart from being able to stretch out and relax, the trip also gave him a chance to unwind with a few drinks to help numb the pain. Well, more than a few, as Phil Hollingworth explained. "Once we were on the ferry, we drank everything from the cocktail menu, from top to bottom of both pages and then reversed it the other way! Kenny didn't drink that often but I'd never seen him as pissed as he was that night!

"He was sat at the bar and resting his leg on crutches when these two big drunken Danes bumped into him and nearly knocked him off his stool. Gareth Perrett, a police inspector in Halifax and a good mate of Kenny's, was with us, along with Pete Garside.

Needless to say, Carter's broken leg was a massive handicap to qualification among the top 11. Under normal circumstances, he would have sailed through what was the penultimate round of the World Championship and he got off to the best possible start by winning his first race.

But it was plainly obvious that he was struggling badly. Looking awkward on the bike, he had a job to manoeuvre around the bends and seemed to be hanging on for dear life. He got tailed off badly in his second ride and gave up before the chequered flag.

He had to call on all his reserves of raw courage to manage three consecutive third places but it was not quite enough. Even then, his title dream over, he somehow summoned the strength for one last-ditch attempt to make it through to Sweden . . . only to lose it to Cradley Heath's Alan Grahame in an extra race that decided who would be reserve for the World Final.

There were 20,000 fans at Vojens but a thoroughly dejected Carter appeared a sad and lonely figure in the pits at the end of a gruelling few days. He said: "One race and I was in agony. I was crying with the pain. I knew then I wouldn't qualify.

"Never again. If I break my leg again, I'll just forget it until I'm better."

Ian Thomas, who helped Carter all the way along the '84 World Championship trail from Oxford to Vojens, said: "I told Kenny that he'd come so far, he had to go out and try and win that race against Alan Grahame – there was still a chance that somebody else would get injured between then and the World Final.

"He gave it one hell of an effort but it just wasn't enough in the end. I thought he took going out of the World Championship much better than I would have expected.

"All that he did that year was achieved against all the odds – the medical people didn't want him to ride and other riders wanted to knock him out of the championship. Plus we were also caught up in that controversy at Oxford at the start of the year when other people were reportedly buying and selling points.

"It was an unusual year for me, because it's not often you get the opportunity to help such a talent who was trying to get through to a World Final with a broken leg."

Vojens was a mountain too far. All the pain Kenny had endured since April, fretting over whether he would be fit enough to take his place in each qualifying round, the extra risks he had taken as the pain from his leg worsened, it had all come to nowt.

So had England's dreams of regaining the World Team Cup. In the most one-sided final to date, Denmark romped to a 20-point victory over England, who finished ahead of a disappointing USA and Poland. Not even a fully fit Carter – who was in Poland to co-commentate for ITV's *World of Sport* – could have denied the dominant Danes in the mood they were in.

In the individual World Final at Gothenburg, it was again Denmark's night, with Erik Gundersen winning the crown for the first time, ahead of his great rival Hans Nielsen and the American Lance King. Simon Wigg, England's only representative, did well enough on his big night debut, scoring nine, but everyone agreed that England's best title hope was laid up back in Halifax wondering what might have been.

Kenny watched the closing stages of Halifax's dismal 1984 season with his leg still plastered up, unable to add to the eight team appearances he made before his disastrous crash at Cradley in April or save the Dukes from slipping three places in the final table to 14th.

Following a welcome holiday in Spain, where he would begin to rebuild the muscles in his leg that had wasted away, Carter withdrew from the indoor gala at Birmingham's NEC in November and vowed to be back fully fit in 1985.

After all the pain and suffering he went through in '84, it could hardly get any worse for him.

Or could it?

Before a difficult year had come to an end, things certainly got worse for Halifax Dukes.

Kenny Carter rocked them with a written transfer request.

Chapter 20

UP IN SMOKE

AFTER six full seasons with his home-town team, it seemed unthinkable that Kenny Carter would no longer be leading Halifax when the 1985 season roared into life.

Eric Boothroyd had been very much a father figure to Kenny throughout his brief speedway career and you could not have blamed him had he felt disappointed when Carter's transfer request dropped through his letterbox at his home early in December '84. Maybe, because of their long friendship spanning seven years, the club skipper felt too embarrassed to speak to his promoter face to face before putting his request in writing, or was he just being businesslike?

There is no doubt that Kenny was genuine when he said that it was the Dukes' lack of success, especially away from home where he usually carried the burden of leading what was a one-man team, left him feeling "depressed" and in search of a fresh challenge elsewhere.

But it was not a good time to be seeking pastures new. In the space of months, the dwindling British League had shrunk by another five teams, from 16 to just 11, with Eastbourne, Poole, Exeter, Newcastle and Wimbledon all jumping ship to the National League. Most tracks continued to report falling attendances, while at the same time riders' costs were going in the opposite direction.

Having lost precious coverage from ITV following the demise of *World of Sport*, and with the national press also rapidly losing interest, speedway was in a period of steady decline. Big name sponsors were becoming increasingly hard to find, although Kenny reached a deal in January with the Morrisons supermarket chain to make 40 personal appearances at their branches in the north.

In putting in for a transfer from Halifax, he cited their lack of success and heat leader support for him as his reasons – and they were perfectly understandable. But was it also about trying to squeeze more money from the management?

Even after Boothroyd had moved swiftly in the New Year to sign New Zealand Champion Larry Ross (on loan) from Belle Vue and retain the emerging Neil Evitts on a permanent deal from Birmingham, and then added Sean Willmott (from Exeter) and Rod Hunter (Newcastle), Carter was still stalling on a new deal.

It prompted renewed speculation that he may turn to road-racing if he was unable to reach agreement with his speedway club. He said: "I'm not threatening to quit speedway for road-racing but I know that if I don't reach agreement with Halifax, then I could switch without too many problems."

His words seemed less of a bluff tactic and gained more substance when he added

Alan and Kenny on parade before the media at their Donnington Park launch.

The Dukes' last season at Halifax, 1985. Left to right: Eric Boothroyd, Eric Monaghan, Larry Ross, Kurt Hansen, Kenny, Neil Evitts, Sean Willmott and Rod Hunter.

that many of the new sponsors he had lined up would back him in either form of motorcycle sport.

While his protracted talks with Boothroyd continued, Kenny kept himself busy building up his next project . . . Team Carter. He had gained the backing of a raft of sponsors, including the Donnington 100 Club, who would support both him and his brother, Alan. As part of a lavish sponsorship launch at the Donnington Park racetrack, the Carter boys posed for publicity pictures wearing near identical new red, white and blue Hideout leathers – the colours Kenny always wore – and sipping from the obligatory champagne bottle. Afterwards, they braved the cold wind to take a few laps of the Derbyshire circuit – but not even Kenny could have stage-managed the shot he unwittingly served up on a plate for the Central TV crew and assembled press photographers, including *Speedway Star's* Mike Patrick.

Much to his embarrassment, he rode into a corner in almost slow motion . . . and slid off his bike! The pictures of him flat out on the tarmac were not what he had in mind, although this time only his ego had been damaged. Trust him to exploit the publicity opportunity to the full!

He had put together an impressive joint sponsorship package. With Dunlop tyres, Mercedes Trucks and Heuer Watches involved, as well as the Donnington Club, Kenny claimed the whole deal was worth a combined £150,000 to him and Alan. Mercedes Benz, through their Bradford-based main dealer Northside Truck Centre, stepped in at the last moment after an Italian company pulled out – but it was a decision they would soon live to regret.

Boothroyd says that while he never had any major fall-outs with Carter, their financial negotiations could be lively and combative.

"One year he came round to our house to thrash out his deal for the following season. He arrived at 9am and we were still arguing at 10 o'clock that night before he finally signed," said Eric. "Bonnie got fed up with all the haggling and left us to it at 9pm – and she said she could still hear Kenny and me bickering at each other from the upstairs bedroom!

"But once we had agreed a deal, he'd stick to it and never gave us a problem."

It was easy to see why Boothroyd played hardball with his top man around the negotiating table before the '85 campaign. The Halifax boss had the memories of the financially disastrous previous season still fresh in his mind. He explained: "We agreed to pay Kenny a big, five-figure upfront sum before the '84 season but when he broke his leg on Easter Saturday it backfired on the club, financially, more than him.

"He never rode for Halifax again all that season. We had to resort to guest riders to replace him but we'd already paid out thousands to Kenny in the form of a big advance."

Boothroyd scrapped the idea of paying his star rider a large amount upfront and in 1985 he restructured their deal to reward Kenny with higher points money instead. With a new agreement finally signed and sealed before the end of February, Carter stayed on to lead the Dukes in what would be their final season at The Shay. He quickly proved he was back to full fitness by scorching to a full maximum in the Shay opener against Belle Vue and showed all his old fight – literally – when Sheffield visited on March 30. The Tigers left with a 42-36 League Cup win.

Feisty Neil Collins, who loved a scrap himself, left minus two of his front teeth after a pits scuffle with Carter.

"Our Neil must have said something to Kenny. I don't know whether Kenny hit him with a bike stand or threw a punch, but Neil lost two front teeth and it cost him a fortune in dentistry fees to get them fixed," said Neil's oldest brother, Peter.

Kenny's friend, Jimmy Ross, reckoned that Neil Collins had asked Kenny 'if he liked the taste of hospital food?'. He said: "Peter made a similar comment to Kenny at Belle Vue a couple of years later, which caused a fight, but whereas PC meant that Kenny would end up back in hospital if he continued to ride dangerously, his brother Neil said it in a way to suggest that he would put Kenny back there himself."

Carter was in reflective mood when he told Richard Bott: "I seem to have trouble with the Collins' because they are brothers. They stick together. And a lot of it stems from what happened at last year's British Final at Coventry. But why drag it on?

"Okay, I admit, I shouldn't have said what I did on TV about the arguments, but I was in a lot of pain from my leg and I was angry because about 10 riders seemed to be ganging up on me.

"Look, if that meeting had been rained off after the first few races, there is no way I would have qualified. I couldn't have gone back for a re-run in my condition. Obviously, because I'd won my first race, I wanted the meeting to continue."

Carter claimed he had taken a long, hard look at himself during the winter of 1984-85 and realised where he had gone wrong in the past. Although winning the world

England's team that won the UK round of the World Team Cup at Odsal in 1985. Standing: Kenny, John Berry and Kelvin Tatum. Front: Chris Morton, Jeremy Doncaster and Phil Collins.

title remained his burning ambition, he would not say publicly that he was going to win the big one at Odsal, in his own backyard.

As England prepared to face world champions Denmark in the three-match Test series in late April and early May, a more reserved Carter even accepted the fact that he would not be re-appointed England captain with good grace.

Successful Ipswich boss John Berry, who led the Witches to another league and cup double in 1984 before being persuaded to enter his third spell in charge of the national side at the expense of Carl Glover, took the unorthodox decision of not naming a skipper. Instead, Berry opted to select his captain on a match-by-match basis and, in fact, the first three to be afforded the honour in the Danish series were home track favourites Kelvin Tatum (at Coventry), Simon Wigg (Oxford) and Phil Collins (Cradley Heath).

Once Berry had ruled out Peter Collins after the former World Champion privately informed him that he was prepared to ride for England in the finals of the Pairs and Team Cup but not the qualifying rounds, he was virtually left with a straight choice for skipper between Carter and Chris Morton. And to appoint either would have invited more of the same kind of trouble that had beset Glover.

In *Confessions of a Speedway Promoter*, his acclaimed first book in 2004, Berry wrote: "I don't know the history of the bad blood between Peter Collins and Chris Morton, on the one hand, and Kenny, on the other. It must have gone deeper than professional jealousy, because the dislike was intense. So intense that it prevented me from doing what I felt I should by choosing an England skipper between Kenny and Chris, for fear of upsetting either. I ran without a captain in an effort to play Solomon."

On the captaincy issue, Berry later added: "When I was faced with the personality clash between Chris Morton and Kenny, and as some might say took the coward's way out by not appointing a captain that season, it was surprisingly Kenny, of the two, who seemed to understand and cope with the disappointment better.

"The only 'strong request' Kenny ever made of me, and it was one I had no difficulty in granting, was that he be allowed to wear the number one on his back.

"Some say he was not a team man but he was passionate about riding for his country, which wasn't always clearly evident with all of his team-mates, and never ever gave less than full commitment to the cause. I said at the time, and I repeat now, team man or not, I would have been delighted to have had seven Kenny Carters in the England team."

Given Berry's pledge to encourage youthful promise instead of continuing to lean on the fading old guard of Peter Collins, Dave Jessup and the recently returned Michael Lee, it was hardly a surprise when Denmark won the series, 2-1. Carter, who top-scored at Coventry but managed just one at Oxford and eight in the last Test at Dudley Wood, forged a tenacious partnership with the spectacular Phil Collins – who says he never got on with the famous brothers? But this was a young and inexperienced England team in the early phase of major transition.

For the World Team Cup UK round that opened the new-look Odsal venue on May 12, Berry went with Carter, Phil Collins and two newcomers in Coventry's big winter signing from Wimbledon Kelvin Tatum and his own track's No.1 Jeremy Doncaster, with his most experienced rider, the 28-year-old Morton, at reserve. Simon Wigg was not an option because he had been banned from all 1985 international FIM-inscribed meetings for his part in the race-fixing nonsense at Oxford in '84. The five-man team was easily good enough to see off Australia, New Zealand and Finland but Denmark were a much different proposition. Even without Hans Nielsen, who was at loggerheads with their autocratic manager Ole Olsen, the superior gating Danes were still a class apart. And yet 'Berry's Babes' came within two points of a series victory in the final match at Cradley.

Australia had also been severely weakened by the tragic death in April of Ipswich star Billy Sanders who took his own life when he was unable to cope with the break-up of his marriage. His wife had begun a relationship in Sydney with his former World Pairs partner, Gary Guglielmi, and, although he had a vulnerable young son to care for in England, the Australian Champion and No.1 drove his car into woods near his Suffolk home and committed suicide through carbon monoxide poisoning.

Carter showed no outward sign of emotion when news of Sanders' death stunned speedway but those closest to Kenny say he lost a friend as much as a rival. Kenny could count on one hand his few real friends among the riders but Sanders was one of them, along with Kelly and Shawn Moran and, possibly, Mitch Shirra.

There were clear parallels to be drawn between Carter and Sanders. Both were fiercely driven individuals, fiery characters with a burning ambition to reach the top but who never quite got there. Maybe they wanted it too much and when faced with a situation or set of problems that they could no longer handle, they lost it all? True, Sanders did not kill anybody other than himself. But is it inconceivable that as Kenny's own marriage started to hit the rocks later in 1985, the disturbing memory of Sanders' tragic fate did not resurface in his own tortured mind?

After the defeat by Denmark, Berry came under close scrutiny again for choosing Carter and the 20-year-old Tatum as England's representatives in the World Pairs, while ignoring the claims of reigning world champions Peter Collins and Morton. Carter and the reliably fast-gating Tatum cruised through the semi-final at Bradford as runners-up to the Americans Shawn Moran and Bobby Schwartz – only Carter's last race engine blow-up against the winners denied the home pair victory. (After Carter's bike packed up, he received a lift back to the pits from Shawn Moran – who says he never got on with the Americans?)

Berry admitted after Odsal that it was more difficult to omit the in-form Tatum, who had bounced back in style after missing most of the previous season due to a broken thigh, than Carter, who was short of his best form at the start of the season. He had finally broken with his buy-British policy and taken the decision to switch from Godden to the increasingly popular GM engine but his gating had suffered in the first few months of the season and it took him time to get the best from the Italian motor.

Phil Hollingworth said: "I think it was a big mistake when Kenny stopped riding Goddens and switched to GM. The Weslakes he had before would sometimes blow up for no reason, whereas the Godden was much more reliable. One of their engines could last all season, and we had four or five bikes at one time, but apart from changing the odd piston once a year, they were like bomb-proof.

"Don said he wanted an English world champion riding his bikes and he thought Kenny would be that man – and he should have been several times over.

"Guiseppe Marzotto had been trying to persuade Kenny to switch for some time and one night he came over from Italy to Halifax to try and clinch a deal. We took him to Flashmans, a night club-restaurant in town owned by Jez Terzak and his brother, the entrepreneur who sold Kenny the Rolls-Royce he drove at my wedding.

"Guiseppe, Kenny and I were in Flashmans – it has since been re-named Bar Eleven – having a few glasses of wine when a big parrot, which used to be kept in a cage but had been let out on this occasion, landed on the back of Guiseppe's hand. At first we were all amused by it but Guiseppe was soon getting a bit concerned. 'Ooh, ooh . . . ouch!' he said, trying not to appear too worried. The bloody macaw was pecking away at his skin!"

As well as switching machinery, Carter also decided to make more changes to his back-up team. The long-serving Richard Pickering had left the team early in 1984, when Hollingworth took on the main mechanic's role full-time. But a year later it was Ollie who was fired after Kenny brought in teenager Bryan Larner, the son of the former Newcastle co-promoter of the same name, as part of a cost-cutting exercise. Youngster Chris Fagan was also part of Kenny's workshop and pits set-up by then.

Ollie explained: "Bryan started working for Kenny under the Youth Opportunities

Scheme and I could see what was happening. I felt a bit like how Richard must have done when I was first brought in – I could see the writing on the wall.

"Kenny said Pam wanted a nanny to help her around the house and it was around the same time that he said he couldn't afford me any more. He had been paying me £200 a week when I'd been previously getting only 60 quid as a joiner, so it was very good money. I obviously wasn't happy at being sacked, especially as I'd put in a lot of hard work.

"While Kenny was in hospital in Stourbridge recovering from his first broken leg in '84, I was on the intensive care ward for a week in hospital at Halifax. The doctors thought I'd had a heart attack at first but then they found out it was a burst ulcer.

"The routine used to be that Richard would cover all the home meetings at The Shay on a Saturday and I'd go with Kenny to the continental meetings at weekends. There was a lot of driving involved and, basically, a lot of bad living – going home to bed at three in the morning, getting up at eight and eating motorway services food. We didn't worry about drinking and driving then.

"I went on the dole for a bit and although Belle Vue's Andy Smith asked me if I'd be his mechanic, I turned him down and took a job with Marshall, a building company. I still work for them today."

It was a building company, Coalite Building Supplies, who brought reinforcement to Halifax in mid-season. There was a new enthusiasm about the place as Eric and Bonnie Boothroyd welcomed the appointment of new directors Bobby and Allan Ham, who sponsored Carter through their construction company, and Chris Dunley, who ran a freight business out of Manchester Airport, to the board of Northern Speedways Ltd. Through their business contacts, the Hams secured a new team sponsorship that saw the team re-named the Coalite Dukes from the start of June '85.

The pre-season signings did at least make the team slightly more competitive on their travels. They still could not manage to win away more than once in 20 British League and League Cup matches all season, but the LC win at Coventry and BL draw at Wolverhampton at least gave the long-suffering travelling Dukes fans cause to remember a couple of awaydays where they managed to avoid defeat. Essentially, though, they continued to be a one-man team on too many occasions away from The Shay.

Before the World Pairs semi at Odsal, Carter had vowed to "drop his leathers" if he failed to score a six-ride maximum. It was common knowledge among the riders who had shared a dressing room with 'King Kenny' that he was "hung like a donkey", so perhaps a rare sense of modesty prevented him from carrying out his promise!

He certainly put on another big show in the British Final at Coventry, rearranged to the Wednesday night after the Sunday washout. This time there was no hint of controversy, no dressing room acrimony and the grippy Brandon track was in a perfect condition as Carter romped to a stylish 15-point maximum.

He did it in thrilling fashion, too. Last from the gate in heat 10, he barged his way

British Champion at Coventry again in '85 – this time without the injury or the aggro.

A tender moment with Pam at the Coventry pit gate.

past John Davis, the man who had beaten him twice at the Shay in previous weeks, including the British semi-final which Carter won after a run-off against the Reading star. And in heat 19 at Coventry, Kenny had to re-pass Phil Collins to retain his title.

A jubilant Carter said afterwards: "Although I came here desperate to win and believing I could, I didn't go round saying I was going to do it. I must have matured a lot since last year.

"Being so badly injured last season woke me up. I have realised that the most important things are my health and my family.

"I've got a beautiful wife, two lovely kids, and since I have been better from my

Kenny and Pam celebrating at Brandon with mechanics Bryan Larner (second from left) and Chris Fagan (far right), with Peter Garside and Gareth Perrett in the background, along with Gareth's then wife.

accident, as long as I am healthy I'm not too bothered about what happens.

"If I'd finished last of the 16 tonight I would have been sick. But I would have woken up tomorrow morning and got on with my life."

The in-form Davis, who dropped his only point to Carter, was joined on the rostrum by Kelvin Tatum whose whirlwind rise to stardom ensured that he and Carter retained their places for the World Pairs Final at Rybnik four days later. Their gating ability was suited to the atrociously wet track conditions but there was more to their brilliant performance in Poland than simply dropping the clutch and winding on the throttle.

In the end, their fine efforts were good enough to earn them only consolation silver medals. They had no answer to Denmark's Erik Gundersen in a decisive heat 10.

Berry recalls the drama of that race in vivid detail. He wrote in Confessions: "I can remember that Pairs final at Rybnik in every detail. Before the meeting it rained and it rained. The track was so bad nobody would have considered starting had it been just another match. It did stop raining, but not before the track had become a quagmire.

"Normal procedure in these events is for the riders in a pairing to alternate their choice between the available gate positions – but Kenny was in for a shock. I pulled him to one side and explained to him that the only chance we had of winning the event was if the fast-starting but inexperienced Tatum took all six inside gate positions, leaving Kenny to make the best of the outside slots.

"Kenny gave me a very old fashioned look. You could hear his mind whirring. I spoke to both riders at the same time. I made Kenny aware I considered him the

The British Champ returns home to The Shay in style.

senior partner and the man to see us home. I might also have mentioned that I had chosen that pairing when the Speedway Star and SWAPA (Speedway Writers and Photographers Association) had thrown their collective weight behind Collins and Morton. In effect, I explained I had stuck my neck out for Kenny and now it was time for him to back me up. He waited until I had finished, looked me in the eyes and nodded.

"It was a big ask in those conditions. These two kids were up against it. Terrible track conditions and a really classy international field including Shawn Moran and Bobby Schwartz; Ivan Mauger and Mitch Shirra; Jan Andersson and Per Jonsson; Phil Crump and Steve Regeling; and the outstanding pairing of Erik Gundersen and Tommy Knudsen. The only possibly weak pairing in the field was that of the home nation, who did at least have local knowledge and support on their side.

"Given the amount of bad comment I had suffered at the hands of the speedway press and others, and given that even I realised I had stuck my neck out by putting in Tatum, I was as pumped up for this meeting as I had ever been for any. Never mind the two riders, I had a point to prove!

"It went like a dream even though the track was dreadful. There was no question of grading it. A tractor would just have bogged down. As the meeting went on, the sticky, grey bog that the track surface had become was thrown out by the back wheels of the bikes, leaving a racing line about 15 feet wide. Kelvin was gating like a train, while Kenny's first turn work was just out of this world. They were never headed after the first turn in their first three rides.

"The crunch heat was just after the interval. We had gates one and three, which was a slight advantage. As I watched on the centre, the tapes went up and Kelvin flew from them with Kenny on his shoulder. Kenny waited long enough to make sure Erik could not double back under from gate four, and then put his back wheel on the edge of the morass that was effectively the outside of the racetrack.

"We had done it! Knudsen had a look to come back under Kelvin as they emerged from the turn. Talking to Kenny after, he said he saw Knudsen making his move and, content in his mind that Erik had been hung up, leaned back on Kelvin to push him tighter onto the line.

"What Kenny, nor me or anyone else in the stadium had taken into account was Erik's bravery, desperation and pure riding ability. Up until that time, I admit I was one of those who thought Erik was 'just a gater'. But at that very moment he won me over forever.

"He should have been in a fearful muddle but he held his throttle wide, hung on and ploughed fully 12 feet wider into the heavy wet clay than anyone had been or would go for the rest of that night. You had to be close up to the track and see its condition to fully appreciate what he did.

"Had Kenny stayed out wide, he would still have blocked Erik's run, but he wasn't even looking because Gundersen had no right to be there. While Kenny, Kelvin and Tommy were having their own little sort out, Erik bolted right around them and was gone. Kenny was caught in no man's land. Did he try to help Kelvin or go after Erik? He tried to go after Erik, leaving Tommy to slip past the unprotected Kelvin.

"It was not the best race I have ever witnessed, but it was the best single move I have ever seen a rider carry off, simply because it contained every ingredient. It was a desperate situation in a critical heat in a World Final. It was bravery beyond compare, and its execution required the maximum degree of skill.

"I was less generous at the time, though. I was so worked up that I ranted uncontrolled at my pair. They had the win in the palms of their hands and, as I told them, had given it away.

"It wasn't true. It had been snatched from them by a bit of genius, and that is not a word I use often.

"There was still the possibility the Danes might slip up, so the England pair soldiered on and finished the meeting without dropping another point. Sadly for us, so did the Danes, who had pipped us by the smallest possible margin.

"At the time, I was devastated and my humour was not improved when the first question I was asked at the post-meeting press conference was if I thought I had made a mistake with my selections, and that Collins and Morton would have done better.

"The speedway press, I don't think, quite reported it so crudely in the UK, but certainly the English pair on that night were not given anywhere near the amount of praise they deserved.

"As I say, at the time, and for a good while after, I allowed my disappointment to dominate. But now I can look back and enjoy in my mind, the great efforts made by the young English pair against top opposition in diabolical conditions. And then admire the sheer brilliance of Erik Gundersen's riding on the day."

Carter would have respected Gundersen's skill, too, for Kenny genuinely liked the friendly, little Dane. He confided to friends that sometimes he felt he could perhaps intimidate Erik by 'showing' him his front wheel in hard-fought first bend clashes, even when he did not set out to do so, but Gundersen certainly was not put off from going round Carter in the rain at Rybnik.

The Yorkshire terrier and the former public schoolboy. It was an unlikely combination but Berry's selection worked and no other English pairing could have gone closer to beating the brilliant Danes that grey day in Poland, especially given the abysmal track conditions. Kelvin Tatum does not recall much of the racing at Rybnik, his first appearance in a world final, from the meeting 22 years ago but he has pleasant memories of his World Pairs partnership with Carter. Now the leading TV speedway summariser and co-commentator for Sky Sports, the articulate Tatum said: "I was well excited to be called up by John Berry in the first place – it was quite a controversial selection at the time. And I was also excited about riding with Kenny, who had built up this aura around him as perhaps being a difficult person.

"But I've got to say we got on really well and I never had an issue riding with him at all. In fact, I found riding with him in those two World Pairs meetings in '85 quite easy.

"When it came to deciding gate positions, there were no egos evident and Kenny was definitely there fighting for the England cause – not just for himself. He wanted us to pull off the best possible result and, under the circumstances, I thought coming second was pretty damn good," said Tatum, whose speedway career had only started at Wimbledon a little over two years earlier.

"It was quite an experience going into eastern Europe. The journey was a bit hectic, being pulled over by the law for speeding in East Germany after me and Kenny had flown over and hooked up with our mechanics. I can remember Kenny getting very irate when the police jumped out with their lollipops and booked us for speeding.

Asked about Carter's mood before and after the final in Poland, Tatum said: "Kenny did change when he was at meetings. As the meeting got closer, I sensed his personality change to a certain degree.

Planning tactics before the World Pairs semi-final at Bradford with John Berry and Kelvin Tatum.

"When he was away from the racing, the spotlight and all the attention on him, he was a pretty easy-going bloke but he seemed to sort of put up his guard when he got to race meetings. At that point, when we were actually at the track, he was certainly not easy to get to know.

"At that stage of his career he was a seasoned campaigner, he'd had his run-ins with the Yanks and he had a real tough veneer about him. It was all still very new to me.

"Obviously he hadn't made a lot of friends among people like Peter Collins and Chris Morton and that gang but, because he didn't have an axe to grind with me, I think our relationship worked well. It was quite astute of John Berry to put us together because I don't think you would have seen the same scenario had Kenny been picked with either Morton or Collins."

Carter and Tatum would soon both pay a heavy price for their trip to Poland. After the two England riders boarded their flight back to Heathrow and, for Kenny, Halifax's match at Reading the next night, their three mechanics – Bryan Larner and Steve Beardswell representing Kenny and Kelvin's spanner man Alan Hambridge – set off in their van on the long journey home by road.

All appeared to be going smoothly until young Larner, who had turned 17-years-old just nine days earlier and was, apparently, driving on a provisional licence, momentarily dozed off at the wheel. Before they knew it, the Mercedes van had left the road and crashed down a ditch.

Luckily, the three mechanics managed to jump clear of the wreckage and apart from Hambridge, who needed hospital treatment for a broken cheekbone, they suffered only a shaking, minor cuts and grazes. "They rolled it over and were bloody lucky," said Tatum.

The bad news was that after they had clambered out, the van burst into flames. The fire destroyed everything inside, including the riders' two bikes (Carter's new GMs and Tatum's Jawas), spares, helmets, leathers, tools and other equipment.

The England pair had planned to meet up with their mechanics at Reading Speedway the next night, but only Carter and Tatum showed up at Smallmead. With still no word from their missing mechanics, Carter appeared for Halifax wearing a pair of old leathers borrowed from Tatum, who had to act as his mechanic. The Weslake bike Kenny rode and scored 11 points on that night was loaned to him by Kelvin's younger brother, Neville, who was riding for Canterbury at the time.

Two nights later, Carter rode a rebuilt GM at Coventry and, wearing a set of brother Alan's road-racing leathers, he scored a maximum.

Tatum said: "The three mechanics got moved to a hospital, where their passports were taken off them and, basically, they were left there for five days. We were obviously concerned because we didn't know where the hell they were. It was only through my wife Debbie's contacts at the freight company where she used to work that we eventually located them in Dresden.

But the news about the burnt out van got worse for Carter and Tatum when it was revealed that they were not insured for any of the equipment wiped out in the crash in Germany. Foolishly, Carter had not bothered to obtain a new green card – effectively an extra payment to insure the vehicle while it was being driven outside the UK. They cost around £30 at the time – but the England stars paid a much higher price for Carter's negligence.

Tatum, still only 20 at the time and brand new to the continental scene, had left all the arrangements for the van and transportation of their bikes and other gear to the more experienced Carter. "I had no idea about how to organise the paperwork and all the gear for such a trip – I was still green round the ears. I left Kenny to do all the organising," he said, "But it turned out that the green card they had for the van was out of date from a previous trip, and therefore invalid.

"It wasn't until the end of that week that we fully realised what had happened and the full consequences of not being insured.

"Because it was my first world final, and you didn't have much kit in those days anyway, I was left with pretty much stuff-all. I'd virtually emptied the garage. I remember getting back home, walking into my workshop and seeing one wheel, some tools and a few other bits and pieces, but really and truly I'd sent pretty much everything I had in Kenny's van to Poland.

I more or less had to start again in order to simply continue riding for Coventry."

The loss of all his machinery and a behind the scenes dispute made up Tatum's mind to switch from Jawa to GM with immediate effect. He revealed: "Jawa had lent me a factory engine to take to Poland and of course in those days you had carnets for everything – but the carnets were all burnt in the van. Jawa didn't believe me – they kept suggesting that I'd sold the engine and they wanted reimbursing for it. We got into quite a slanging match over that and the RAC were also involved because the carnets had come from them . . . and they had seen everything go out of the country and nothing come back! There were a few photographs of the van knocking about but not much hard evidence of what had happened. The police and authorities, in what was still an eastern bloc country then, didn't really want to get involved either. It was quite a saga.

"I didn't have to re-pay Jawa in the end but we fell out over it. Even later on, when I was competing for the world long-track title, they refused to help me.

"I calculated that the loss of all my equipment in the fire cost me between £10,000 and £12,000, which was a lot of money then."

Tatum does not recall having another specific conversation about the insurance problem with Carter, although his comment that it was "an oversight" on Kenny's part smacked of understatement. I didn't see much of him that season and, you have to remember, I was still young and didn't feel I had the confidence to go tearing into an established international rider. It was slightly awkward for me."

Kenny would also pay a hefty price for not following the correct legal procedures when his van set off from England. The management at Northside Truck Centre of Bradford, who supplied the Mercedes van, were furious and immediately withdrew their sponsorship of both him and brother Alan, who had been given an identical van for his use.

Kenny estimated that the accident had cost him personally around £18,000 and, between them, £30,000.

Carter immediately launched a 'Disaster Fund' to try and raise money to cover

Top: The Brits did well to finish second, behind Danes Erik Gundersen and Tommy Knudsen but ahead of Americans Bobby Schwartz and Shawn Moran.

Left: Kenny and Kelvin sheltering from the rain.

Below: With their mechanics and equipment marooned in East Germany, Kenny had to wear a pair of Kelvin Tatum's old leathers for Halifax's league match at Reading.

England's World Pairs representatives in league opposition as Halifax face Coventry at The Shay, 1985.

their losses. He appealed to speedway supporters everywhere when he said: "It's a terrible blow. We hope the British fans will get behind us and help us to replace the lost equipment. After all, we were representing our country in Poland."

Fans were invited to pay cheques into a Disaster Fund bank account in Halifax. Former Newcastle co-promoter, Robin Stannard, got the ball rolling with a gift of £100 and the Halifax riders even walked among the crowd on the terraces at The Shay to collect donations. One former team-mate of Carter's, who was injured at the time and there simply to watch the racing, had a swift rebuke ready when the fund-raising riders reached the part of the stadium where he was standing. "F*** off, that prat's got more money than me!" he said.

The Disaster Fund appeal was received much less sympathetically by thousands of others in the Bradford community who were still mourning a genuine disaster that had stunned the city just 35 days earlier. The tragic, appalling death of 56 football fans who perished in the fire at Bradford City FC's Valley Parade ground on May 11, 1985 did not bear comparison to Carter's van going up in smoke.

John Berry said: "When I found out what happened I spoke with both riders and then tried to get the BSPA to chip in with some financial help. I think we had a World Team Cup meeting the following weekend, so I concentrated on that. To be honest, as far as I know the BSPA gave no help at all."

Tatum confirmed that no help from the promoters' association was forthcoming and so the riders were left to bear the cost of the crash themselves.

Berry added: "I think Kenny was very money-orientated and tended to do things on the cheap. Bryan Larner is an obvious example. Having said that, I cannot say I ever saw him caught out on track through poor organisation," said Berry.

Who could have imagined then, in June 1985, that Kenny had just ridden in his last-ever world final.

Chapter 21

HEART-BREAKER

KENNY Carter and Kelvin Tatum did not have time to dwell on the financial implications of their burnt out van ordeal. A week later they resumed World Team Cup duties with England at Vojens, where no-one was surprised that England had to settle for second place behind the rampant Danes, who filled the one automatic qualifying passage to the final.

Carter – again wearing his brother's tatty leathers – and Tatum were forced to borrow bikes from team-mates. Carter rode Phil Collins' spare machine, while Tatum borrowed the recalled Chris Morton's second bike.

The runners-up in Denmark had to go on to contest the Continental Final round at Neustadt, Germany to book their ticket to the final in Los Angeles. England, with Cradley Heath boss Colin Pratt assisting Berry, could afford to finish a comfortable second to Sweden this time to ensure their place in California on August 10, alongside the Danes and the Yanks.

Before the team event reached its conclusion, however, there were two more qualifying rounds of the individual World Championship to cram in to a bewilderingly hectic schedule of FIM events. Carter was the odds-on bet to follow his second successive British Championship success with victory in the Overseas Final at Odsal but a brilliant piece of intelligent riding by the mercurial Shawn Moran saw him outwit Kenny in the decisive run-off.

Only five more rides and Carter would be back at the Bradford track, just seven miles from his Bradshaw home, to launch his assault on a long-awaited first world title. All he needed to do was finish in the top 11 qualifiers from the Inter-Continental Final at Vetlanda on August 3.

He started with an acceptable second place behind Tommy Knudsen in heat 4 – but then disaster struck again. This time not a van bursting into flames, but his world title dreams going up in smoke. The jinx that had struck Carter at Wembley in 1981, at the Los Angeles Coliseum in 1982 and throughout a pain-riddled 1984, returned with a vengeance.

There had been doubts whether the penultimate qualifier at Vetlanda would go ahead after torrential rain had left a top surface of water on the typically flat and distinctively wide track. The start was delayed for 30 minutes while extra shale was added to try and soak up some of the water. In some respects conditions looked as bad, if not worse, than the infamous British Final of 1984. Referee Graham Brodie admitted: "I did have doubts about the meeting going ahead. Things were only 50/50."

This time, though, everybody just got on with it . . . until Carter could go on no more.

The worst victim of a spectacular three-man pile-up at the first bend in heat six, he lifted slightly on the inside, piled into the back of John Davis' bike and cartwheeled across the track. Shawn Moran raced clear as Davis and a third Brit, Andy Smith, also came down in the carnage. But while those two were able to pick themselves up, Carter lay ominously flat out on the Vetlanda shale, covered in muck from head to toe.

He managed to get to his feet but then he was carried into the ambulance and on his way to hospital, where he stayed overnight. Doctors immediately diagnosed a broken right leg – the same one he bust at Cradley 18 months earlier.

John Berry, who was in Vetlanda to oversee the efforts of the five-strong English contingent, said: "Kenny knew the leg had gone and the pain was all over his face, but as he lay there on the track he was already issuing instructions to his mechanics as to what they should do.

"Later, in the hospital, when it was clear he had been robbed of winning his World Final at Bradford and the pain and disappointment had mixed together, I don't think I have ever seen a rider looking so grey and sad."

Carter was taken to one hospital for consultation and then another, some 30 miles from the Vetlanda track. He received a visit from the English press corp and explained to them: "I hit a bit of dry track, picked up and took off. I hit John's bike and went over the top."

It was yet another devastating blow in a young life that had already been filled with heartbreak, pain and bitter disappointment. How could he keep possibly bouncing back up off the canvas like a punch-drunk boxer who had taken too many bad knocks? Would Vetlanda prove a challenge too far even for the indestructible Kenny Carter?

"I was absolutely sure I was going to win the World Championship," he said. "Things had been going so well. I had three bikes and they were so fast. I won the Golden Hammer on one, the 16-lapper at Ipswich on another and scored 18 points in the World Games (a pairs event, partnered with Halifax team-mate Larry Ross) at Wimbledon on the third.

"I would have bet everything that I could have won the World Final. I wanted to win, more than anything else, especially at Bradford."

And then, defiant as ever, he added in true Arnie Schwarzenneger style: "I'll be back!"

As soon as he returned from Sweden, Carter sought a second opinion from speedway's best known medico Carlo Biagi at the Peel Hospital in Galashiels, Scotland, where generations of speedway riders had travelled in their droves searching for an instant miracle cure. Carter thought he had come to the right place and was hugely relieved to be informed by Biagi that his leg had not been broken, as first feared, and that he had escaped this time with only bruising to muscles and ligament damage.

According to Biagi, it appeared that the doctors in Sweden had been confused by the results of x-rays that revealed the four previous broken bones from Kenny's

Down and out again . . . crashing spectacularly in the wet at Vetlanda, with John Davis and Andy Smith.

crash at Cradley Heath in 1984.

When Kelvin Tatum fought the battle of a lone Englishman on the afternoon Erik Gundersen retained his individual crown in front of 31,000 fans at Odsal Stadium, Kenny Carter's role was that of Dave Lanning's co-commentator for ITV.

Just when it seemed Carter's year could not possibly get any worse, it did. Some seven weeks after returning from his crash in Vetlanda, and having struggled around on crutches and trying to rebuild his fitness, a visit to another specialist confirmed, once and for all, that his right leg HAD been re-broken!

Kenny explained: "I was pig sick when I found I had been walking around for seven weeks with my leg broken. No wonder I was in agony. And I cannot understand how it wasn't discovered before.

"I spent a week in hospital but I was told it was probably a trapped nerve that was causing the trouble. I was taking tablets to clear up an infection, too. But I was in so much pain I decided to see another specialist."

Carter found the answer much closer to home, at the Bingley clinic run by Dr Jempson.

"He examined my leg and I could see the bone moving. It was a hell of a shock. I'd been out cycling and doing all sorts trying to get fit. Now the leg is back in plaster up to the knee. I could be in plaster for anything from two to four months."

A depleted England, without Carter, were badly defeated in the World Team Cup Final at Long Beach, California, where Denmark retained the trophy 24 points ahead of Berry's beleaguered Brits. Not even Carter's enormous presence at Long Beach would have made much difference – except perhaps to have fired up the American team, managed by Bruce Penhall, a bit more.

Berry has always recognised and respected Carter's contribution to the England cause. Outspoken and never afraid to tread on toes or upset those he believes needed upsetting, Berry perhaps saw something of a kindred spirit in the straight-talking Carter.

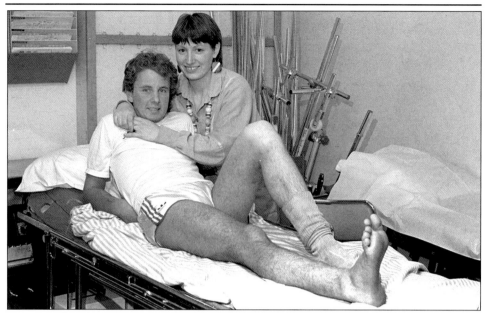

Pam gives Kenny a consoling cuddle as he recovers in hospital after his Vetlanda crash.

"In my role of England manager, I had got to know Kenny far better – and from the first time until the last, he was a joy to have in the team," said Berry. "I always found him to be quiet, professional and pleasant to deal with. In short, he was the very opposite of his reputation.

"None of the practical jokes or clowning around normally associated with speedway lads, or lads of any sport really. Kenny used to leave the letting down of hair to the others and would keep himself to himself, often just reading books to relax.

"He was far more single-minded than his England team-mates but I never saw any problems between him and the others, including riding partners. Most times at that level, riders tend to alternate gate positions. Sometimes I would step in if I felt it was important for the team to have riders on different gates, and I cannot ever remember a time when any rider, including Kenny, didn't accept this.

"Kenny rarely showed much external reaction at losing, in the case of either himself or his team. However, his intensity was always there.

"Never once did he ever give less than everything he had for the cause. He was proudly, fiercely, patriotic."

Carter ended the season recuperating in the sunshine while looking after the interests of his brother. Firstly, he and Alan travelled to Spain, where the younger Carter signed a new deal to join the J.B. Colbas road-racing team. Then they both headed for Australia, where Alan competed in the Swan road-racing series. "I'll be staying with him during the series and then have six weeks to recover from my injury before coming back on February 1," said Kenny.

Despite suffering yet another major injury blow and whatever else may have been going on in his mind as the year of 1985 drew to a close, he was as bullish as ever on the outside.

He said: "I'm going to go for it next year. You can't keep a good man down!"

Chapter 22

THE FINAL RACE

AFTER another traumatic end to the year, 1986 could not have started much better for Kenny as he soaked up the Aussie sun and continued to re-build the muscles in his right leg by running and swimming Down Under.

He had not intended to ride at all during the winter but on January 31 he received an offer he could not refuse. Carter marked his return to the track with an 18-point maximum for England against Australia in a one-off, unofficial Test match at the Redcliffe Showground, near Brisbane, where a capacity crowd of 14,700 supported the bikes-only event promoted by Clive Featherby junior. Simon Wigg, Jeremy Doncaster and Marvyn Cox also rode for the tourists in their 66-42 win.

Most importantly, Carter's leg – broken for the second time in 18 months when he crashed out of the World Championship the previous August – stood up to the rigours of the third-of-a-mile circuit.

It was just as well that Kenny and his fellow riders got paid out at the end of the meeting, though. For the cash takings on the night were later stolen from the offices of Featherby's silent partner and sponsor, Harry Van Der Zlam, with a reported $50,000 missing!

Back in England, Kenny had his business head on too. Despite giving Eric Boothroyd repeated assurances that he would be devoting all his energies to speedway in future, he continued to have his fingers in numerous other pies. He could no doubt see the writing on the wall in British speedway following the demise of World of Sport and a host of problems that continued to plague the sport in this country, and still do today.

At the end of February, he set up Kenny Carter Promotions within the vibrant, new Dean Clough industrial complex in Halifax, a modern business park built on the grounds of an old carpet mill As head of the business employing five full-time and two part-time staff, Kenny said his agency was a consultancy company offering clients a range of services, including sports management, marketing, public relations, television, personal appearances, sales and promotions.

"I'm hoping to sign up several riders – a bit like Barry Hearn did in snooker," said Kenny, revelling in his new role behind the managing director's desk.

"But I'm planning to get people from all sports on my books, even complete teams.

"It all started last year when I became manager of my brother, Alan – the road-racing scene is very big.

The businessman getting down to work at his Dean Clough office and (inset) signing up Tessa Sanderson.

"But there's much more scope and what I need now is to be World Speedway Champion myself to really get the business going. And that's what I'm after."

To ensure he looked the part, he treated himself to a £31,000 white Lotus Esprit turbo, with red upholstery and gold wheels. It was also fitted with the latest in-car telephone – well before the days of mobile telephones – and bore the personalised number plate KC W1N.

And with typical Carter cockiness, he added: "Injuries? They're all behind me. This is going to be my lucky year!"

Kenny was never slow to project himself, of course, but people beyond speedway had to sit up and take him seriously, too, when he announced his first big-name signing – popular Olympic gold medal winner Tessa Sanderson. She had triumphed in the javelin event at the 1984 Los Angeles games and went on to become one of the UK's best known athletes, making a record six appearances at the Olympic Games. She retired from competitive athletics in 1997 to pursue a successful media career and is also now vice-chairman of Sport England. Ms Sanderson has been honoured with the MBE, OBE and CBE.

The irrepressible Carter recognised talent when he saw it – and the chance to raise his profile even more.

The flash Lotus was originally ordered by Kenny for Tessa Sanderson's use but he then decided to take on the £400 per month lease-purchase payments himself – and that was another big mistake. While he believed that driving a sleek sports car around town would get him noticed even more than before and enhance his new high-flier image, it was crippling him financially.

And Tessa Sanderson would never find out what he could do to help her develop her career.

With the promotions company not taking off to anything near matching his lofty expectations, he vowed to himself to battle on and keep his worries to himself.

As March began, Kenny had to turn his attention back to speedway – and another career move. He would still be skipper and No.1 and start his ninth consecutive season as a Dukes asset. Not at Halifax, where speedway had sadly closed after 21 years, but at Bradford, a track he had mastered in international meetings the previous year.

Cash-strapped Halifax Town FC had been at loggerheads with Calderdale Council over who should pay for alterations to the speedway track. With an already excessive rent and reported ambitious future plans for a 'super stadium' that was unlikely to feature speedway, the Coalite Dukes' management were left with little alternative but to call time on The Shay. They also abandoned their 'white elephant' emblem that had first appeared on the Dukes' race jacket since 1949 when they took their show five miles up the road to a venue that had not staged league racing for 11 years.

Eric Boothroyd felt confident that his main man would be able to put the injury problems of the past two years behind him and look forward to a change of good fortune.

After squeezing in another business trip to Spain, Carter was ready to do the business for Bradford in their opening meeting at Belle Vue on March 22. Boothroyd admitted that for the first time since he packed up riding in 1968, the Dukes had three genuine heat leaders to spearhead them. Carter was joined by Neil Evitts and the new, big winter signing from America, Lance King, who returned after a season out of the BL and came on loan from Cradley Heath. Larry Ross completed the strongest top four seen in Dukes' colours since their one and only league championship triumph at The Shay in 1966.

If anybody questioned how seriously Kenny was taking speedway at this time, he answered those doubters with an all-out assault on the new season.

Or, to be more accurate, an all-out assault on his old foe, Peter Collins.

One of the reasons given for scrapping the old second half format is that after the main 13 or 15-heat match had finished, neither riders nor supporters took the follow-up event very seriously. Riders would withdraw on the flimsiest of excuses, fans would head for the bar or the exit gate.

In wintry conditions at Belle Vue's famous, old Hyde Road home on the opening night of the season, they witnessed a brutal battle that erupted into violence.

There had never been any love lost between Peter Collins and Kenny Carter, a simmering rift that exploded in the changing rooms at the 1984 British Final. But this took their mutual antipathy to new depths.

Carter had scored a maximum for Bradford and beaten PC twice in their 40-38 League Cup victory over the Aces when the night turned nasty when the two England heroes met in the top scorers' Golden Sash second half final. The prize in this new winner-takes-all finale was a pitiful £30, but money was not on Carter's mind this time.

Collins has not been comfortable discussing Kenny since his death but he recalled: "I can't remember what lap we were on but we were using those new, poxy tyres without any slots on them – they were dreadful and everybody was having trouble with them.

"I was leading as we went over the start-finish line into the top bend, and as I began to turn into the corner, he came right up the inside of me, got in trouble and he just bailed out. He let his bike go, it hit me and sent me cart-wheeling from the start of the corner right into the fence.

"We'd had a lot of heated situations on the track before – he'd had me in the past and I'd had him – but who knows what was going on in his head at times like this?

"Anyway, the referee excluded him for knocking me off – it was dangerous and dirty riding and not my fault."

After losing the England manager's job at the end of 1984, Carl Glover returned to speedway as Belle Vue team boss, under promoter Stuart Bamforth, from the start of the '85 season. Glover was in the Hyde Road pits that night and recalled: "Kenny absolutely T-boned Peter in the middle of the first and second bend. We had to pin Bammy to the floor because he was going to kill him!"

It was what PC said on his return to the pits that sparked ugly scenes and led to both riders being hauled before the Control Board to answer serious charges.

Collins explained: "I had damaged ligaments in my knee, so they brought me back into the pits on a stretcher. Coming into the pits, I'm not sure now whether I was in the process of just getting off the stretcher or was still actually on it, but Kenny was sat down on the right as I came back in.

"My comment to him was, 'Kenny, you must like hospital food because the way you're going, you're gonna end up back in there'. They were my exact words to him. I didn't say I was going to put him in hospital, but maybe he thought I had said that – I don't know.

"But while I was sort of being helped off the stretcher, he jumped on me, head-butted me and then punched me. "

Glover confirmed: "I've never seen Peter lose his rag or show as much anger as he did that night. After we picked him up and got him back to the pits, he turned to Kenny and said: 'You must seriously like hospital food'. But he didn't mean it as a threat towards Kenny – he was simply referring to the reckless way Carter had ridden that night.

"Next thing, it all kicked off and mechanics were going in all directions. Bammy laid into one after the other as they came at him.

"What is it about little men that makes them feel they have to prove themselves all the time? I couldn't get through to Kenny when I was England manager and I don't think anybody else could either. He was paranoid that everybody was against him."

The trouble did not end there, though. Collins decided to take a shower before getting his damaged knee treated properly and says that when he left the changing rooms, Carter was waiting outside to attack him for a second time.

He said: "I was going to go to the hospital to get my knee looked at, but I decided that I would take a shower and get changed first. My mechanic, Rob Hignett, and our team manager, Carl Glover, were with me in the dressing room.

"It took me quite a long time to get ready – I was one of the last to leave the changing rooms – and when I went back outside, there was Kenny, who had already got changed, waiting for me. As I came out, he jumped on me and started punching me again, even though I couldn't even walk properly and virtually needed crutches. Carl and Rob, who's a big lad, soon pulled him off me and Kenny went away shouting.

"What really got to me at the time, was the fact that he had people backing him up and trying to justify what he did to me in the pits. One who really surprised me was the Bradford promoter, Eric Boothroyd, who said that Kenny had every right to do what he did because I'd threatened to put Kenny in hospital.

"But that wasn't what I said to Kenny – his people misinterpreted my words. I just couldn't understand how Eric could back him up after all he'd done . . . cart-wheeled me into the fence, for which he was excluded and fined by the referee . . . head-butted and punched me . . . and then jumped on me again while I was being helped out of the changing rooms! I was very, very surprised by Eric's attitude.

"We made an official complaint to the referee – basically Kenny was up on an assault charge. The Speedway Control Board was going to hold an inquiry that Kenny and I were meant to appear at. I had three witnesses who were going to speak for me at the Control Board in Pall Mall and there was no way Kenny would have won that case."

Collins says he still suffers the legacy of his last skirmish with Carter 21 years on.

"I really struggled to ride again in '86 after that, the ligaments were badly damaged and I had to wear a knee brace for a while. I was never the same again, averaging six-and-half points or something, and in fact that was my last season.

"That crash caused by Kenny virtually finished my career. And I still have problems with that left knee today."

The Odsal season opened a week later than schedule after a rain-off and it was a strangely subdued Carter who managed just two race wins on his way to nine points in the Coalite Dukes' third successive League Cup success. After the Wolves had been sent packing, 56-22, he explained: "It's been an upsetting few days for my family, as we have been devastated by the death of our close friend, Richard Oldham, in America."

Richard was the 18-year-old son of Ron Oldham, a great family friend of Kenny's. Ron's Ripponden plastics factory made crisp wrappers for leading brands, and Kenny was impressed by his business acumen and obvious wealth. Oldham also had business interests in Florida. It was while he was in the States that his son died of a genetic heart disorder. Phil Hollingworth said of Ron Oldham: "He was a genuinely nice guy and the only millionaire I've known who would buy a round of drinks."

A minor burglary at Grey Horse Farm had not improved Carter's mood and two wins against World Champion Erik Gundersen at Cradley Heath, including victory over the Dane in the Golden Helmet, provided only temporary respite. Many were surprised to see Carter lose the match-race title at Odsal to Ipswich's Jeremy Doncaster in his first defence. Afterwards Kenny complained: "I have been suffering from flu' and with all the work I've been putting into my new business – he followed Tessa Sanderson by signing up a female judo champion – I've been tired

With his favourite American, Kelly Moran, before Bradford's early season visit to Sheffield, 1986.

out.

"But within the next two or three weeks I'll have all my machinery sorted out," he vowed.

There was more disappointment for Carter when Eric Boocock and Colin Pratt, the new joint team managers of England following John Berry's winter resignation, ignored his claims to regain the captaincy. They turned, instead, to the effervescent Simon Wigg when announcing their 10-man squad for the Sunbrite-sponsored Lions' series against Denmark, with Oxford rider Wigg replacing Kelvin Tatum as Kenny's new World Pairs partner.

Carter publicly pledged his full support to Wigg, saying: "Now Simon is captain I can concentrate on being No.1 for my country. I'm confident that I'll get on well with Simon and we'll make a good partnership for the Word Pairs."

Carter clearly had so much on his plate by then that being overlooked for the England captaincy had become an irrelevance.

He may still have been wearing the No.1 body colour but in reality he was no longer the dominant force for either club or country. After his opening night full house before it turned nasty at Belle Vue he failed to manage another full or paid maximum in his following eight matches – and failed to make double figures in consecutive home meetings at Odsal.

He recorded just one heat win in six races against Denmark in the Sunbrite Lions' narrow first Test defeat at Cradley Heath where, partnered by Belle Vue's Carl Blackbird, he was passed by both Erik Gundersen and Jan O. Pedersen in the first race. Kenny admitted: "It was embarrassing . . . making the start and then having people go flying past."

With Neil Evitts in impressive form and guests to cover the injured Lance King, the Coalite Dukes maintained their encouraging start to the season. But Carter, who formed an opening heat pairing with Sean Willmott, had to borrow bikes from Evitts and guest Simon Cross to win his last two races in the home win against Sheffield on May 5.

Carter blamed his poor form – by his own high standards – on a lack of power from his GMs, so he headed for Norwich and tuner Trevor Hedge in search of the answers. "He came down in his white sports car," recalled Trevor. "He seemed all right and we always got on well. He was always professional and very good to deal with."

However, a thorough examination of Kenny's Italian engines found nothing wrong with them. It was reported that the problem had been traced to a 45-gallon drum of methanol fuel that, when tested, was shown to have a high water content. Was this the real reason for his lack of power or another smokescreen for the shambles unravelling away from the track?

Kenny was grateful, though, to have Phil Hollingworth lending a hand in the workshop again. Ollie explained: "Kenny had problems with his bikes, his form had suffered and he just wasn't performing. I think he'd been taking his eye off speedway by doing too many other things.

"He asked Gareth (Perrett) to build two bikes for him just hours before a meeting at Bradford. But Gareth was struggling to get the work done so he called me at about one o'clock in the afternoon and asked if I would come up to the farm to give him a hand. Kenny was borrowing stuff from everywhere to put a bike together and I noticed that things in the workshop weren't organised as well as they used to be. It had been possible to build up 10 bikes from all the equipment, so I don't know what had happened after I was sacked.

"I was helping Gareth in the Nissen hut when Kenny came up at about half-past four, just as we were finishing the bikes, and he seemed gobsmacked to see me. 'What are you doing here?" he asked.

"And I replied: 'What does it f****** look like!"

"Gareth said: 'Don't you two start again . . . '

"But Kenny wasn't about to cause trouble. He said: 'No, it's good to see you again'. We talked and I told him he'd been fannying about like an old woman and it was about time he got his act together again.

"He asked me to come to the meeting with him that night but I said I couldn't, as I was going out with my wife and friends for a meal later.

"Anyway, he insisted I came with him to Bradford and said I could borrow one of his cars, a Renault 5 Turbo, to ensure I got away from Odsal and off home straight after the meeting so that I wouldn't be late for the meal.

"I'd never been with him to Bradford before and I think he scored a maximum and cleaned up in the second half too. That night it seemed just like old times between us." In fact, a flat tyre on the final bend, which allowed Phil Crump to pass him, deprived Carter of a maximum in the home match against Swindon on May 10.

"A few days later Kenny phoned me from his office at Dean Clough and invited me down for a chat. When I got there, he asked if I would come back and work for him again, full-time. He was fed up that his bikes had kept going wrong. I'm not blowing my own trumpet here – it was more the fact that, in the past, the Goddens machines I mostly worked on rarely went wrong.

"I explained to him that I now had a young family to think about and that I needed more job security and stability, so I turned down his offer. He then asked if I would at least go with him to the big meetings and I said 'no problem' to that – I always enjoyed the craic abroad anyway. That was the fun part of the job and I could fit it in with my full-time work for the building firm."

As it turned out, Carter made only one more overseas appearance. The day after returning to his old form in the League Cup against Swindon, he went off to Lonigo, Italy – GM country – for the World Pairs semi-final. He was not quite at his tigerish best on the scorching hot day the FIM introduced their much-maligned and short-lived six-rider races to the Pairs format but he and the more impressive Simon Wigg won the round eight points clear of the USA to qualify for the final at Pocking on June 15.

Eric Boocock recalls sitting next to Carter on the flight home from Italy. Booey said: "I sat with Kenny and listened to all the problems he had, although not any personal ones. He was telling me how this business wasn't going well and that wasn't going right, but that he was still going to make it.

"He never mentioned his marriage on that flight at all, though. Maybe that was part of the problem. If he could have let it out to somebody he could trust, things might have turned out different in the end. The problem with Kenny was, though, that he wouldn't trust anybody."

Despite qualifying with Wiggy at Lonigo, Carter was still not satisfied with his GMs and shocked quite a few people by arriving at Belle Vue for the second England versus Denmark Test five days later with two new overhead cam Weslakes – an engine he had not ridden for almost three years. Kenny revealed that he had signed a two-year deal earlier that day with Weslake agent Bill Davies.

The Hyde Road match, in which Kenny would win his 57th senior international cap, was one England fully expected to win. Boocock and Pratt decided to partner Carter with his Dukes team-mate Neil Evitts and the night began well when Gundersen was excluded at the tapes to gift the young Lions a 4-2 over Jan O. Pedersen.

But after beating Hans Nielsen and then finishing second to Tommy Knudsen, Carter's night went downhill rapidly. He crashed into the pits wall when his footrest snapped and, bizarrely, did exactly the same thing in his next ride on his second bike! Carter had been embarrassed again on a track where he was always so hard to beat.

Bitterly disappointed to see his team go down 45-63, Boocock was unhappy with Carter's part in the defeat. He told reporters at the Manchester track: "Kenny Carter has come here tonight with two new Weslakes and he's been going well enough on GMs. I told him if he wants to experiment he should do it in a league match, not in a Test match."

Neil Evitts said: "In the two years that I rode with him at Halifax and Bradford, I formed the opinion that his bikes could have been a lot better then they were. In fact, he borrowed my bike more times than I used his.

"But he used to win, so that just shows how good he was.

"Kenny's equipment didn't compare well against that of, say, Hans Nielsen. I think he just wanted everything for free and didn't necessarily use the best machinery available to him.

"He once told me that he just went out for every race, looked across the start line and thought to himself: 'They aren't good enough to be on the same track as me'. It didn't matter what the weather was like, rain, sun or snow, he went out to race with just one tear-off on his peak and one on his goggles – that's all.

"He just convinced himself that he knew he would win."

Kelvin Tatum said that he noticed a change in Kenny from the more communicative man he had ridden successfully alongside in the World Pairs a year earlier. "I remember he turned up for that Belle Vue Test dressed in a blazer, shirt

Deep in thought while waiting for the action to begin in the first England v Denmark Test at Cradley Heath in the opening match of the 1986 series?

Left: With World Pairs partner Simon Wigg before the second Danish Test at Belle Vue.

Final appearance for England. Above: On the outside of John Jorgensen and Hans Nielsen in the Test match at Belle Vue. Below: Eric Boocock and skipper Simon Wigg try to raise his spirits.

and tie and you couldn't get through to him. He seemed to have changed, as if he had a lot going on in his mind – he wasn't the same person I'd been with and got to know the previous summer."

The day after his two embarrassing falls at Belle Vue, Carter was beaten by Malcolm Simmons and Michael Lee at King's Lynn. But at least his 12 (paid 13) points helped Bradford to a well-earned draw that kept them hot on the heels of Coventry at the top of the League Cup table.

Trevor Hedge remembered: "I was in the pits that night and Kenny kept coming up to me and shaking my hand. It was as if he knew something that I didn't."

Despite his return to Weslake for the Test match at Belle Vue, Carter reverted to GM for the British semi-final staged on his home track the afternoon after King's Lynn. The switch from one engine make to another, and then back again, in such a short period indicated that, in his troubled state of mind, he did not really know what day it was.

Jimmy Ross revealed that his son, Wayne, who was riding for Boston at the time,

FINAL MEETING

Top: Diving between Simon Cross (inside) and Carl Blackbird at the first bend in his first ride of the British semi-final at Odsal on May 18, 1986.

Middle: After tangling with Alan Mogridge, Kenny receives medical attention.

Right: An anguished Kenny sees another World Championship disaster looming, but as we know there were many other more serious issues going on inside his head by this time.

received a call from a flustered Kenny at around 10 o'clock on the morning of Sunday, May 18 – just hours before Carter was due to compete in the afternoon British semi-final at Bradford – pleading with him to come to the farm to help build a bike for him. Wayne was living in Halifax and while he quickly headed to Grey Horse Farm to help work on Kenny's machines, he could only stay a while before heading off to Boston for their home NL match against Stoke that night.

"While 'Young Un' was at Kenny's place, they were going to have something quickly to eat but when they looked in the kitchen cupboards, all they could find was a tin of peas. Kenny had been buying his food from the chippie every night"

At Bradford Kenny looked more like a novice than the home No.1 who was expected to sail through as one of the top eight qualifiers, if not win the meeting itself to set up the possibility of completing a hat-trick of British Championship successes at Coventry in 14 days' time.

Another clear sign that all was far from well with Kenny came when he crashed in his first ride at Odsal after tangling with Canterbury's Alan Mogridge on the opening lap of his first ride. Kenny needed medical attention from St John's staff and was flat out on the ground for several minutes after jarring his back and arms.

Carter's pain turned to anger when he saw that referee John Eglese had excluded him from the rerun as the prime cause of the stoppage. Kenny protested and said afterwards: "The referee put the phone down on me without giving me a chance to put my case. Mogridge ran straight into me."

The double British Champion then faced two successive rides, in heats eight and nine, but continued to struggle even when he borrowed Evitts' bike for his third outing. That left him down in 12th place after all 16 riders had taken three rides each.

While Carter, his mind in total turmoil, was staring shock elimination from the World Championship in the face, main Weslake agent Bill Davies was busy in the pits building up a Wessie for him to use. Another engine change only added to the bewildering chaos that had engulfed Kenny – but this time the switch worked.

He won his last two programmed rides, the second in front of team-mate Evitts – who was hardly going to eliminate him from the title race – to force a run-off with Carl Blackbird and Louis Carr for the last two places in the British Final. He won that, too, and had qualified for the next round at Coventry by a whisker.

A relieved Carter said: "If it hadn't been for the Weslake it would have been the end of the story. I would have been finished!

"I couldn't even breathe properly after my crash. Thank goodness I'm through . . . but we all start equal at Coventry!"

Under normal circumstances, qualification would have been a formality for the Odsal track specialist.

But as events would rapidly reveal, these were anything but normal times for Carter.

He had already ridden his final race.

Two nights later, on Tuesday, May 20, he was due back at Odsal to lead Bradford against champions Oxford in a rearranged League Cup fixture. Carter appeared in

Struggling badly for qualifying points on his home track, a body colour-less Kenny is left behind in third place (above) by Jeremy Doncaster and Simon Wigg.

This time (left) it's Paul Thorp and Chris Morton who leave him trailing.

the pits and said he would not be able to ride because of a broken finger. In fact, no one took to the track that night – the bad weather that had blighted the early weeks of the season caused yet another postponement.

As the Bradford riders and management trio, Eric Boothroyd, Bobby Ham and Allan Ham, said their goodbyes and prepared to leave the West Yorkshire bowl much earlier than expected, none of them could possibly believe that they would never see Kenny Carter alive again.

Kenny Carter's 1986 record – his last 13 appearances for club and country

As this brief resume of Kenny's final season shows, apart from his opening night maximum in that violent clash at Belle Vue, he failed to record another full score and his form had clearly been badly affected by his lack of focus and non-speedway events events unfolding off the track.

March 22 Belle Vue 38 Bradford 40 – 12 points (maximum)

March 27 Sheffield 36 Bradford 42 – 11 points

April 5 Bradford 52 Wolverhampton 26 – 9 points

April 12 Cradley Heath 41 Bradford 37 – 11 points

April 26 Bradford 39 Ipswich 39 – 10 points

April 28 Wolverhampton 37 Bradford 41 – 8 points

May 3 England 53 Denmark 55, 1st Test at Cradley Heath – 10 points

May 3 Bradford 50 Reading 28 – 8 points

May 5 Bradford 44 Sheffield 34 – 10 points

May 10 Bradford 47 Swindon 31 – 11 points

May 11 Lonigo, World Pairs semi-final – 22 (+ 3) points – 1st place

May 16 England 45 Denmark 63, 2nd Test at Belle Vue – 8 points

May 17 King's Lynn 39 Bradford 39 – 12 (+ 1) points

May 18 Bradford, World Championship British semi-final – 8 points

THE FINAL PICTURE

Kenny needed a favour here from team-mate Neil Evitts to get through, but he never rode another meeting.

Chapter 23

LAST HOURS

ON the afternoon of Wednesday, May 21 at Lymm in Cheshire, the other side of the Pennines from Halifax, Peter Collins was at home preparing himself, mentally, for a trip to London the next day. PC had to attend the Speedway Control Board hearing into his violent pits encounter with his arch rival Kenny Carter.

The Belle Vue legend fully expected to win the case after being physically attacked by Carter in two separate pits incidents during the first meeting of the season at his home track.

Collins said: "I had made arrangements to leave my place at six o'clock on the following Wednesday morning but there was no need to go to London for the hearing after I saw the news of what had happened to Kenny on Teletext the previous night.

PC was no longer required to attend the hearing at RAC headquarters in Pall Mall, because the case had suddenly been dropped.

Kenny Carter was dead.

At just after 6.30pm, Pam's father Bob Lund and his son, Adrian, were at their farm in Bradshaw when they were alerted by neighbours who heard gunshots coming from the Carters' home just a few hundred yards up the lane. They drove the short distance as fast as they could and discovered the most horrifying scene imaginable.

Bob's daughter, Pam, was lying dead on the gravel outside her house.

When police arrived at 6.45pm, they broke through the front door and found Kenny dead on the couple's bed upstairs.

Both had died of shotgun wounds.

Police knew what had happened – they were not looking for anybody else in connection with the shootings.

Bob Lund also realised the devastating truth of what had happened – he knew about his daughter and Kenny's marriage problems and, in fact, the couple's two children were staying with him and his wife, Veronica, at the time of the deaths.

An inquest, held two months after the death of Pam and Kenny at Grey Horse Farm on the hillside above Bradshaw, unravelled much of the background to the tragedy.

What nobody in the speedway world knew until the facts behind the horrific events of that night emerged was that the marriage between Kenny and Pam Carter had broken down and that the Bradford and England star could no longer cope with the situation.

Kenny's Alsatian Gypsy standing guard outside Grey Horse Farm.

Bob Lund told the inquiry how, in mid-May, he went up to the farmhouse, off Taylor Lane, with his wife after a telephone call from Pam. Following an argument with Kenny, police were called.

Pam took their two children, Kelly Marie (three) and Malcolm (nearly two), and moved out of the family home into her parents' place, Black Castle Farm, just a short walk down the hill towards the quiet, semi-rural village.

Accompanied by her cousin, Martin Abel, Pam returned to the couple's home, which she and Kenny had shared for the past five years, two days before the shootings to collect some clothing. She took Martin with her because she was afraid of her husband. There was another argument and although he did not want to interfere, Mr Abel confirmed: "She was terrified. She said Kenny was going to get her."

The Range Rover she used for the short trip was filled with expensive designer dresses and shoes she had accumulated in the recent years. Had it been 'comfort buying' on the part of Pam? Or was the bulging wardrobe a symptom of Kenny's belief that he could 'buy' her affection with money and material things when the love ran out? Not only did Pam spend freely on herself and the children, who were also both dressed in designer outfits, she spared no expense in having her hair done regularly at Vidal Sassoon's salon in Leeds.

If that was his intention, it did not work in the end.

Pam had visited her solicitors the day before the killings to secure an injunction to keep Kenny away from her and their two young children.

At the July inquest in Halifax, a close friend of Pam's, Miss Elizabeth Healey, told Coroner James Turnbull that Pam had said she wanted to leave Kenny. Miss Healey said: "She had told him she wanted to leave him. He said he wouldn't let her leave. She told me he said he would kill her if she tried."

Miss Healey, a former work colleague who had known Pam since 1979, also said how Kenny used violence against his wife and made her life a misery. "Before they married she told me that he had a violent temper and in arguments he had a tendency to hit her," she said.

Miss Healey said it was Kenny who stopped Pam attending karate lessons in Halifax. Miss Healey continued: "He was unhappy because the karate instructor and all the other people there were male. He contacted the instructor and told him she wouldn't be able to come any more.

"He seems to have had some concern about her coming into contact with other men without him being there," she added.

Mike and Sue Condon bought Kenny's previous home in Brickfield Lane from him at the end of 1981. The couple had remained good friends with Pam, who had regularly stayed over at Kenny's before they bought Grey Horse Farm together. Mrs Condon last spoke to her just three days before her death when she was a spectator at a kung fu tournament in Wakefield. Mr Condon was quoted in the *Halifax Evening Courier* as saying: "He was turning her away from him by his attitude to anything she wanted for the house or what she wanted to do."

Pam had been a member of the weekly kung fu beginners' class at North Bridge Leisure Centre, Halifax, soon after she married. Mr Condon said Pam enjoyed herself at the classes but claimed Kenny stopped her from attending after just a few weeks. He also stopped her selling soft drinks on a round he had originally set up for her near their previous Holmfield home.

Others not called to give witness statements at the inquest, have spoken of 'Pam's luxury farmhouse becoming her prison' and how she was unable to leave without Kenny's permission. "He did become very possessive of her in the last couple of years. Pam could hardly ever get out of the house," said one friend who did not wish to be named.

Another said that Kenny had confided in him one day and said how Pam once told him: 'You make my skin crawl'. Had she signed her own death warrant with that remark?

There were unsubstantiated rumours, six months before the killings, that Pam had been having an affair, and there are people who still believe the she had been 'carrying on' behind Kenny's back. But Miss Healey told the inquest that Pam denied she was having extra-marital relations when they discussed it.

Pam's father had heard the rumours, too, and spoke to his daughter about it. He told the inquiry: "I talked to Pam. She said she had never been out with anybody else. I believed her.

"I mentioned it to Kenny. He said it had been a big mistake. I think he accepted that this was the truth."

Tragically, as events proved, he clearly did not.

Pam was out shopping when Kenny called at the Lunds' home at 4pm on that Wednesday afternoon to leave her the keys to Grey Horse Farm. She had already removed most of her and the children's clothes and belongings from the home but there were still some other items she needed to collect.

Bob Lund had been so concerned for his daughter's safety that he had visited the

Carters' house a few days earlier to remove Kenny's shotgun. He said Pam was afraid for the children and wanted to be apart from Kenny for a few days to think things over.

Mr Lund said: "She said, 'he will get me if I go away', She was concerned and I took it seriously."

But Kenny had assured him that the couple's home would be empty when Pam called there later. He left his father-in-law saying he intended to drive to his office at Dean Clough and then on to visit his grandmother, Katie, for tea that evening. Kenny was very fond of his grandma and had been very close to her late husband, who lived at nearby Illingworth. Katie said that Kenny had been heartbroken over the recent death of his grandfather, Lionel Hanner, who had passed away, aged 79, just a month earlier. "He and Kenny had been very close," she said.

When Kenny saw his grandparents for the last time, he gave them his valuable collection of Royal Dalton china, as if it were a gift to remember him by. He knew they would appreciate it, as he had no further use for it himself.

Whether Kenny suddenly changed his mind at the last minute or this was all part of a premeditated plan, we will never know. But he drove back to his home and parked his car in the garage, out of view, before going inside the house.

Believing that Kenny would not be at home, Pam declined her father's offer to accompany her when she left her parents' farm at just before 6.30pm and set off on the very short car journey to collect the last few bits she needed for her and the kids.

Mr Lund explained: "She went to collect the clothes. I wasn't happy. I said I would go with her but she said 'no'. She went on her own."

Pam told her father that if she saw Kenny's car parked in the driveway she would come back immediately.

Bob Lund would never see his daughter alive again.

As Pam opened the front door, we can only imagine how she would have been gripped by sheer terror on finding her husband waiting inside . . . with a fully loaded Remington 12-bore shotgun. He had parked his car in the garage, out of sight, and let himself in with a spare set of keys.

Even though Kenny's father-in-law took away his shotguns for the safety of his daughter and grandchildren, he would stop at nothing to find another firearm from somewhere. The inquest was told by John Whitworth, of Salendine Nook, Huddersfield, how Kenny called on him the day before the shooting but because he could not produce his gun licence he refused to lend him a gun.

Only three hours before he killed Pam, Kenny visited Brian Hinchcliffe, of Holmfirth. He borrowed his Remington automatic, capable of storing four bullets in the magazine and one in the breach. Mr Hincliffe said he lent it to him because Kenny said he wanted the gun for pigeon shooting the next day – former manager Peter Garside had introduced him as a member of Huddersfield Rifle Club. Kenny also bought three boxes of cartridges to make his story seem more plausible.

It was this gun Kenny used to blast his wife to death with five shots, two or three of them fired at point-blank range.

In her sheer desperate panic to try and escape she collapsed, face-down on the patio before somehow crawling to the gravel-covered yard next to the house. She

Picture of Happiness . . . Pam, Kenny, Kelly Marie and Malcolm.

had been shot in her back and under her right arm. At 6.30pm a doctor pronounced her dead from shock and haemorrhage.

Kenny then made a desperate final telephone call to his dear friend, Ron Oldham, who was still grieving following the recent loss of his 18-year-old son, Richard. "He seemed very distressed. He said:' I've shot Pam and I'm going to shoot myself'," said Mr Oldham, recalling the conversation that lasted no longer than 90 seconds.

"Kenny said: 'Be quiet, I want to tell you about the children. There's lots of money. Get it and make sure the children are taken care of'.

"He said the kids were up the road and that he was going to shoot himself. 'You won't hear from me again. Look after the children. Goodbye'," he said.

Mr Oldham rang Kenny back immediately but there was no reply.

He said Kenny had been at his house the previous night. "He seemed quite normal," he added.

After killing Pam, Kenny went back upstairs to their master bedroom and reloaded the shotgun. He sat on the edge of his bed, positioned the weapon between his legs and lent his body forward to press against it. He died from a single gunshot wound in the left side of his chest. This had pierced the left lung and gone through his body

– he was found lying on his back on the bed. Dog handler, PC Peter Galvin, of Halifax police, said at the inquest that he believed Kenny was, technically, still alive when he entered the room.

Neighbour Mrs Patricia Ellison, who lived just 200 yards from the Carters, raised the alarm. She drove to the entrance of Grey Horse Farm and although she was not sure if it was Pam's body lying in the yard, she knew something was wrong and drove on to alert the Lund family.

Bob Lund and his son, Adrian, who ran the village milk round, drove up to the house. "When we saw Pam I tried to get into the house with the keys that were in the Range Rover but I couldn't get in," said Mr Lund, who stayed with his daughter's body while his son returned home to call the police. Police told him Kenny was dead inside the house when they arrived.

Hardened Yorkshire police detectives learn to cope with tragedies of this horrific nature but to one officer the discovery of the two bodies was particularly harrowing. Detective Inspector Jim Crossley of Calderdale CID, who identified the bodies at the scene, had been a personal friend of Kenny and Pam's and attended speedway meetings with him. He had last seen Carter at a speedway social function held at The Shay Sporting Club on March 24.

Details of a suicide note found next to Kenny's body were also revealed at the July inquest. The handwritten note was written to the couple's close friends, Ron and Margaret Oldham, who had known Kenny since he was a teenager.

It read: "I want Ron and Margaret Oldham to look after the kids. All assets and money to go to them for life. I love Pam and I can't live separate. I'm going to kill myself now.

"Please bury us together. She did love me. I'm going to join my mum. Tell my brother I love him. Don't tell the kids what happened."

Mr Oldham said the two families were to keep custody of the children but after the shocking events at Grey Horse Farm that day the Carter and Lund families could not conceivably agree to anything again. A custody battle ensued and a court decided that three-year-old Kelly Marie and two-year-old Malcolm would live and be brought up by Pam's family. Pam's younger sister, Heather, has been credited with playing a particularly prominent role in the children's development.

Coroner James Turnbull said it was unusual to disclose the contents of suicide letters but he wanted it to be seen that Kenny loved his wife.

"In his last moments Kenny was saying he loved his wife and he believed she loved him," he said.

Phil Hollingworth, who had only recently been reunited with Kenny to help him prepare a bike for a meeting at Bradford, could not take it all in when he heard what had happened. "The night before he died he phoned and asked me to come to the farm. He said he had 'some trouble' with Bob and his son, Adrian, who had apparently nearly kicked the front door in trying to get to Kenny.

"I didn't know what had happened, I think Kenny had been having a 'do' with Pam and whether he'd hit her or what I don't know, but Kenny said he'd been 'scrapping with Bob'. I guess they had gone there to sort him out.

"But I told Kenny I couldn't possibly leave my house at that time – my wife was out and our young daughter, Kate, was asleep in bed.

"After Bob and Adrian had left, Kenny couldn't get his door to shut – it was broken off the hinges – so I told him over the phone how to take the lock out and then put the bolt on the back of the door as a temporary measure. I told him I'd see him the next day to fix the door properly.

"I was just about to go up to his place at tea-time on that Wednesday when I got a call from my mate, who was the friend of a local copper, who told him what had happened. My mate said to me 'You'd better get up to Kenny's'.

"When I got there, I saw Pam lying dead in the yard and the police had cordoned the place off. I knew then what must have happened.

"Kenny had told me the previous night what had gone on at his house and, thinking back, I guess he phoned me because he wanted someone to talk to.

"It bothered me for a long time afterwards, wondering if it could have all been avoided if I'd gone up to see him that night he phoned, but not any more. I was still fairly young, 28, when it happened and I just thought, 'what a waste'."

Jimmy Ross recalled his final meeting and conversation with Kenny, the kid who considered him a father figure in his youth. Although they didn't speak for a couple of years, when Kenny surrounded himself with others, they had resumed their close friendship before Kenny's death.

Ross revealed that he received a phone call from Kenny the day before the shooting, asking him, in his capacity as an executive for Scottish Legal Life, if he could arrange a new mortgage for him. Kenny finally confessed that all was not well between him and Pam and that divorce was inevitable.

Jimmy said: "Kenny looked really down and, unusually, started to open up about him and Pam's problems. I asked: 'Is it bad?' He said: 'Worse'.

"I tried to soften the blow by reassuring him that he would still be able to see his kids at weekends, or when he wasn't riding, and by pointing out that millions of couples get divorced each week. I tried to make him realise that just because his marriage had failed, it didn't make him a failure."

It appears that Kenny had accepted that he and Pam would split amicably when he asked Jimmy Ross to arrange a mortgage on a new property for him.

"He said he had seen a bungalow he liked the look of at Mount Tabor, just round the corner from where his brother, Alan, was living in Halifax. He said he would be signing the farm over to Pam and asked if I could arrange a £32,000 mortgage for him to buy the bungalow.

"I assured him that regardless of the surveyor's report and anything else, it would be no problem – I said I could get him a staff discount of 2.5% when I think the going mortgage rate at the time was more like 12%. I told him to consider it done and we agreed that I would pop up to the farm at six o'clock the next evening – Wednesday, May 21 – to give him all the mortgage application forms to sign. When I left him that night he seemed OK but I never saw him again.

"The next day I had to go up to Workington on business and was late getting back to my office in Huddersfield. I can't remember exactly, but it was probably sometime between half-past five and six when I arrived back there – and then I noticed that on my letterbox was a Kenny Carter sticker.

"Kenny had obviously visited my office some time during the day and, when he found I wasn't there, left a sticker to let me know that he'd called. I considered this a bit strange, as we'd previously agreed that I would be going up to see him at the farm that night to fill out the forms.

"After doing a few things in the office, I phoned his house some time after six o'clock. We all know now why Kenny didn't answer his phone.

"I have often wondered if things would have turned out differently had I been in my office when Kenny called to see me that day. It probably wouldn't have changed anything – he might have done what he did a day later or perhaps the day after that. We'll never know."

Summing up at the inquest, Mr Turnbull went on to say it was a particularly tragic case of a couple who had been happily married for a number of years.

"It seems that trouble had arisen between them because Kenny may have suspected Pam when he had been told that she had been unfaithful to him.

"There is not the slightest shred of evidence that the suspicion could have been founded on any sort of fact," said Mr Turnbull. He said Kenny's mind had been affected by his suspicion.

"That sort of insidious suspicion can act upon people's minds and cause them to do things that in normal times they would not do.

"There is evidence that something was preying on Kenny's mind."

Mr Turnbull said Pam had no reason to think Kenny would be at home lying in wait when she went to collect her clothes.

"It seems plain he must have gone straight to the house and put the car in the garage so she would have thought he wasn't there," he said.

Mr Turnbull asked the families not to tell the children what had happened to their parents until they were older.

Those at the inquest, which lasted 90 minutes, included Kenny's father Mal Carter and his brother Alan, who was in Germany preparing to race in the 250cc Motorcycling Grand Prix when he heard of the tragedy. Pam's father, Bob Lund, was accompanied by his son, Adrian.

Mr Turnbull recorded that Pam had been unlawfully killed and that Kenny had killed himself.

Chapter 24

A STATE OF SHOCK

MORE than 21 years on from this awful tragedy, people who loved and knew Pam and Kenny are still struggling to comprehend the events of that appalling day when the two 25-year-olds, who both seemingly had so much to live for, died so needlessly and in such shocking circumstances.

As far as the wider speedway community was concerned, reports of their deaths started to emerge within hours of the double tragedy.

Suddenly, the 'small' sport that most sections of the media had turned its back on was big news again. Millions watching television at home on the evening of Wednesday, May 21, 1986 will never forget the moment Kenny Carter's face appeared on the screen during ITV's News At Ten programme and the unthinkable became reality.

Could it really be true? Kenny and Pam Carter. . . *dead?*

As the basic facts filtered through, those who knew Kenny best – family, friends, promoters, team managers and riders – jammed the phone lines connecting all corners of the world. Everyone who knew of the double British Champion tried to make sense of it all.

Phil Hollingworth said: "The national press were everywhere. They were camped outside our house and we were getting phone calls from them at all times of the day and night, wanting to find out what they could about Kenny. I was in the pub and the phone would start ringing with enquiries from the press. I couldn't believe the media attention. There were TV vans around and every time you turned on the television, especially Yorkshire TV, it was big news.

"I was in a state of shock."

Eric Boothroyd remembers how he heard the unbelievable news about his best rider, the lad who had been almost like a son to him for the best part of nine years.

He says he sensed nothing of the terrible events that were to unfold when Carter phoned him at home on the day of the shootings.

"He called me at around nine o'clock that morning and seemed fine. He'd been injured again, having crashed in the British semi-final at Odsal, but said he'd definitely be OK to ride for Bradford that coming Saturday. That was the last time I spoke to him.

"Later that afternoon, I left my wife Bonnie at home to attend a supporters' meeting in Bradford. It was strange, because as I drove past the end of the lane that led to Kenny's farm, I saw a policeman standing alone. I just drove on past him and thought nothing more of it. I had assumed he was there to investigate possible

N/B   THE STAR: Thursday, May 22, 1986

SPEEDWAY ACE IN DOUBLE SHOOTING HORROR

THE bodies of British speedway champion Kenny Carter and his wife Pam were found last night at their home.

The couple, both 25, had gunshot wounds. Police said they were not looking for anyone else in connection with the double killing.

Pam was found outside the couple's home in Taylor Lane, Bradshaw, Halifax, and Kenny was inside the house. A double-barrelled shotgun was lying nearby.

Their two children, a girl aged four and a boy aged two, were staying with Pam's parents, who live nearby.

Sweethearts

The couple had been childhood sweethearts and were married five years ago. They moved into their home about a year ago. It was a former pub which Kenny modernised.

Kenny was the skipper of the Bradford Dukes speedway team and had been British champion for the past two years.

But on Sunday he crashed in the first ride at his home track and only just managed to qualify for this year's British final.

Kenny was well on the way to become...

The family mill...

Kenny Carter tragedy

By CAROLE MALONE

World championship had always eluded him. He missed the last two years because of injury.

In 1981 he fractured his jaw when he took a tumble and was off the scene for months.

Again in 1982 he was rushed to hospital with a punctured lung after a crash.

In 1984 he broke a leg and was out for a long time.

And in 1985 he broke his leg for the second time, which finished his chances of winning the world championship.

In Sunday's crash he suffered a torn shoulder muscle and had to pull out of the England team to ride against Denmark at Wolverhampton tomorrow.

Stunned

The Bradford promoter, Eric Boothroyd, said last night: "What has happened has not yet sunk in. I know Kenny has been under a lot of pressure recently and he may have been worried about his recent performances.

"But he and Pam were childhood sweethearts and as far as I know were very much in love.

Last night neighbours were too stunned to talk about the double tragedy.

To them the man who drove around in a £31,000 white Lotus Esprit looked as if he didn't have a care.

But for Kenny Carter, success and wealth in the end were not enough.

● Carter is the second speedway ace to kill himself in little more than a year.

In April last year Ipswich Witches skipper Billy Sanders, 29, was found dead in his car with a hose leading from the exhaust. His wife had left him for another man.

The jinx he could not shake off

KENNY CARTER could never shake off the jinx which prevented him from winning speedway's world championship.

Only three days before his death, Kenny put spectators on the edges of their seats when he came a cropper in his first race in the British Championship semi-final at Odsal.

scathed after the crash with American Bruce Penhall. Kenny protested that Penhall was responsible for his fall but the referee disagreed, Kenny was excluded from the re-run and Penhall won the title.

In 1983, with no injuries to dog his progress, Kenny looked set to snatch the world championship crown in Norden, West Germany. But it was not to be.

He complained that the decision...

Pam's life of hell with superstar husband

PAM CARTER told friends... Mr. Mike Condon, who... and from the one we knew... drinks on a round he organised for... "They wanted to delay the move...

Daily Mail, Friday, May 23, 1986

ACE RIDER 'TOO BUSY' FOR A MARRIED LIFE

Track star killed wife who walked out on him

By RICHARD TAYLOR

SPEEDWAY star Kenny Carter shot his wife dead and then killed himself after she left him, it was revealed yesterday.

Pam Carter, 25, packed her bags on Monday and went home to her parents. She returned to her £75,000 home near Halifax to collect more belongings on Wednesday and came face to face with her furious husband also 25.

As she fled down the drive after a row, the British champion shot her twice in the back. Then he turned the shotgun on himself.

Neighbour Diane Riley said: 'There had been a lot of problems between them. Kenny ate, drank and slept speedway and did not have time for married life.'

A 13-year-old neighbour, Matthew Mensah, of Cloth Hall Farm, Bradshaw, told how two men arrived by car outside the Carters' home shortly before the shots.

'A car screamed up,' said Matthew, 'and one of the men jumped out and ran towards Kenny's front door.

'Suddenly there were two shots and the man ran back to his car, jumped in, and sped off.'

Matthew's mother, Lily, said: 'It seems Kenny had rung someone to tell them what he was about to do.'

Pam's parents, Bob and Veronica Lund, live just 200 yards from the Carter home. Last night they were looking after the couple's children, Kelly-Marie, two, and Malcolm, four.

Happy day: The Carters at their wedding in 1981

Kenny Carter in action

complaints from neighbours about the noise from the scrambles course that Kenny had built on his land.

"I didn't know the truth until Bonnie saw what had happened on News At Ten and then phoned me at the meeting. I couldn't believe it.

"Looking back, if I'd have been a psychiatrist I might have seen it coming. After he died, I thought about it and reckoned that Kenny's brain had been racing 10 times faster than his body, if you know what I mean. He had a lot on his mind, what with starting his new business and his marriage problems.

"Kenny and Pam had been arguing a lot and someone told him she had been spotted in Bradford with a male friend. I think he lost it from that point."

Eric and Bonnie Boothroyd were like surrogate parents to Kenny and Pam. Bonnie is godmother to their daughter, Kelly Marie.

"They lived about a quarter-of-a-mile away and would often pop round," said Eric. "Kenny was a good, friendly kid. So was Pam. We never had children of our own, so they were like son and daughter to us. And I suppose they saw us as grandparents. Kenny would often ring up for advice on non-speedway matters."

By Friday morning, two days after Pam and Kenny had died, the national press went into overdrive with the story of how England's top rider had murdered his wife and orphaned his two children. The story dominated the front page of the red-top tabloid papers, who were not surprisingly quick to seize on unfounded rumours surrounding the couple's marriage problems. The *Daily Star* quoted 'a friend' as saying: "It was an open secret that Pam had another man and that Kenny had started a regular relationship with an attractive contact. I understand the girl became pregnant. Kenny began to act a bit strange when he found out."

Friends of Kenny's now insist the report was complete nonsense.

And when the *Daily Star* approached Bonnie Boothroyd with their claims, she strongly dismissed them as "cruel gossips."

But given the overwhelming evidence of the latter stages of the couple's unhappy marriage that emerged more clearly at the inquest, and from what others close to the Carters have said since then, could anybody really have blamed Pam Carter if she had begun a new relationship apart from her husband?

Trying to explain the ending, Eric said: "I think there was another big argument between them and when Kenny couldn't accept Pam's explanation, he shot her outside the farm and then went inside to kill himself. He couldn't have coped with the idea of spending the rest of his life in prison.

"You can't forgive anybody who did what Kenny did but I think he must have gone schizophrenic. His mind had blown."

Phil Hollingworth admits even his name was one of those falsely linked by rumours to Pam, but he laughed them off as "ridiculous." Phil and his former wife, Debbie, had the awful task of returning to the farm just days after the shooting.

He explained: "I had to sort out the funeral arrangements as best as I could. A few days after Pam and Kenny died my wife and I had to go back to their house and clean up all the mess and get the place ready to be sold. Kenny used a pump-action shotgun, so there were marks all over the house.

"Pam's dad asked me if I'd make the funeral arrangements. Bob and Veronica lived only 50 yards down the road but they were obviously devastated, and Mal (Carter) was also in shock. As I'd been one who had been the closest to Kenny, and almost everybody else had shunned him after what happened, we felt we had to help out.

"I'd been used to seeing dead bodies from my days working as a joiner and making coffins for a firm of undertakers, but this was surreal. To be clearing up after one of my best friends had killed himself and his wife, and considering the fact that we were just getting back together again, well . . . " Phil's words trailed away.

He recalls an innocent conversation with Carter en route to Germany. The man who spent so many hours with Kenny as a mate and his mechanic said: "Some while after he died, I remembered a chat we'd had while in Bremen for the Golden Key meeting a year or so earlier. Kenny had won the meeting and him, Richard Pickering and me were sitting passing the time in the hotel bar, drinking a few glasses of Piesporter and just chatting about nothing really.

"Then Kenny suddenly asked me: 'What would you do if Debbie pissed off and left you?'

"I shrugged my shoulders and brushed it off by saying: 'There are plenty more fish in the sea . . . '.

"Kenny could have had any bird he wanted, especially abroad where there were always plenty available and willing.

"When he asked that question I didn't think for one minute that he and Pam had any marriage problems – it hadn't entered my head. Kenny didn't have many people to talk to and I just put it down to friends having a chat over a few drinks. Even if he did have a problem, he wouldn't admit it to many people, if any.

"If you saw him a bit down and you asked him what was the matter, he'd just say: 'Nothing'. He would bottle things up inside.

"But he said to us that night: 'I'd kill her if she left me'.

"I took it as a flippant remark, the type of thing many blokes have said about their wives. I thought nothing more of it, it was just a figure of speech.

"The way things panned out, I think that's the main reason why things happened the way they did. He didn't kill Pam because he couldn't get another woman. I liked Pam but she wasn't Miss World. And he could have had Miss World if he'd wanted her, because he had everything going for him.

"But I just felt he couldn't bear the humiliation of being dumped. I reckon he thought to himself: 'Who do you think you are to dump *me?*'

"But he also knew that Pam loved him. She wasn't after him because he was Kenny Carter, speedway star. When she first met him he was just a schoolboy, a nothing.

"He got very possessive with her in the last couple of years, she could hardly get out of the house. Pam phoned me about it a couple of times.

"Kenny died of a broken heart. She was leaving him and he knew it was all over."

Despite discussing Kenny's application for a new mortgage and plans to buy a bungalow the day before he died, Jimmy Ross recalled a solid vow his friend had made to him after feeling so badly hurt at the break-up of his parent's marriage when he was a teenager. Ross said: "Kenny told me: 'There will NEVER be another divorce in this family'."

Chapter 25

VILLAGE IN MOURNING

THE quiet, sleepy village of Bradshaw, nestling at the foot of the rugged hills overlooking Halifax, had never known scenes like it. On the damp and dreary afternoon of Thursday, May 29, they came in their hundreds, from far and wide, to attend the funeral of Pam and Kenny Carter.

In accordance with Kenny's last wishes, and following much deliberation by Pam's family who fought against the idea, the couple were buried together.

There was more than just a little disquiet among some of the local villagers who, appalled by the shootings, did not welcome the addition of Kenny's body to God's sacred earth. After the funeral, the parishioners compiled a petition demanding Kenny's body be exhumed.

But Pam and Kenny were joined in death just as they had been in matrimony, at the St. John's Parish Church where their wedding service took place in November 1981.

"This is the biggest funeral we have ever seen around here," said one villager as cars swarmed onto the narrow streets around the church and quickly filled up the car parks of the nearby Fleece and Bradshaw Tavern pubs.

Police officers had to divert vehicles away from the church to ensure the smoothest possible traffic flow through the picturesque, old village as scores of speedway fans, journalists and TV crews converged on this usually tranquil community.

As a mark of respect, villagers drew their curtains and stood on their doorsteps as the cortege arrived. Pam's coffin was carried by her relatives and friends. Kenny's by his former Bradford and Halifax team-mates, including John Louis, Sean Willmott and Larry Ross. Brothers Kelly and Shawn Moran, two of the American stars who did battle with Kenny in those memorable Test matches from the early 80s, were also there and clearly more distraught than most.

The funeral was conducted by Reverand Clifford Haynes, who had spoken out previously of his concerns that the occasion could be turned into a media circus. "I do not want it to turn into an extraordinary event," he said, but of course that is just what it was.

Cameras were banned from the church, where the congregation crammed into the 200 pews.

Outside hundreds more, many of them Dukes fans sheltering under umbrellas and wearing Kenny Carter Racing anoraks, listened to the service via loudspeakers.

As requested by the families, the congregation sang *The Lord's My Shepherd* and family friend Sam Sorono sang a solo, *With This Hand*. Mr Haynes read a lesson

Large crowds gathered to pay their last respects.

from the 12th chapter of St. John.

Two large heart-shaped wreaths from Kenny's family stood either side of the altar. One bore Pam's name, the other Kenny's. During the normal half-hour Anglican service a wreath of carnations lay between the coffins. It read: 'With Love To Our Mummy and Daddy. Love Kelly Marie and Malcolm'.

The children did not attend the service.

The mourners, led by Mal Carter and his second wife, Janet, and Pam's parents, Bob and Veronica, led the congregation outside to the burial plot where their children were laid to rest, side by side. A grief-stricken Alan Carter had to be comforted by his fiancee Nicola Dickinson. He was pictured in tears at the graveside the next day by the *Evening Courier*.

Others from the speedway world who attended were Eric Boothroyd and former England managers Eric Boocock and Ian Thomas. A third ex-England boss, John Berry, also put on his black suit and tie, drove the three-and-a-half hours from Ipswich to Halifax, sat in his car outside the church while the funeral service was conducted – not wanting to be thought of a someone who had turned up to see and be seen – and then drove home again. He did it simply to pay his respects to the lad who never gave anything less than 100 per cent for him in an England race jacket.

Among friends who were present included Richard Dunn, the former British Heavyweight Boxing Champion. Tessa Sanderson, Kenny's first client for his short-lived promotions business, sent a floral tribute. Lots of flowers were also sent from speedway clubs and fans from all over Britain.

Adrian Lund laid flowers with the message: 'To My Brother-in-law Kenny. May God Forgive You. Adrian'.

The headstone inscription simply reads: 'Pamela and Kenny Carter, Died Together May 21, 1986. To our Mummy and Daddy – Kelly Marie and Malcolm'.

Chapter 26

'REMEMBER MY NAME'

ONE of the most brash slogans spray-painted on the side of one of Kenny Carter's vans turned out to be his epitaph. It simply read: 'REMEMBER MY NAME . . . KENNY CARTER'.

So, how will he be remembered? In life, as in death, Kenny continues to divide the speedway community like no other personality the sport has known. There is not another rider, whose short career began and ended in the 70s and 80s, who can still provoke the vast volume of words or ignite passionate debates about the rights and wrong of that era than Carter does today.

Log onto the internet and visit the British Speedway forum website at www.speedway-forum.co.uk. Key his name into the search window and watch as numerous recently-aired threads appear.

Love him or hate him, he is difficult to ignore. Even now.

Phil Hollingworth said that despite his friend's image in speedway as an abrasive and cocky loudmouth, Carter did have a well-hidden caring side to him, too.

Ollie said: "Behind the scenes he was a caring person. But he could be a selfish, hard-nosed bastard if he wanted to be. Very few people got close to him and most of those he met were through speedway – and either they all wanted a piece of him or they were hangers-on.

"Once you got to know him he would do anything for you. My daughter, Kate, absolutely adored him and whenever I went up to Kenny's place, she always wanted to come with me.

"He was the classic Yorkshireman who said what he thought.

"I painted the graphics on the side of one of his vans and as I was doing it, Kenny said: 'Go on, write England's No.1'. He loved winding people up, and telling the world he was going to beat everyone in his next meeting. But it was a front.

"He gave speedway a high profile back then and he was good for the sport."

As if the appalling deaths of Kenny and Pam Carter were not enough to leave a lasting imprint on Phil, he touched tragedy again as one of the heroic survivors of the Asian tsunami that claimed around 200,000 lives and destroyed hundreds of towns and villages when it struck with such devastation on Boxing Day, 2004. Phil and his girlfriend, Christine Shaw, were on holiday in the Maldives and eating breakfast in a restaurant when the first wave came and swept the Sri Lankan restaurant owner out to sea. A stunned Phil bravely swam after him but was unable to save the man who had been eating at the next table just seconds earlier. Luckily, Phil managed to cling to an upturned surf board and swim back to safety towards

Christine before the second wave came to wreak more death and destruction.Courageous beyond belief and humble with it, Phil simply did what he thought was the right thing to do and he was genuinely embarrassed at making front page news in the *Halifax Evening Courier*.

With fully justifiable understatement, he said: "After what happened to Kenny and Pam, and then being caught up in the tsunami, Christine and I do tend to look at life as never knowing what's around the corner."

Six times speedway World Champion **Ivan Mauger** (below), who was manager and mentor to Kenny Carter throughout 1981 and 1982 when Kenny went closest to winning the title, said: "He was a true Yorkshireman, a real tough character and I believe he was a talented rider. He was very determined to be World Champion.

"Kenny was easy to teach and he could comprehend compressions, ignition timing, gear ratios, clutch settings, fork spring rates and heights, wheel bases, tyre pressures and all the other very important things about setting up the bike for different tracks and conditions.

"He could grasp whatever I told him almost instantly and he understood exactly why we had to do certain things, so he was very good technically. He could come back into the pits and give an accurate assessment on any changes we had made. I knew plenty of world class riders who did not have that ability.

"We worked on a lot of aspects of his gating and riding techniques and, next to Ole (Olsen), he was probably the most receptive and understanding of any of my training academy riders, so he had plenty going for him.

"I showed Kenny how I kept my record books on the gearing needed for every different track, which I still have, and told him he had to be honest with himself in whatever he recorded.

"He had the ability to ride the bike and had everything about him to win big meetings.

"The thing about him was that he could actually win races when he really had to. I remember something Briggo said after Kenny had won the British League Riders'

final at Belle Vue. It was a real sticky old track that night and I was helping Kenny in the pits. Briggo said: 'Be careful what you tell that kid, because he does absolutely everything you tell him to do'.

"He also did a few things that I didn't tell him to do as well. He knocked Dennis Sigalos off in another BLRC – and I had nothing to do with that!

"It was unfortunate about Kenny. Without his injuries, he probably should have won the World Final in 1982. People don't realise how badly injured he was in Los Angeles – he hadn't ridden in England for weeks due to a punctured lung and ribs.

"I was proud to work with him."

Eric Boocock (right) will never forget the contribution his fellow Yorkshireman made to British speedway.

Booey said: "I knew Kenny both as a team-mate – at Halifax when I made my comeback in 1983 – and as a manager when I was in charge of the England team with Colin Pratt three years later.

"He was just coming into his prime in '83 and I enjoyed riding with him. It brought back a lot of memories and I loved his attitude – it was something we're short of in English speedway today. We need another Kenny Carter on the scene – rapidly!

"On one occasion when we were lining up for a second half race, I decided to teach him a little lesson. He was next to me at the starting gate and wanted me to move over. I was having none of it so, just as the tapes were about to go up, I stamped on his foot. He was the king of the kids and I was an old stager, so it was like giving a puppy a little smack.

"After that we laughed about it a lot but he wasn't best pleased at the time. Mind you, I wasn't best pleased that he thought that, because he was No.1 and I was just an old fart, I should move over.

"As for whether he was popular with his other team-mates – well, he's not here to answer that question but it didn't matter to him anyway because he was that kind of lad who didn't care what anybody thought about him.

"He was very self-opinionated and he was going to be the best – and was the best! His attitude was 'why should I worry about you? You worry about me!'

"In a funny kind of way he wasn't being big-headed - it's just how he was. He was tough as nails and his attitude was, 'look out for me, I'm coming and I don't care what you do to me because I'll look after myself'.

"He was popular with the fans, though – they paid his wages and the promoter's wages so that was the main thing. He was super with the fans and he loved the adoration. He played his part as a good No.1.

"He was good for Halifax Speedway. When he came back from his loan spell at Newcastle he was not only vying to be the top man at Halifax but the top man in the country. Halifax had got a top rider who had come from nowhere.

"I already knew Kenny before we teamed up at The Shay because Diane, my wife, and I had a spares shop. We lived not far from each other in West Yorkshire, so he was a regular customer. He had his engines tuned by Phil Pratt in London but all the running bits like handlebars, wheels and tyres, he got from me.

"He always used to phone up at about six o'clock in the evening – he had his finger in so many pies that there was never enough time in the day. He told me that by the age of 25 he'd be a millionaire. He wasn't being big-headed when he said that, he was just being Kenny.

"If he called we'd maybe go and have a drink – nothing wild or anything, just a pint, because neither of us were drinkers. We'd just go somewhere to have a chat. Or sometimes we'd just sit around the kitchen table for an hour and a half yakking about things. He always used to come to the house before we went to the shop.

"A few years later I was his joint team manager with Colin Pratt in the England set-up and he was an absolute dream for us. When he put that Union Jack on, he was just so proud to be English – something we miss today.

"There was always plenty in the press about Kenny hating the Yanks. I don't know whether he did genuinely hate them or not, but he was English and that was the over-riding factor. These blokes were coming over here and taking money off him! It was his job, and he wanted to beat them. I don't think it was a hate relationship, it was just that as a sportsman, he had to beat them.

"He was very introverted and kept everything to himself. If he'd had a shoulder to cry on maybe – and we'll never, ever know – it wouldn't have happened.

"The last time I saw Kenny was five days before he died. He was riding for England against Denmark in a Test match at Belle Vue. He fell twice when the footrest broke each time, but you couldn't knock him for that – it's terrible when a footrest breaks and it always seems to happen at the wrong time, just as you are going into the corner with all your weight on it.

"Then, at about midnight, five days later I was in bed when I got a phone call from a newspaper in Australia – the Sydney Herald, I think it was. They asked me what I knew about Kenny Carter because they believed he'd been shot.

"Obviously we were devastated. I was shocked because I never thought something like that would happen. I don't think I was particularly close to Kenny, but I was probably about as close as anyone could get. That's what upset me. If only he'd said something on the aeroplane coming back from the World Pairs semi-final in Italy just over a week before. A problem shared is a problem halved. He could have come over, talked to me or talked to Diane and maybe we could have helped him if he'd let us.

"It was just so tragic – tragic for the family mainly but also for the sport of speedway. The loss to British speedway at the time was massive – most of our top names had retired or were coming to the end of their careers and he was the new lad coming through. We have genuinely never replaced him – we think we have, but we haven't.

"We've certainly never replaced him with anyone who has the same attitude. Remember that British Final in 1984 when 15 other riders didn't want to ride because of the track conditions? Well, Kenny wanted to ride and went out and won it. He had a broken leg as well, but he called all the other riders wimps to their faces in the changing rooms. I know that because I was there. 'I'm riding', he said. 'You can all please yourselves but you're all soft'. That was the attitude he had.

"I personally thought he was a good guy and a good guy for speedway. I liked him a lot, and my wife certainly had a lot of time for him too. Maybe there was just that something missing. Whatever it was, we'll never know."

Sadly, it is not easy to find former rivals of Kenny's with too many good words to say about him, but **Joe Owen** is very happy to talk of Carter as an old mate he

Good mates Joe Owen and Kenny, with Ian Cartwright in 1980

shared many laughs and experiences with in their younger days.

A legend at Newcastle before Kenny came to Brough Park, Joe became his opponent in Yorkshire battles between Halifax and Hull, the senior league club Joe joined in the late 70s and early 80s. And it was immediately after Carter crashed at the Vikings' notorious rough Boulevard track one night that the two English youngsters got to know each other very well.

Joe said: "Kenny was lying on the track, moaning about how his bike had been 'pop, pop, popping' before he crashed when I walked over to him and helped him back on his feet. I took the mickey out of him a little bit by asking him to repeat his 'pop, pop' explanation for the fall. We became friends from that moment and I always got on well with Kenny."

Joe recalls "chaperoning" Kenny, who was four years younger than him, when they were both members of the England team's two-match tour to Poland in July 1979 – Kenny's first overseas trip as a rider.

But before setting off from home for the matches at Bydgoszcz and Gdasnk, where Michael Lee was outstanding and Malcolm Simmons acted as rider-coach, Joe and Kenny got to know each other much better away from the track.

Talking recently from his Lancashire home, Joe explained: "Kenny came to my dad's farm in Ormskirk the night before we left for Poland and we went shooting pheasant in nearby fields – I'm not proud to say it now, because I'm against it, but we didn't see it as being wrong back then. Kenny liked guns and he was a good shot, too.

"After we'd been out shooting, he stayed over at our place but he had turned up with what looked like only one change of clothes in a poly bag. At the end of the night he took off his pants, gave them to my then wife and said, 'wash those for me please, will yer?'!

"He used to make me laugh but he was a pain in the arse all the way to Poland on that trip. He could be naive about things and spent the while journey asking me one question after another – it was all new to him and he wanted to know everything about anything. I told him, 'will; you shut the f*** up, you're driving me mad'. He was like a parrot on my shoulder!

"But I could say things like that to him because we got on really good and were mates. Kenny was all right but you just needed to know how to handle him. I think that's where the riders who didn't get on with him went wrong – they took an instant dislike to him, for whatever reason, and never got to find out what made him tick.

"If he ever got too hard with me on the track, I'd have a word with him and that would be the end of it.

"I suppose I've always tried to see the good in people. I've had a few mates who are a bit rogue-ish but I tend to get on well with them.

"It's like Kenny dad's Mal. I always got on all right with him, too. He was a typical, hard Yorkshireman but underneath it all he had a heart of gold and I liked him. He was a nice guy."

So, too, is Joe Owen, who recalls a memorable day out in Derbyshire with Carter senior and junior.

"Mal and Kenny invited me to go road-racing with them to Donnington Park and we had a great day. We set off with the shotguns in the boot – that sounds terrible, but you know what I mean. Anyway, on the way there we stopped off in a quiet, little lane in the country to shoot pheasant and rabbits. Mal was a good shooter, too.

"At the race track, I rode a 350cc Yamaha, I think, but Kenny was brilliant on a big 500cc Honda that he was trying out, riding neck-an-neck with the great Ron Haslam. I didn't particularly like road-racing but Kenny would have been very good at it if he hadn't ridden speedway instead."

Joe asked Kenny to appear in his testimonial meeting at Newcastle in July 1983 and the England and Halifax No.1 was only too pleased to oblige his friend. Joe still has the video footage of the meeting. On a subsequent occasion, he also agreed to support Joe at a fund-raising function.

"Kenny asked me to pick him and Pam up on the way from my place, so we de-toured to Halifax. I noticed that night that he wasn't the same happy-go-lucky kid I'd known all those years earlier. He had definitely changed.

"Kenny sat in the back of my car with Pam but he said very little on the journey – they hardly spoke a word to each other all the way to Newcastle and back. I thought to myself, 'what's up with him?' and I sensed then things weren't too good between them. The rot had set in."

Joe's successful speedway career ended tragically when he crashed while starring for champions-elect Ellesmere Port at Birmingham just before the end of the 1985 season. It left him paralysed and by the time he left hospital, Carter's own personal problems were already spiralling out of control.

"Kenny didn't visit me in hospital, which was a bit of a surprise," said Joe, "but he did keep in touch and phoned my first wife two or three times to check how I was doing.

"I was awfully upset when Kenny died – it was a hell of a shock and I never thought he was capable of doing what he did.

"To me, he was a really nice guy – not the bad lad that some said he was.

"But what he did was so unnecessary. He could have had a good life but he killed his woman because he loved her and obviously couldn't bear to live without her."

Richard Bott, the respected Lancashire-based journalist, recalled his last encounter with the man whose *Speedway Star* column he used to 'ghost' for him.

"Among my speedway souvenirs is the laurel wreath that Kenny was presented with when he won his second British Final at Coventry in 1985. I bought it in the auction that was held at Denny's, the Halifax night club, to raise money for his kids. If they want it back, they are welcome to have it. It has been on my office wall ever since, alongside souvenirs of world finals and, in particular, Peter Collins' triumph in Poland in 1976.

"So is the programme for Kenny's last-ever meeting, the World Championship British semi-final at Odsal on Sunday, May 18, 1986, a couple of weeks before he hoped to complete a hat-trick of British Championship wins.

"How he struggled that afternoon, going into the interval with only two points from three rides and his World Championship dreams seemingly in tatters yet again. But he bounced back to win his last two programmed rides and a run-off with Carl Blackbird and Louis Carr for the last qualifying place.

"He said to me: 'Bloody hell, Dick, I nearly made a mess of that', as he uncorked a bottle of champagne back in the pits. He nearly put my left eye out as well, because the cork hit me just below my eye. I had a lump the size of a marble for a week. I don't know who was more relieved that day, Kenny or me.

"Unbelievably, it was the last time I spoke to him. Three nights later, I got a call at home from the *Daily Express* news desk to tell me he had shot himself and his wife and could I write them a quick obituary. That's how it is in the media. No time for sentiment. Just do the job.

"I didn't keep the cutting but I seem to remember that my tribute ended with the words: 'Deep down he just wanted to be a winner and he knew he was good. But what a hell of a way to lose his last race.'

"And what a mess he did make of it. Impetuous in life as he was in his racing career. And others will have much stronger opinions.

"But he was a genuine talent and British, too.

"PC will always be my favourite British rider of all time and not just because of my association with him as his business manager for seven years and our ongoing friendship. But I had more time for Kenny Carter than most, including PC probably, because he had the same desperate ambition to be World Champion that Peter had had in the 70s and that Ivan Mauger seemed to have every year!

"And like PC he was a true patriot, proud to ride for his country and sick of the domination of the Danes and the Americans.

"The difference was that Kenny talked the talk before he walked the walk and his cockiness, a bit like three Yorkshiremen who did walk the walk, Geoffrey Boycott, Fred Trueman and Harvey Smith, often rubbed people up the wrong way.

"One of Kenny's favourite expressions was: 'If you think you're the best, why say owt else?'. He had a sign painted on his van which read 'Kenny Carter – England's No 1' before he was. But he believed it.

"I got to know him when he was riding for my old pal, Ian Thomas, at Newcastle and then, of course, at Halifax and Bradford.

"I interviewed him many times for *Speedway Star* and also for the *Sunday Express* and one of the stories he told me was about the shock he gave Eric Boocock when Booey was driving home up the M1 on a filthy night after they had been at a Test match at Wimbledon. Eric suddenly saw a ghostly figure waving at him outside the car window and it was Kenny, going flat out in the rain on his Honda 1100, heading for the airport to fly to another meeting.

"One day I went to Kenny's luxury farmhouse up on the moors when he was hopping round the kitchen without a pot on the leg he had broken a month before. He was more bothered about whether I was impressed that he had two stone lions at the end of his drive to illustrate how proud he was to be English.

"Bruce Penhall and Kenny clashed big-time in LA at the 1982 World Final and the rest is history. To quote one of Kenny's famous sayings: 'I had no chance'.

The harsh truth is that his wife had even less on that fateful night 21 years ago. But, judged purely on his track talent and his entertainment value, Kenny Carter was good for British speedway. Tragically, he was always chasing a dream that eventually turned into a nightmare."

Bruce Penhall was not keen to contribute his thoughts to a book about his old enemy when I called him, at home in Los Angeles. The 1981 and 1982 World Champion shares the thoughts of most others when he says that what Kenny did to Pam is something he could never forgive and, predictably, he had some very strong words to say about the man who very nearly denied him his second world title.

"I really don't want to say two words about Kenny Carter," said Penhall. "In my eyes he was an absolute mental coward for the way he went and left his kids without parents. There are probably stronger words I could use, but that's what comes to my mind right now.

"The only reason I agreed to talk about him for this book is that the book is going to make some money for his kids. So good luck with the book, I hope it goes well.

"I am a true father, with four kids, and I couldn't, even on my worst day, imagine doing what he did, therefore I don't have one bit of respect for that kid."

Surely the former blue-eyed boy of American speedway must have had some respect for Carter as a top international who served his club and country so successfully?

"Kenny was like me – his heart was in racing. I don't care if it's racing motorcycles or a swimming competition, if guys have the heart, I truly respect that because I know what it takes to be a competitor, whether it be Kenny Carter or Peter Collins.

"At the time I raced against him, I did have respect for him as a racer. But, of course, the tables turned when this ugly tragedy happened.

"When it's all said and done, he wasn't all there upstairs. It proved it in the end. The kid wasn't dealing with a full deck at any frickin' time of his racing career while I knew him

"I'm a pretty easy guy to get along with. Of course, we had strong feelings on the track. But off the track, you have to be civil. Kenny wasn't my only rival – I had dozens upon dozens.

"I remember once travelling with him on a bus from a meeting at Treviso in Italy – and yes, we talked. Kenny didn't really have any friends, even among the English riders, and he was pretty much the black sheep. It just so happened that somebody had to sit next to him on the bus and that day it happened to be me. I spoke to him – I never just turned away and ignored him. My family raised me to have respect for everyone and that's the way I treated people."

Penhall was no stranger to family tragedy himself. He lost both of his parents in an aeroplane crash before he had even begun his five-year stint in the British League career.

Ironically, Carter and Penhall could have been team-mates in Carter's first season of speedway and Bruce's debut year in the British League. In 1978, Eric Boothroyd made enquiries about bringing the highly-rated Californian to The Shay but he subsequently signed for Dan McCormick at Cradley Heath instead.

Penhall looks back and shudders at the thought. He said: "We could have been team-mates at Halifax. . . and it would have been just as bad between us, probably worse.

"Even when I brought Bobby Schwartz to England, to ride on the same team as me at Cradley, we wanted to do the best we possibly could for our team. But you've got to remember that we were there as individuals as well, trying to win the mighty World Championship. If one of your friends gets in the way, it'll cause problems. You have to get through all that, beat your best friends and not blink an eye to it.

"The only difference between Bobby and Kenny is that Bobby was an intelligent guy and Kenny was not all there. He was a demented young man.

"It would never have worked if Kenny and I had both ridden for Halifax. There would have been a problem because he was all out for himself at all times. I've never seen him actually team-ride and I'd gladly give you a dollar for every time it happened.

"Even when he was racing for England, he went out there to win heats on his own – no-one wanted to ride next to him. Yet you saw some amazing team-riding involving the Americans and Danes. Not with Kenny Carter."

Speedway is still trying to replace Carter in terms of a superstar with huge box office appeal, who would draw fans from all corners of Britain to see him take on the rest. Does Penhall believe that Kenny would have made a good World Champion had he lived to fulfil his dream?

He said: "There are two ways you can look at it. When I was World Champion I wanted to be good to others, give the media as much as I could and to be a little less controversial. And, on the other side, there was Kenny, who wasn't all there. He could have really upset the media, which, in a way, maybe would have drawn even more media attention to speedway and helped the sport.

"Speedway always loves a bad guy as well, it's the good cop/bad cop thing. I was a bad guy for a while for some of the decisions I made. There are guys who people love to hate and, for the most part, Kenny was one of those.

"I always wanted to be the good World Champion who would give back 100 percent of my time to the media, but I don't think Kenny would have done that if he'd become World Champion. I think he would have said: 'I don't give a stuff'. In fact, he was quoted a million times as saying 'I wanna get out of this effin' sport, I hate it. I wanna go road-racing. So he could have won the World Championship and then said, 'now it's time to go road-racing'. You'll never know.

"But as far as his mental capacity goes, I don't think he had what it took to be a good World Champion."

It seems that you cannot talk about Kenny Carter's contribution to speedway and the imprint he left on the sport without mentioning Bruce Penhall in the next breath, and vice-versa. Much as Penhall will hate this to be the case, their speedway careers will forever be intrinsically linked.

Finally, Penhall was asked for the umpteenth time to recall their most brutal, well chronicled clash of all – the heat 14 incident with Carter in the 1982 World Final that still provokes lively and conflicting debate today. His anger about the manner of Carter's demise resurfaced in his voice as he said: "I've seen that incident with Carter from hundreds of different angles, from footage taken by the people filming for *CHiPS*, and it clearly shows from the back angle that I never hit Kenny when he fell.

"But, you know what . . . the way I look at it now, after what he did to his wife and children, I wish I would've frickin' put him up in the middle of the grandstand."

Malcolm Simmons, the former world No.2 and a team-mate of Kenny's when he made his international bow at Swindon in 1979, agrees with Penhall's view that Carter was not suitable World Champion material. Simmo said: "If Kenny had won in the Los Angeles Coliseum that night, I don't think he would have gone on to dominate speedway for long. He would have burnt himself out very quickly, because that was the nature of the guy.

"I don't think he had the temperament to stay at the top. I don't believe Kenny could have won a World Final unless he did everything absolutely right and things also went wrong for his main rivals. Michael Lee could have put 10 very good races together at any given time, but Kenny could always blow a fuse . . . especially if there was an American in the race.

"It's a great shame, but he was his own worst enemy in the same way that Michael was.

"I don't care what anyone says, to be able to go as fast as Kenny did and to be as good as he was, you have to have quite a lot of ability. He had ability as well as a screw loose."

Peter Collins, the 1976 World Champion and Kenny's World Pairs partner in 1982 and again when they won the title together in Sweden a year later, said: "I'm a firm believer that you reap what you sow at the end of the day.

"Kenny upset so many people. When we used to go and ride in open meetings,

Before it turned nasty . . . Peter Collins and Kenny after winning the World Pairs Final in Sweden, 1983.

people would sacrifice their own chances of winning as long as they beat Kenny and stopped him winning the meeting. That's how it was with a large amount of riders, especially the Americans.

"He had that much resentment against him, which he had created himself.

"To some extent, when Kenny and I rode in the World Pairs together, it was at the stage when our relationship wasn't so badly frayed. I didn't like the things that he stood for or how he'd gone about getting to where he'd got – that wasn't my way at all. It wasn't my idea to trample on people to get to the top. I still get on with just about everybody from my racing days – there are only a few that I don't get on with, rider-wise.

"Kenny was a thorn in my side but, then again, he had a lot of aggro with other people, too. He had confrontations with so many people – I was just one of them. I suppose because I'd been England No.1 and captain before him, he was after what I'd already achieved."

"Would he have made a good World Champion? Kenny's history just answers that question – it tells you everything.

"I think he struggled to cope when he was injured and couldn't win the world title at Bradford in '85. That was a big downer for him. I remember seeing a picture of him at the start of the '85 season, sitting on his bike at the top of the banking at Odsal, with the track and the stadium behind him. He didn't actually say 'this is where I'm gonna win the World Championship in September' in as many words but you sensed that was what he was thinking. But we all know it doesn't work like that.

"He probably thought that was his big chance and he possibly never got over it.

"I think he was having trouble living with himself at the end of the day and there were certain things he just couldn't accept. He had a lot of demons upstairs and, to be fair on him, I think that was his main problem. I knew about his mother and, I suppose, that's why you just about have to give him the benefit of the doubt with most of it, but . . .

"It's all very sad and the fact that other people are having their say in this book makes it a little easier for me to speak about him now. I don't want his kids to read stuff that I've said about somebody who can't answer back. I don't want to rubbish him but there are things that are healthy to say about him, without going too deeply into it.

"I just feel for his kids – their well-being is more important than anything anyone is going to say about Kenny."

Chris Morton, PC's long-time Belle Vue team-mate and friend, acknowledged Carter's importance to speedway in his autobiography. Mort was parked at the Hilton Park Services on the M6, on the way home from Cradley Heath with his mechanic Ged Blake, when a supporter approached them with the news of Kenny's death.

Morton, the 1983 British Champion, wrote: "Although he was an abrasive character, some say you either loved him or hated him, but I believed it then and I believe it now – that he was great for speedway."

Andy Grahame, the 1982 British Champion, said: "I rode with and against Kenny because, as well as being rivals in the British League, we rode in the same England team and toured Australia with the national side.

"He was a very talented rider but, as a person… He would have had more friends and been more highly thought of if he'd had a level head on his shoulders.

"He could have gone on to be World Champion if he'd been a more sociable person, because people would have helped him more. Instead it was all me, me, me all the time.

"When we were on international duty it wasn't the England team, it was Kenny Carter and the England team. The only person Kenny Carter was interested in was himself. He thought he was Mr Big and was going to win everything. He was a very talented rider, there's no doubt about that, but he was also a big head.

"He always spoke his mind but he upset a lot of people.

"It's a shame, because he'd got that much talent that he didn't have to be the way he was."

Nigel Flatman has much happier memories of riding with and enjoying the laid-back Aussie way of life with Carter. He said: "I knew he was going to be good from when we made our first trip to Perth together (1979-80).

"We lost touch later in Kenny's career. We'd talk to each other if we were riding in the same meeting, Halifax v Ipswich, but he became much more serious and was completely different to the guy I used to know from our early fun days in Perth. He became very business-orientated.

"His brother, Alan, came to see me and Tracey when he visited Australia about three years ago. We got on great, he's a good bloke, and it was such a shame that we didn't have enough time to talk properly. He was obviously sad about what happened.

"I've got some great pictures of Kenny jumping off a roof into a pool when we were both still youngsters having fun. I'd love to pass copies of them on to his two kids – and to meet them."

Dave Jessup, Carter's former England colleague, saw a less intense side to Kenny when they rode together on international duty. He said: "If Kenny saw me sitting alone in my van before a meeting, concentrating and getting myself psyched up, he would occasionally come and join me for a quiet chat. He'd either sit in the front seat alongside me or on the step by the open door.

"I got on well with Kenny and never had any problems with him."

Former England boss **John Berry** had a lot of time and respect for Carter, the rider he awarded a first cap to and managed him in all three of his spells in charge (1979, 1982 and 1985). He said: "If Kenny had been born a dog, it would have to have been a Jack Russell Terrier. Small, snappy, aggressive and often bad tempered, but with strong loyalty, no fear and never a thought of taking a backwards step.

"I don't pretend to know in any detail the young Kenny's early teenage years. All I do know is that they were not easy times. Tragedy and consequent disharmony and then further tragedy beset the Carter family during his adolescent years. At an age when he should have been growing up, Kenny was forced into self-reliance and having to face problems most of us never have to.

"Personally, I suspect it was a mixture of this, added to a rather domineering father, and a younger brother who had become no mean motorcycle racer, that gave Kenny an almost unhealthy determination to win at all costs. In fact, I am sure that those medicos who study such things would describe him as being 'driven'.

"Being potentially so good, so young is not always such a good thing. It doesn't hurt to show talent early on but if enough people around you keep telling you how good you are, it can put tremendous pressure on you. There's no place to hide and do the normal growing up most 16-year-olds are free to do.

"Champions like Ove Fundin and Ivan Mauger thrived in the role of crowd villain but they had served their apprenticeships and started to shave before having to carry that kind of pressure.

"Sadly, there is a fine line between determination and obsession. There were so many similarities between Kenny and Billy Sanders. Their desire to become World Champion became unhealthy and both became driven men. No doubt, their obsessive behaviour played a large part in both marital break-ups.

"Of course, it is possible that even had the decision gone the other way in Los Angeles in '82, Kenny might well still not have finished as the world champ, and his bad luck continued when he broke his leg just before the Bradford World Final in '85 which he was expected by many to win comfortably."

And to repeat his earlier assertion: "I am convinced that had he been crowned World Champion on that day in Los Angeles, or even at Bradford, his life and attitudes would have changed, and those tragic, horrific, nightmarish events which haunt us all would not have taken place."

Ian Thomas, co-promoter at Newcastle when Carter burst onto the speedway scene at the start of 1978, said: "Kenny's temperament never changed from when I first knew him – from that season at Newcastle to him being in the England team managed by Booey and myself and then when I looked after him in the '84 World Championship through to his untimely death. He was always 'Kenny Carter', do you know what I mean? He was always going to win everything.

"He was precocious and cocky when he was 17, but that never worried me. I was probably one of the few people who got on really well with him. I never had a problem in any of my dealings with him.

"The only thing I didn't like about him was his bloody Alsatian dog!

"I think it would be wrong to do a true comparison between Kenny and the likes of PC and Michael Lee, because Kenny didn't have a full career. Nobody will ever know what he would have achieved.

"And while I always liked the kid and got on well with him, what he did was dreadful and nobody could ever condone it. I'd never been to a double funeral before and it was 'ticket only', so to speak. That knocked me sideways," said Thomas.

Carter rode three different makes of machinery used by the British League stars of his era – Weslake, Godden and GM, but never Jawa – so what did a couple of his engine tuners make of him?

Phil Pratt (below), who prepared the Wessies Kenny rode in all three of his individual world finals (1981, '82 and '83), said: "The aggressive, loud-speaking person the public saw, and the way he has been portrayed by so many people, was not the Kenny Carter I knew and dealt with on a daily basis.

"I found him to be a complete gentleman. I didn't have any arguments with him at all and never had problems over money either.

"He came to my home, and sometimes he brought Pam with him. She was a shy type of girl, very reserved, but on the many times I went to Kenny's house she

couldn't do enough for you.

"On a one-to-one basis, socially and at home, away from racing, he was a totally different person than the one most people in speedway knew him to be. To be perfectly honest, I just loved the guy to bits. And as a couple, I couldn't fault them.

Pratt only ever tuned Carter's Weslakes and was very sorry to see him leave for the newer British-built Godden engine at the start of 1984.

He said: "At the time I worked with Kenny, I was probably the best Weslake tuner. But when he switched to Godden, Don would have realised that his technical know-how was very limited and he probably said to him that he would look after those engines to make sure Kenny had the best available to him.

"I think he moved there because Weslake weren't developing enough for the future. I mean, they gave him a single overhead camshaft engine which, quite frankly, was absolute crap. Nobody rode the things, they were no good, so I don't think Kenny saw his future with a company that wasn't trying to take it forward.

"And Don was probably offering him more than he was going to get from Weslake. It was my loss, for sure. Of course I was disappointed that he went to Godden. But at the end of the day, I took Kenny from someone else and somebody else took him from me – that's the business we're in."

"But to be honest, Kenny could have got on a JAP and still won races.

Don Godden, whose GR500 bike Kenny used to win the British Championship for the first time in 1984, said briefly: "I would say Kenny was one of the top three or four speedway riders who would make the best of what you gave him to ride.

"I never had any problems with Kenny. We got good feedback from him and he was always good to deal with."

Bob Radford, the first national speedway reporter to interview Carter as a 17-year-old at Wolverhampton in 1978, recalled: "I remember chatting at Phil Crump's home over a glass of red wine when the news broke on ITV's News At Ten. Phil was talking but I kind of heard what was said on telly. Phil wondered if I was off my trolley but of course it was soon up on Teletext, too.

"For me, Kenny became far too belligerent for his own good. It had been an immense strength but became his weakness and probably led to his ultimate downfall.

"He was actually good to deal with and friendly for interviews or over the radio mike. That said, even today I regard Penhall as the most charismatic speedway rider of all time next to Briggo – in terms of making it exciting and talking the sport up. You might imagine that did not go down well with Kenny."

Former England international and world finalist **Doug Wyer** said: "What a guy! He was obviously flawed in some way, but what a sad way to go.

"I spoke to him at Bradford in a World Championship round not long before he died and he was having a bad time. I asked him what was up and he said it was this and that, but he had something on his mind, I could tell.

"I told him to concentrate. He still had three more rides left and I told him he could walk it – he had two points already and he could get nine points easily. But he only just about scraped through and I thought he seemed a bit strange.

"And the next thing . . . that was it. My mate phoned me up and asked me if I'd heard the news. It was such a tragedy, not just for him and his wife but for speedway, and I was among those at his funeral. He could have been a world champion, I think he definitely had it in him.

"It was such a shock to me. He lived in Halifax, I lived in Sheffield and we were a generation apart so we didn't socialise, which meant I didn't know what was happening in his private life.

"There have been lots of jack-the-lads in speedway. He probably had tons of women, but as soon as she wanted another bloke, that was it for whatever reason.

With Neil Evitts before the 1985 British League Pairs at Wolverhampton.

"But I was told afterwards that he'd threatened to shoot his wife a few times and that her dad came to his house and took his guns away. In the end he borrowed a gun to shoot her."

Exactly a week after Carter died, his Bradford team-mate **Neil Evitts** produced the performance of his career to win the British Championship at Coventry. Evitts had not been happy with the Coalite Dukes' management who, after asking him to stand in as skipper for the best part of the two seasons when Carter was out with a broken leg, immediately handed the club captaincy back to Kenny on his return to fitness at the start of the 1986 season.

But Evitts had no personal axe to grind with Carter and said: "Kenny's death definitely gave me extra motivation to win the British Final that year.

"Riding with him definitely improved me as a rider," he continued. "Not many people liked him because of his attitude but when you did get to know him, you realised just how good he actually was.

"I had to admire Kenny. If you could compare him to anyone, it would have to be the Gallagher brothers in Oasis. As far as they're concerned they are the only musicians in the world. Kenny used to think the same way in speedway terms.

"He was very confident. I was also confident in my own ability but I knew my limits, and you have to know them. Also, I wasn't as good as Kenny anyway.

"It was such a tragic waste. I knew he had a problem in his life but because he was the type of person that he was, he never told anybody else what his problems were. He didn't discuss personal matters with others but you knew there were things going on in the background.

"The last time I saw him was at Bradford the night before he died. He came down to the pits and told us he wouldn't be riding that night because he'd broken his finger. We had a quick laugh about something and that was it – I saw no more of him.

"The Bradford meeting was rained-off on the Tuesday and I heard the news of his death when I got home from Cradley's meeting the following night. Terrible."

Rob Woffinden remembers his good friend. He said: "I met Kenny in Australia the first time I went over there with my bike – my dad lives out there. Kenny was the resident rider at Claremont so I got to know him and became quite a good friend to him. I was one of the few he didn't fall out with over the years – he lost a lot of friends in speedway but I was a friend right up until the end.

"Kenny was a good friend. He was a bit rude sometimes but I told him straight. If he asked me to do something and didn't say 'please', I would tell him I'd do it but there are such things as manners. I think that got us off on the right foot.

"He was always arrogant and keen – he was No.1 and that was it.

"I didn't socialise with him apart from on the odd occasion. He used to come to my house and we practiced together at Scunthorpe before some of his big meetings. We used to do some starts together – I wasn't in the same class as him but I was someone to start with.

"I'd call him a close friend but I wasn't someone he would confide in. I don't think Kenny confided in anybody.

"Kenny used to run a car sales business and although I wasn't involved in that, he wanted me to become involved in his promotional business. He rang me and asked if I wanted to help him out and do some work, but that hadn't been going long before he died.

"But in any case I didn't want to work with him – I wanted to keep my friendship with him. I thought it was going to be a friendship that would last for life, but obviously not.

"In Australia I used to go on the back of his motorbike because he'd got a licence and I hadn't – well, I *think* he'd got a licence!

"We used to do a trip to Claremont to pick the wages up and just sort of hung around on holiday really.

"Dave Cheshire was staying at my house for the season when I heard the news that Kenny had died. We were in the shed doing our bikes one night when my mum walked in and told us it had been on the news. We were very shocked.

"We went to the funeral, although there weren't many riders there. Four riders carried the coffin, I think, but there were only another four or five riders there."

Perhaps **Eric Boothroyd** sums up the impact his top rider had on the sport best when he said: "Kenny was obviously a very driven and fearless rider but he was also a natural talent – I'd say he was absolutely gifted.

"He had the heart of a lion and was determined to be the very best, to become World Champion.

"He was only a little bloke, with a small frame, and he took a lot of hard knocks. He rode for two years with a broken leg that hadn't healed properly.

"A majority of the fans did like Kenny – and the supporters at Halifax and then Bradford loved him. We immediately lost 500 people a week off our crowd at Odsal after he died.

Kenny and his Bradford promoter Eric Boothroyd drink a good luck toast at the opening of Kenny's promotions company at Dean Clough in February 1986 – three months before he died.
With Kenny on the picture hanging from the wall behind them are Heather Lund and Phil Hollingworth.

"I always think Kenny was like a meteor. He flashed on to the scene, was brilliant for a short while . . . and then he disappeared just as suddenly as he arrived," said Boothroyd.

Kenny Carter has been dead for more than 21 years. But at least one of his wishes came true.

'Remember My Name'.

Epilogue

UNANSWERED QUESTIONS

WHY? That is the question we still ask ourselves, after more than 21 years and countless thousands of words and diverse opinions have been expressed. Why did Kenny Carter, a young man idolised by so many, who apparently had so much to live for, reach the point where he ended it all the way he did?

We will never know the definitive answer. Instead, we practice being amateur psychiatrists in an attempt to at least make some sense of this terrible tragedy.

A tragic life that turned devastatingly sad when he was just nine-years-old and ended 16 years later in the needless waste of two, young lives.

Would it have turned out all so differently if only Christine Carter's car had not suffered a puncture and spun out of control?

Would it have made an ounce of difference to Kenny's view of the world and his driven personality if his dad had not left the family home when he did, with his former wife paralysed and condemned to a life of suffering and misery – a short life that lasted only another nine years, until she could take no more.

What if Kenny had won the World Championship he craved so much, when he was so obviously good enough to have won it in 1982, 1984 or 1985? Would I now be reaching the end of a book about a celebrated speedway legend who went on to conquer the world more than once, instead of searching for the right words to say at the end of an incredibly sad story with two few highs (considering Kenny's ability) and far too many heartrending lows? That is the book I would have much prefer to have written – one brim full of illustrious on-track achievements, remarkable acts of courage, typical outspoken opinion and laced with many entertaining anecdotes. In totally different circumstances, only the beginning and the end of this extraordinary story would change.

But those 'what ifs?' just keep recurring whenever you hear or mention the name, Kenny Carter.

What if Tore Kittilsen had put his finger of blame on Bruce Penhall's blue exclusion light instead of the white one that signalled heartbreak for Kenny in LA?

And what if Penhall had not been so desperate that night in Los Angeles that he wanted to win the world title even though just minutes later he would be retiring from speedway for good? A bitterly disappointed and frustrated Kenny spoke to his friends afterwards and asked: "Why do that to me when he knew he was finishing with speedway? Why rob me when he was giving up anyway?"

Why?

Kenny probably took as many unanswered questions to his grave as he left for others to ponder in his passing.

Penhall and Carter . . . you just can't talk for long about one without mentioning the other. Many will be saddened – possibly angered – by the bitterness Bruce still feels towards Kenny but perhaps we should not be surprised by it. The way he probably sees it, he sadly had no say in whether or not his parents perished in an aeroplane crash before he was barely out of his teens, whereas the mindless, callous act of his old arch rival was totally unnecessary and could never be condoned by anyone.

So what on earth possessed Kenny to shoot Pam? Why, oh why? The questions keep coming.

Did he have firm evidence that she was cheating on him, or was he simply reacting to rumours – still categorically denied by those who knew her best – in the worst way possible? Whatever the answer to this one, the result could never be justified.

Thousands of marriages end in divorce every week. Wherever we turn today it is a sad by-product of modern society that families split up and the lives of mums, dads and children are rebuilt under new roofs. Life goes on – or so it should. Which begs the obvious question: why couldn't Kenny, no matter how deep and genuine his love for Pam was, accept that she no longer wanted him and move on to start again like most other men in his situation do every day?

Kenny's closest friends believe that he just could not bear to lose the woman he married and the woman he had been obsessed with since they were both in their early teens. And if he could not have her, then as far as he was concerned nobody else could either. Remember what he told Jimmy Ross: 'There will NEVER be another divorce in my family." And the apparently innocuous remark Kenny made to Phil Hollingworth on the way back from the Golden Key of Bremen meeting in Germany: "If Pam ever left me, I'd kill her!"

Kenny had clearly lost his mind on Wednesday, May 21, 1986 and Ross said: "He was a winner. But the fear of being a loser – shown up and embarrassed in front of others – was equally strong and not acceptable to him."

None of us should underestimate the financial, as well as emotional turmoil Kenny had put himself under. An intensely proud man with a luxury farmhouse to pay for, a wife and two young children to support, he was never going to confess to anyone that his ambitious promotions company, which he started just 12 weeks or so before he died, was already floundering and haemorraghing his cash.

A £400-a-month sports car that he did not need only added further weight to a financial strain that had grown after he had missed virtually two complete seasons while recovering from serious injuries, in 1984 and 1985. While the title of British Champion was something he had worked relentlessly and courageously to achieve, and it certainly appealed to his ego, the financial rewards were relatively minuscule.

Two British Final victories did not put food on the table while he missed virtually two full seasons for Halifax and was unable to capitalise on his England No.1 status. Instead of snapping up the many open meeting invitations that would have naturally flooded his way, both at home and abroad, Kenny was lying in a hospital bed or at home recovering with a plaster on his leg. These serious injuries were particularly

Waving goodbye to the fans?

sickening and frustrating to him because they wrecked his dreams during his peak years.

As well as the psychological blows there was also a large financial price to pay for such long, enforced absences. Insurance pay-outs helped ease the burden in '84 but, by all accounts, he had only £100 a month coming in when he re-broke the same right leg in August '85 – nine months before his death.

If only it had not rained in Vetlanda that night and he had come through that semi-final round unscathed, then gone on to win the Bradford World Final. World Champion in his own Yorkshire backyard.

'If only' again . . .

A shortage of money also led him to mistakenly cut corners on the mechanical side, firing one of his few trusted friends and his main mechanic and replacing him with an inexperienced young lad. The catalogue of machine failures he suffered at the start of his last season was surely no coincidence.

Kenny had clearly taken his eye off the ball where speedway was concerned, totally consumed as he was by a driving ambition to become rich and famous as quickly as he possibly could. Maybe the succession of debilitating injuries finally convinced him that his future lay outside racing sooner than most of us thought? He was certainly shrewd enough to see for himself that the sport was drifting towards a new, steady decline that had started when his own career did and deepened through the 80s.

His friends are adamant that he allowed himself to be too easily distracted by the 'hangers on' who introduced him to a more pretentious new image of smart jackets, fast cars, white wine and American self-help manuals that seduced him with promises to make him 'a millionaire by the time you're 30'. Kenny's well-meaning acolytes from the world of business had made plenty of money themselves but how much did he need them? If he had got himself fully fit again, managed to stay out of trouble for longer periods, and built himself a property portfolio based on his earning capacity as the top English rider of his era, he could have made it to the millionaire bracket before he was 30 simply by doing what he had always done best.

Who was he trying to prove himself to? His father, who had made his own fortune, or was he driven by nightmare visions of his mother. "I'll win the World Championship for mum," he stated after she was taken from him.

Instead, Kenny left very little behind. Grey Horse Farm was put on the market for £79,000 (and bought by a haulage boss from Bradford) but there was little left over for the children. Pam and Kenny's son, Malcolm, was perturbed in later years to discover that some of his dad's prized possessions, including his Tag Heuer watch, his wedding ring, the Golden Key he won at Bremen and two Golden Hammers he collected with great glee at Cradley Heath, went missing from the farmhouse and were never, ever found.

There was speculation that Kenny might have had some money secreted offshore in an Isle of Man bank account, set up for him by one of his wealthier associates, but it would probably not have amounted to much had the rumours been true.

He did not need yes-men around him. He needed the few genuine friends he had known and grown up with for years, the people he occasionally treated like a pair of discarded, old trainers until he realised his mistakes too late.

Jimmy Ross said: "Kenny looked ill – thin and drawn – when I saw him towards the end of his life but he was getting back to being the old Kenny in his last few weeks. I think he realised then what had happened to him and felt as if he'd been mugged.

"He'd come a long way from being the 18-year-old Lucozade-and-Lion bar kid I used to drive to meetings.

"But, after a painful period and lessons learned, I think he could have got back to being the top rider he had been in speedway before 1986."

But . . . and there is always a but where Kenny Carter is concerned.

Another problem for him was that he was a natural wheeler-dealer, buying and selling cars and anything else he could get his hands on before he was out of his teens. He was not the type to be content with winning races for England, pursuing world titles and leading a one-man Dukes team which, in his own provocative words, he viewed as "me and six other tossers." He was never content, always relentlessly chasing that elusive pot of gold at the end of the rainbow.

Too many questions left agonisingly unanswered. Questions the Carter and the Lund families will no doubt continue to ask themselves forever more.

Kenny's legacy lived on in speedway for a while at the start of the decade, when his son Malcolm had a go at riding for the Sheffield Prowlers junior team. Malcolm, who it is said has his mother's black hair and dark eyes and his father's unflinching bravery on a bike, saw his tenacious efforts curtailed by a broken leg. But he should have no regrets about failing to make the grade on shale – he is by no means the first son of a former world class rider who has not been able to follow successfully in his father's tyremarks. Thankfully, he now has a much more sensible job!

Young Malcolm has overcome his own personal problems and it is good to hear that he is now doing well for himself, while I believe his sister Kelly Marie, 24, is happily living in Hull having qualified as a martial arts teacher. She has attended Scunthorpe Speedway in recent years to hand out the prizes at a junior meeting run in memory of her father.

If Malcolm, now 23, needs anyone to remind him just how tough a career in speedway can be, he has only to ask his elder cousin, Wayne, who maintained the famous Carter name in the sport after Kenny died. And like Kenny, he suffered a very serious injury at a very early stage in his career – a road accident, near his Halifax home in May 1992, left the then 21-year-old Wolverhampton prospect with a badly broken knee joint that almost led to amputation.

Thankfully, although he had to adapt his racing style, Wayne went on to enjoy a good

Malcolm Carter with Sheffield Prowlers in 2000.

career and received a well-deserved testimonial in August 1999 while on loan from Wolves to Isle of Wight. Wayne – whose dad, Alan, is the brother of Mal Carter – was only 14 when Kenny died, although he recalls watching him race at The Shay and lending a hand to Kenny's mechanics in his workshop.

We should not let Kenny's speedway achievements overshadow the brilliance, at a very young age, of his younger brother, Alan, who never fulfilled his undoubted promise. Some say his temperament let him down at crucial times, and he probably joined the wrong teams at the wrong time, but there can be no denying his skill on a bike at high speeds or his ability to ruffle the feathers of some of road-racing's true greats during the 80s.

Alan still has a place in road-racing history books as the youngest ever British rider to win a 250cc motorcycling grand prix, and it's a delight that he is back on track again, but away from racing, running his own business as a supplier to florists.

Nor should we forget that Alan, the more outgoing of the two brothers, also suffered the same family tragedies – the loss of his mother and younger brother – very early in his young life, just as Kenny did. Kenny loved 'Our Nip' and he would be proud of him now.

It is Mal Carter's strong, resourceful and very capable second wife, Janet who is credited with helping Alan get a foothold on the business ladder after his racing career finished. She is described as a 'rock' for the Carter family. Janet is the driving force behind the mobile home and leisure park that she and husband Mal run, which is reputedly valued at in excess of £2million.

As I said at the start of the book, my biggest hope is that both Pam and Kenny's families can enjoy the rest of their lives in peace, the best possible health and happiness.

Finally, the thoughts of people from the speedway fraternity reading this will inevitably turn back to Kenny. All things considered, we can but wonder if Kenneth Malcolm Carter was simply jinxed from the start? But this is, again, yet another lingering question that no-one can possibly answer.

Jimmy Ross and Phil Hollingworth have provided us with a brilliant insight to Carter the man, as well as the speedway superstar. One very poignant and private conversation Jimmy had with Kenny in his younger days perhaps reveals just how deeply troubled he was by the loss of his mum, Christine, and how her own enormous suffering played its part in his own fate.

Ross, who still visits Pam and Kenny's churchyard graves every week, said: "Kenny never got over what happened to his mum and he told me several times after she died that he had 'seen' her at the end of his bed. Pam also told me that she had seen Kenny's mum, appear before them.

"He was haunted by the vision. Many people would interpret this experience as a kind of 'calling' from the spirit of the person concerned – in this case Christine. Kenny would tell me what he'd seen and say, 'you do believe me don't you, Jimbo?' He mentioned this experience to me on several occasions.

"He loved his mum so much, in the end he just wanted to be with her."

KENNY CARTER'S CAREER RECORD (1978-86)

WORLD CHAMPIONSHIP

Individual World Final
September 5, 1981 – Wembley Stadium, London, England
3   2   3   EF   3   11 points (4th)
August 28, 1982 – Los Angeles Coliseum, California, USA
3   3   3   FX   1   10 points (5th)
September 4, 1983 – Norden, West Germany
2   3   3   1   1   10 points (4th)

World Pairs Final
December 11, 1982, Liverpool. Sydney, Australia
Runner-up (to USA), 22 points – Peter Collins 15, Kenny Carter 7
June 17, 1983, Gothenburg, Sweden
Winner, 25 points – Kenny Carter 15, Peter Collins 10
June 15, 1985, Rybnik, Poland
Runner-up (to Denmark), 27 points – Kenny Carter 14, Kelvin Tatum 13

World Team Cup Final
August 16, 1981 Olching, West Germany
29 points (England finished 2nd to Denmark, 36 pts) – Kenny Carter 9
August 12, 1983 Vojens, Denmark
29 points (England finished 2nd to Denmark, 37 pts) – Kenny Carter 8

British Champion 1984, 1985

Leading Lance King
during the 1983 World
Team Cup Final at
Vojens.

LEAGUE & KNOCKOUT CUP RECORD

NEWCASTLE 1978

	M	R	Pts	BP	TPts	Ave
Tom Owen	36	169	450	7	457	10.82
Robbie Blackadder	32	120	259	14	273	9.10
Kenny Carter	**41**	**181**	**296**	**47**	**343**	**7.58**
Robbie Gardner	39	159	261	33	294	7.40
Graeme Stapleton	37	55	212	42	254	6.56
Kevin MacDonald	3	11	15	3	18	6.55
Rod Hunter	38	151	219	28	247	6.54
David Bargh	5	12	15	0	15	5.00
Robert Maxfield	3	12	10	3	13	4.33
Neil Coddington	34	97	86	15	101	4.17
Nigel Crabtree	9	27	18	6	24	3.56
Chris Prime	1	1	0	0	0	0

HALIFAX 1978

	M	R	Pts	BP	TPts	Ave
Ian Cartwright	37	162	315	23	338	8.35
Mike Lohmann	36	154	282.5	18	310.5	8.07
Mitch Graham	27	95	158	19	177	7.45
Mick McKeon	33	133	179	27	206	6.20
Eric Broadbelt	31	115	153	19	172	5.98
Chris Pusey	33	118	144	28	172	5.83
Kenny Carter	**16**	**60**	**68**	**13**	**81**	**5.40**
Phil Collins	1	4	5	0	5	5.00
Klaus Lohmann	32	114	112	25	137	4.81
Tom Godal	1	3	2	1	3	4.00
Ian Robertson	1	6	3	1	4	2.67
Colin Ackroyd	1	3	1	0	1	1.33
Alan Stansfield	2	4	1	0	1	1
Mick Blaynee	1	3	0	0	0	0
Martyn Cusworth	1	2	0	0	0	0
Peter Wilson	1	2	0	0	0	0
Dave Allen	1	1	0	0	0	0

HALIFAX 1979

	M	R	Pts	BP	TPts	Ave
Ian Cartwright	36	148	320	11	331	8.95
Kenny Carter	**35**	**150**	**272**	**33**	**305**	**8.13**
Mike Lohmann	33	138	222	40	262	7.59
Tormod Langli	35	142	221	25	246	6.93
Mick McKeon	38	149	225	31	256	6.87
Klaus Lohmann	22	88	101	13	114	5.18
Merv Janke	17	57	54	15	69	4.84
Steve Wilcock	28	90	77.5	18	95.5	4.24
Alan Stansfield	3	9	6	1	7	3.11
Paul Sheard	6	16	8	0	8	2
Graham Plant	1	2	0	0	0	0
Ian Robertson	1	2	0	0	0	0

HALIFAX 1980

	M	R	Pts	BP	TPts	Ave
Tormod Langli	1	4	8	1	9	9
Kenny Carter	**33**	**157**	**338**	**12**	**350**	**8.92**
Ian Cartwright	32	154	284	21	305	7.92
Mick McKeon	29	126	172	34	206	6.54
Merv Janke	34	142	187	28	215	6.06
Piotr Pyszny	28	109	133	25	158	5.80
Craig Pendlebury	31	121	146	17	163	5.39
Les Sawyer	13	40	28	7	35	3.50
Ian Westwell	4	14	12	0	12	3.43
Alan Stansfield	8	21	12	3	15	2.86
Paul Sheard	3	6	2	1	3	2
Jorn Haugvaldstad	4	8	0	0	0	0

HALIFAX 1981

	M	R	Pts	BP	TPts	Ave
Kenny Carter	**31**	**142**	**352**	**9**	**361**	**10.17**
John Louis	45	222	418	16	434	7.82
Ian Cartwright	45	220	405	24	429	7.80
Craig Pendlebury	22	79	103	23	126	6.38
Piotr Pyszny	21	80	83	23	106	5.30
Doug Wyer	45	193	232	17	249	5.161
Dave Trownson	12	49	49	8	57	4.65
Martin Dixon	1	6	6	0	6	4
Steve Baker	45	151	110	24	134	3.55
Billy Burton	2	6	4	1	5	3.333
Rob Ashton	11	43	24	8	32	2.98
Rob Woffinden	1	2	1	0	1	2
Trond Skretting	13	42	12	4	16	1.52
Guy Wilson	3	10	2	1	3	1.20
Ian Westwell	7	13	2	1	3	0.92

HALIFAX 1982

	M	R	Pts	BP	TPts	Ave
Kenny Carter	**38**	**169**	**465**	**1**	**466**	**11.03**
John Louis	42	176	315	16	331	7.52
Ian Cartwright	37	145	237	27	264	7.28
Merv Janke	20	72	100	15	115	6.39
Martin Dixon	12	53	63	10	73	5.51
Doug Wyer	43	162	188	29	217	5.36
Steve Baker	43	151	153	35	188	4.98
Rob Ashton	43	130	120	33	153	4.71
Mats Olsson	5	16	12	4	16	4.00
Kenny Young	2	5	2	0	2	1.60
Rob Tate	8	20	3	1	4	0.80
Eric Monaghan	1	2	0	0	0	0

HALIFAX 1983

	M	R	Pts	BP	TPts	Ave
Kenny Carter	**41**	**184**	**464**	**9**	**473**	**10.28**
Steve Baker	38	155	222	32	254	6.60
Doug Wyer	42	168	244	15	259	6.17
Steve Finch	42	165	209	29	238	5.77
Martin Dixon	40	163	189	39	228	5.60
Craig Pendlebury	31	102	117	21	138	5.41
Gianni Femari	19	59	43	9	52	3.53
Eric Boocock	23	65	37	2	39	2.40
Glen Parrott	2	7	4	0	4	2.29
Mats Olsson	5	13	5	2	7	2.15
Mark Gallagher	4	7	1	1	2	1.14
Peter Nightingale	1	3	0	0	0	0

The above statistics relate to official National League, British League and Knockout Cup matches only.
Courtesy of The Complete History of the British League by Peter Oakes, published 1991.

HALIFAX 1984

	M	R	Pts	BP	TPts	Ave
Kenny Carter	**8**	**33**	**75**	**1**	**76**	**9.21**
Neil Evitts	37	173	293	29	322	7.45
Steve Baker	39	169	220	37	257	6.08
Eric Monaghan	44	173	190	33	223	5.16
Doug Wyer	38	155	177	15	192	4.96
Steve Finch	39	138	139	21	160	4.64
Craig Pendlebury	18	55	51	12	63	4.58
Kurt Hansen	25	84	64	10	74	3.52
Gordon Whitaker	5	12	3	1	4	1.33
Eric Knudsen	4	11	2	1	3	1.09
Peter Clegg	2	5	0	0	0	0

HALIFAX 1985

	M	R	Pts	BP	TPts	Ave
Kenny Carter	**27**	**120**	**301**	**3**	**304**	**10.13**
Neil Evitts	41	168	277	28	305	7.26
Larry Ross	42	165	223	50	273	6.62
Rod Hunter	42	149	208	22	230	6.17
Sean Wilmott	40	142	164	28	192	5.41
Eric Monaghan	42	149	165	36	201	5.40
Kurt Hansen	33	107	107	31	138	5.16
Doug Wyer	13	43	40	5	45	4.19
Gordon Whitaker	1	3	0	0	0	0

BRADFORD 1986

	M	R	Pts	BP	TPts	Ave
Kenny Carter	**10**	**41**	**102**	**1**	**103**	**10.05**
Neil Evitts	37	154	345	14	359	9.33
Lance King	27	118	234	8	242	8.20
Gary Havelock	15	65	98	20	118	7.26
Sean Wilmott	41	160	199	53	252	6.30
Larry Ross	39	151	197	30	227	6.01
Eric Monaghan	4	13	12	2	14	4.31
Gordon Whitaker	41	125	114	16	130	4.16
Paul Stead	1	4	3	1	4	4
Paul Evitts	1	3	2	1	3	4
Michael Graves	43	134	108	22	130	3.88
Anthony Hulme	2	6	1	0	1	0.67
Robin Archer	1	3	0	0	0	0
David Clay	1	3	0	0	0	0
Jim Graham	1	3	0	0	0	0
Paul Whittaker	1	3	0	0	0	0
Bruce Cribb	1	1	0	0	0	0

BL TOP TEN FINISHES

Riders who finished the British League season with a final CMA in excess of 10.00 points. Kenny was the last English rider to top the final national BL averages when he achieved the feat in 1982.

1981

	M	R	Pts	BP	TPts	Ave
1 Bruce Penhall (Cradley)	23	96	261	5	266	11.08
2 Kenny Carter (Halifax)	**25**	**112**	**287**	**7**	**294**	**10.50**
3 Phil Crump (Swindon)	29	124	313	9	322	10.39
4 Michael Lee (King's Lynn)	22	99	251	5	256	10.34
5 Erik Gundersen (Cradley)	28	115	289	6	295	10.26
6 Chris Morton (Belle Vue)	27	117	292	8	300	10.26
7 Jan Andersson (Reading)	28	123	306	2	308	10.12

1982

	M	R	Pts	BP	TPts	Ave
1 Kenny Carter (Halifax)	**23**	**105**	**289**	**1**	**290**	**11.05**
2 Erik Gundersen (Cradley)	25	106	280	4	284	10.72
3 Hans Nielsen (Birm'ham)	25	111	289	2	291	10.49
4 Bruce Penhall (Cradley)	15	62	152	9	161	10.39
5 Dennis Sigalos (Ipswich)	22	96	236	9	245	10.21
6 Bobby Schwartz (Reading)	25	110	276	2	278	10.11

1983

	M	R	Pts	BP	TPts	Ave
1 Dennis Sigalos (Ipswich)	26	111	298	7	305	10.99
2 Hans Nielsen (Birm'ham)	26	120	321	2	232	10.77
3 Erik Gundersen (Cradley)	27	111	277	17	294	10.59
4 Michael Lee (Poole)	26	117	300	5	305	10.43
5 Mitch Shirra (Reading)	27	111	280	8	288	10.38
6 Kenny Carter (Halifax)	**28**	**125**	**319**	**4**	**323**	**10.34**
7 Billy Sanders (Ipswich)	27	111	279	6	285	10.27
8 Chris Morton (Belle Vue)	28	120	293	12	305	10.17

OTHER INDIVIDUAL UK SUCCESSES

1979
Canterbury	British Junior Championship

1980
Halifax	Dews Trophy
Halifax	Autumn Classic
Halifax	Northern Riders' KO Trophy
Wembley Arena	King of the Concrete

1981
Belle Vue	British League Riders' Champs
Birmingham	Second City Trophy
Halifax	Dews Trophy
Ipswich	Metro Stadium Trophy
Sheffield	Owlerton Open Handicap
Sheffield	Northern Riders' Champs

1982
Belle Vue	British League Riders' Champs
Cradley Heath	Golden Hammer

1983
Coventry	Brandonapolis
Ipswich	Marathon Classic
Leicester	Golden Gauntlets

1984
Halifax	Halifaxapolis

1985
Cradley Heath	Golden Hammer
Ipswich	Marathon Classic

Above: After beating Danes Erik Gundersen and Hans Nielsen to win the 1985 Golden Hammer at Cradley Heath.
And in the same season (below) Kenny is with meeting sponsors Pam and Trevor Hedge after winning the
GM/Daily Mirror 16 Lap Marathon Classic at Ipswich.

Index

More speedway nostalgia
from the publishers of *TRAGEDY*